CW01021038

To my dear friend,
Joe
Best wishes.
Brian

HIS MASTER'S VOICE

BRIAN McLAUGHLIN

First published in 2023 by
Brian McLaughlin, in partnership with whitefox publishing

www.wearewhitefox.com

ISBN 978-1-915635-19-8
Also available as an eBook
ISBN 978-1-915635-20-4

Designed and typeset by Typo•glyphix, Burton-on-Trent DE14 3HE
Cover design by Simon Levy
Project management by whitefox
Printed and bound by CPI Group (UK) Ltd, Croydon CR0 4YY

To Sue, my children and grandchildren,
Dave Wilde, James Tyrrell, Eric Nicoli,
Fr Stephen Holford OSB, and Alan Johnson

FOREWORD

At first meeting, and even after many meetings, Brian Finbar McLaughlin is an unlikely captain of industry – but a captain of the entertainment retail industry he most certainly became.

But if we consider the characteristics necessary to sustain success in business and, indeed, in life – loyalty, honesty, integrity, hard work, courage and imagination and, crucially, humility, then it's no surprise at all that he achieved all that he did. Brian also has a well-developed sense of humour and an ability to laugh at himself – and there's quite a lot to laugh at – and this, perhaps, helps explain our close and enduring friendship.

My vertically challenged, stroppy, hairy-arsed friend, as I'm inclined to call him, has had to live with more shortcomings than most of us. Being a life-long Portsmouth fan is tragic enough, but given a very limited formal education and a short fuse when provoked, Brian's determination to be the best that he could be and to win – perhaps because Portsmouth rarely did! – made him a hugely effective team captain and leader of his troops at every level of management.

I met Brian in 1999 when I was appointed Executive Chairman of EMI Group plc, which was the former owner and still part owner of the HMV music retail business. Along with the book retailer Waterstones, HMV made up the recently created HMV Media Group, and Brian's role at that time was the day-to-day running of HMV in the UK. I had taken up one of EMI's two seats on the HMV Media Group board and later was asked to step up to be Chairman of that board. It was in that capacity that I was able to see at first hand Brian in action as a world-class retailer, which made my subsequent decision to ask him to take charge of all of our music and book stores an easy one.

At the turn of the millennium, high street retail was beginning to be significantly challenged by online retail, with Amazon, in particular, competing aggressively in book, CD and DVD retailing, putting HMV and its high street competitors under significant pressure. Brian's drive and passion to maintain HMV's market-leading position in the UK shone through. His inspirational leadership of his team engendered loyalty and extraordinary commitment from his colleagues while he cleverly developed close and respectful relationships with his suppliers, skilfully using – but never abusing – his power as the leading retailer.

Over the years that followed, we saw the rapid advance of technology and the digitisation of content along with the development of broadband which facilitated the distribution of music, film, games and books to be consumed on iPods, smartphones, tablets and laptops – first via downloading, quickly followed by streaming – to the point that the relevance of high street retail in these sectors was questionable.

In quick succession, a number of famous retailers of entertainment products such as Woolworths, Tower, Virgin Megastores and Zavvi disappeared from the high street, and yet HMV remains today. Brian McLaughlin can take pride and considerable credit for HMV's survival. His willingness to adapt in a dramatically changing marketplace combined with a relentless pursuit of improvement and the ability to motivate a passionate team were at the root of HMV's success.

HMV continues today to be an important partner of UK music companies, and it is a measure of the respect in which Brian was held by the entire UK music business that, in 2001, he received the Music Industry Trusts Award which honours an individual's contribution to the UK's musical and cultural landscape. Other recipients of that award include Sir George Martin, Lord Andrew Lloyd Webber, Peter Gabriel, Sir Elton John and Bernie Taupin, and Sir Tom Jones among many other icons of the industry.

Brian's story is a compelling tale of what can be achieved from humble roots with dedication, focus, courage and determination. His passion for his work has been exceeded only by his love for his family. He acknowledges the super-important role played by his wife Sue, who supported him through tough times and who now is enjoying with him his richly deserved retirement.

I'm proud to call Brian a friend.

Eric Nicoli, April 2023

Chapter 1

I was so nervous. On stage there were already some of the greats of the music industry, not just in the UK, but from around the world. There were also 1,000 people in the audience, and not just any people. These were some of the greatest names in the music business, some I had worked for, some I had worked against! And now they were all gathered together for the prestigious Music Industry Award – an award given to someone who had made an outstanding contribution to the music industry. Previous winners included the great Maurice Oberstein, Ahmet Ertegun, John Barry, Sir George Martin, Lord Andrew Lloyd Webber.

As I looked out on the sea of faces, I could see so many worthy winners of this award, the ultimate accolade in the UK music industry. I could have sat you down and told you a thousand reasons they were more qualified than me to get such an honour. After all, confidence had never been my strong point, and more than once I'd felt like a fraud being part of this business. But on this night, I had to put all of that aside, or at least try to! Because there was nothing I could do about it now. They were going to present the award – in fact Lulu was. That alone made it surreal, as I had met her backstage many years ago at the Portsmouth Guildhall, and her real name was McLaughlin!

She announced the winner, and the winner was me.

Perhaps this sounds like a dream, and in one way it was. But it was also all too real. We all have our dreams, we all have our journeys, but to my astonishment mine had not so much come true as exceeded every expectation. I wasn't born to believe that anything like this could happen to me and even as I stood backstage, unable to pee but ready to be handed the trophy, I couldn't help but look back on where I'd come from, and the amazing combination of luck and hard work that had got me to where I was.

I know – everyone who wins a big award thinks they started from nothing, and thinks that it was their own sweat that got them where they are. That's part of the reason I'm writing this book. To admit to myself and the world that mine was no smooth journey, and that along the way there were as many disasters as triumphs.

Did I have support? Yes! My wife Sue especially, but also all of those people who opened doors for me, who guided me through the good times and the bad. Did I have to fight every inch of the way? Yes!

But that struggle was made easier as I was fortunate enough to have worked with some of the most dedicated and hardworking people in the world. It was their energy, their belief and their amazing support that ensured I would not let them down. Many of them were just like me – mad on music, uneducated – but we all knew we were part of something special, something that had enormous potential, and what we achieved together over those years was down to their dedication, drive, determination and sheer hard work. It was an honour and a privilege to have known them and worked so closely with them.

At all of those board meetings, every time that I was renegotiating huge deals, I knew something that the other people around the table didn't – that the man playing hardball was in reality just a little boy from Portsmouth who had lost his mother young, and who had been brought up in chaos. Each time I opened the door to go into those rooms I was taking that little boy in with me. Sometimes

I told him it would be OK, they wouldn't guess who we were, sometimes he was the one who told me.

And now, this night, we were going on stage together. John Lodge from The Moody Blues, Sophie Ellis-Bextor, Bruce Dickinson from Iron Maiden were there holding the trophy, and so many of the HMV managers, my friends and family were applauding. As I accepted it, I raised it above my head, like I'd won the World Cup. I raised that trophy towards the left-hand corner of the room, where all the HMV managers and staff were sat. That gesture was my thanks to them for being there with me on the long journey to success.

But the little boy from Portsmouth was there too. It was him, all those years ago, who had started the Billy Fury Fan Club, deciding that music was the most important thing in the world. It was him who had applied for a job at the Co-op, and him who had quit that and gone to a small company called HMV. It was him who had been daring enough to have jumped into the back seat of a car owned by a girl called Jean in order to kiss her friend Sue, and it was him who had married Sue and had three wonderful children.

It was also him, more often than not, who had been at those meetings, feeling like a fraud but being driven by a passion to make his company number one, an aim I achieved as MD. Even then I had to fight chronic pain that nearly saw my efforts come to nothing, and if not for fate I would have resigned.

It is still that young boy, in many ways, writing this book. If that boy I was had met a man like me, with my success, I would have thought we were from different worlds. But we are not – I try and remember that every time I meet a child who looks at me that way. Who knows what they may become?

I lowered the trophy, took a deep breath, and made my speech, thanking those I should thank. It was well received, and we partied hard into the night, as we so often did.

But the speech wasn't what I really wanted to say. What I really wanted to say was this . . .

Chapter 2

I was born in Portsmouth on 21 August 1949. My parents, Frances O'Sullivan and Patrick McLaughlin, married in 1938, I believe in Worthing. In 1939 their first child arrived, Patrick, and in 1941 their second child, Christina. I am not sure where they lived during the war, but while my dad was in the army, I gather my mum and grandma were living in 'digs' somewhere up North.

My dad's family were all from Donegal in Ireland and, as far as I know, very few of them came to England until after the war. My mum's family, on the other hand, mostly left Ireland to come to England. Like my dad's family, my mum's family was large and, I believe, Mum was one of twelve!

Family history is sketchy as a lot of our documents and photographs were destroyed in the 60s but I'm fairly certain my sister Frances was born in 20 Brompton Rd on 8 September 1948. Brompton Rd was my birthplace too and remained my home until around 1969. Brompton Rd was in what you might call a less salubrious part of Portsmouth called Mile End. It was a very long road with terraced houses on both sides, but I would describe them as *Coronation Street*-type houses, with proud housewives on their knees each morning polishing the step with some form of duster used to brighten up the red shining colour.

Generally, as I recall, people were nice, good and decent and everyone looked out for each other. We had a corner shop that sold most things and what they didn't sell would be available in Sultan Rd, just around the corner from us.

Our house had a kitchen, middle room and a front room downstairs. Three bedrooms upstairs and a cellar. There was an outside toilet and a small back garden, there were also steps giving access to the cellar from the garden. There was a back gate that opened out to a long passage, or alley as we called it, and its name – Brompton Passage – still exists today.

I don't think Mum and Dad were much into gardening, but I have to this day the most wonderful memories of a rose tree that filled our little garden with colour and I spent a lot of time just lying down by it on the grass in the summer, waiting for my mum to wake up.

Portsmouth as a city was heavily bombed during the last war, and most of the lovely buildings were destroyed. What remained were eventually replaced by new housing developments and offices that left a lot to be desired. As a resident though it had a lot going for it, a great and famous dockyard, easy access to beautiful countryside near Petersfield, a great football club, and Southsea, with its long history and lovely beaches. The Isle of Wight was ten minutes away by hovercraft.

As far as I can recall, Dad was a labourer and worked on several building sites in and around Portsmouth. He was short, shorter than me, say about 5′5″, and I loved him to bits. He was always up early in the morning, say 5 a.m., and I remember not wanting to miss him leaving the house without saying goodbye. He was kind and caring and worked very hard even after he broke his thumb in a cement mixer at the Guildhall. He rarely went out during the week; my mum, her sister, Babby, and their mum, would be out most nights at the local pub. Dad used to sit indoors with us.

I don't have much recollection of my brother, Pat, and my sister, Christina, in Brompton Rd, although Pat eventually went in the army. At the weekends, Dad used to put on his suit and hat and go to the cinema, often on his own. Frances and I would be sent off to church at St John's Cathedral, and Mum would stay home and make lunch.

I don't recall much happiness to be honest, there were lots of my mum's family visiting all the time and they tended to be noisy and drank a lot. Mum was my mum, I adored her although she was very strict with us and wouldn't hesitate to use a broom handle to us should we misbehave.

Later on in life I discovered she was an epileptic and that would explain the fits I witnessed in different parts of the house. I was so scared when she had one, as her body shook uncontrollably and often she was foaming at the mouth. Apparently, this all started just after I was born, when it is alleged she dropped me, and it had a terrible lasting impact on her. The downside, apart from the shaking etc., was that the medication they put her on would make her sleep, and as often as not she wouldn't get up most days until past lunchtime.

Frances and I got into all sorts of bother in the mornings, the worst being when we filled up every conceivable container in the kitchen with water and launched them one by one up the long passageway leading to the front door. I can still see my mum coming down those stairs with nothing much more than a corset to hide her modesty, shouting and screaming at the pair of us. I guess we got a good beating and rightly sent to our rooms for the day.

I suppose the medication Mum was on made her feel tired most of the time, so we never went anywhere. We never went for family walks, family holidays, in fact I don't recall us being much of a family at all.

As Frances and I got older we began to notice the influence my mum's family was having on our lives. They were all big drinkers and at the weekends especially, we would be standing outside various pubs in Portsmouth while they were all inside getting pissed. The trouble though usually started when they got home, as one of my uncles would invariably bring a case of Guinness with him from the pub and they would stay up most of the night drinking it.

Dad, I guess, went to bed early, he didn't drink with them that much, and they didn't like him. He was a timid man, unable to stand up to them or my mum. We noticed when they got home – they would have sailors with them, and they too would be in our house all night.

Amidst all this gloom, Christina used to play records on her radiogram and I, to this day, always recall her playing 'Poor Little Fool' by Ricky Nelson. It had a lovely melody and there was something about it that allowed me to escape the unhappiness Frances and I were experiencing. Once you eventually got off to sleep you were never sure who was in the bed with you, often as not they weren't family and they stunk of Guinness.

I guess this became the norm and eventually it led to my mum being arrested by the police for openly encouraging behaviour that led to a charge of running a house of ill repute. One of my nephews discovered this terrible news only recently by trawling through the local Portsmouth paper, but more shocking was the fact that in court the magistrate referred to her charge as the second time she had been arrested. She was fined heavily. God only knows where she got the money to pay it.

I can recall church on Sunday. St John's was a wonderful church and the atmosphere in there was electric. Frances and I would walk to school each day, which was the Catholic school, also St John's, next to the cathedral. Teachers were strict. No, not just strict, brutal, hitting you across the knuckles with a cane. I don't think it was the cane that prompted my mum to storm into our class one day, shouting at the teacher and ordering us out. To this day, I still don't know why we were pulled out, but it had a silver lining for us as the school we were moved to, Flying Bull Lane, was much kinder and friendlier. The one downside, however, is that Mum insisted we keep up our Catholic teaching and therefore after school each day, Frances and I would have to go to the convent in Commercial Rd for catechism lessons.

Prior to all this, Mum gave birth to another child, a son, Thomas Charles, on

17 April 1953. So that would make me nearly four years old and Frances nearly five. All I recall was a baby screaming in Mum's bedroom but have little other recollection of him at this time.

During the school holidays, we ended up playing on bombsites at the back of Commercial Rd, it was fun. There were a number of broken-down cars that we could play inside, lots of other kids would join us too.

When we weren't doing this, we would play in Victoria Park behind the Guildhall. It has fond memories for me, for it was green, with the most wonderful trees and flowers. Something you didn't see a lot of in Mile End. I recall vividly they had a bird sanctuary, which was fascinating, and they had a cheeky parrot that kept most of us amused. The Guildhall itself was an amazing building, rebuilt after the war and apparently is a similar design to the one in Bolton. On either side of this massive, impressive building sat two lions; word has it that if they growled after a young lady went by it was to signal that they were virgins!

We spent most days in the same area, utterly unsupervised and to a certain extent unprotected. Frances and I went to the toilets at the Guildhall one day, only to find in my toilet a horrible man with an erect penis in his hand asking me to stroke it. I told Mum, who I believe called the police but never knew if they ever caught him.

Opposite our road, Brompton Rd in Mile End, was a cemetery and a place called Whale Island. It was a naval establishment and, I think, a firing range, as Frances and I used to collect the shells that were lying about. Whether we were meant to be there or not I don't know but then I don't think anyone was that bothered about us.

I remember having to go to the hardware store, Ben Grubbs I think it was called, and I was so excited as I had my brand-new raincoat on. Mum asked me to buy a tin of paint and told me to be careful carrying it home. Well, I wasn't. I fell over, the paint – white paint – went all over me and the brand-new raincoat. In frantic tears, I recall heading towards Whale Island where some boats were moored asking anyone if they could get the paint off my new mac. I went into two or three boats, they were all foreign, but no one could help me. I was terrified of the beating I was likely to receive when I got home and I was not to be disappointed. On top of my beating, I was sent to bed, no food or drink.

I used to be friends with the son and daughter of the owner of the local corner shop and envied the life they had compared to mine. Their parents seemed normal and jolly nice and they spoke to their children with affection.

I recall with fondness the ABC cinema on Commercial Road. Just out of curiosity, I decided to go there, using my pocket money, and the film they were showing was *Moby Dick*. I still laugh now that it wasn't until I went a second time to see *I Was Monty's Double* that I realised that the seats could come down – I used to sit on the top of them!

My mum went on to have her last child, Enda, on 1 August 1955. Like Tom's arrival, I haven't got any early memories of her. I was, however, to spend more time with both of them in the years to come.

So, overall, my life became generally unhappy – the drinking culture at home seemed to get worse and many more parties involving Guinness and male strangers seemed to increase. Bank holidays were to be dreaded, as Mum, and possibly Dad, would be in town drinking all day and carrying on well into the night once they got home. My mum and dad never appeared close and I can never recall seeing them kiss each other. I since found out that he left her after the court case, but returned home for the sake of the children. I suppose, deep down, I felt sorry for him, you knew he wasn't in charge, and you knew all he wanted was a quiet life.

To lift our spirits, somehow Frances and I convinced our mum to take us all to Hayling Island one Sunday. I didn't even know what Hayling Island was but Frances said it had a sandy beach and we could build sandcastles. Come the chosen Sunday, Mum was sleeping heavily as usual, due to the tablets she was taking. We desperately wanted her to wake up so we could go on our trip, but she woke and said she wasn't going. I don't think I ever cried so much. Somehow I had built this trip up in my mind over and above reality, but I knew it involved going on a bus and then a ferry. I was shattered and literally heartbroken.

We had never been anywhere before as a family and I had never been to the seaside. Well, I must have had an impact on her, for she eventually got up and got dressed and off we went.

It was like going to Disneyland for me, it was a beautiful summer's day, and the short hop on the ferry at Eastney to Hayling Island was just bliss. I don't think we stayed on the beach long, but we did make sandcastles, and we may have even had a drink. The point was, for the first time I could recall we went on holiday, it was the only time in my life to date I felt happy to be alive.

My children ask me about what I recall about Christmases but apart from one or two, not a lot. I recall waking up one morning with some toy soldiers in my bed, which I was thrilled with, and the second recollection wasn't as good, as it looked at one time as if Christmas Day might be cancelled. Mum had gone missing. We woke up to no presents, no stocking. Eventually she turned up, but by then I think I was past caring. Do I remember a lunch, fun, games, laughter? Most certainly not.

For instance, I woke up one morning to a lot of commotion in the kitchen. Looks as though the police were there with Mum, and various aunties. It transpires that my Auntie Rooney was coming back from the pub on her own after closing time and was attacked by a man down the alley that leads to our back gate. Apparently, she was in hospital, as the man had smashed a glass into her face and she was badly injured. Once the police had left and life returned to normal I ventured out into the garden and collided with an enamel, blue bucket. The bucket was full of Auntie Rooney's blood, a terrifying sight for a boy of my age to witness.

For some unknown reason Frances and I were continually falling out, fighting like cat and dog, like brothers and sisters often do! We would be wrestling all over the floor in the kitchen, shouting and screaming at each other. I guess Mum was concerned about this and presumably spoke to our doctor. I don't recall having any tests or seeing anyone other than our doctor but the next thing I know is that I was whisked off to St James's, the local mental hospital. I guess I was seven or eight at the time. The hospital was huge with vast grounds, and I was in a house along with other children of my age. There were two nursing sisters running the house, one I liked immensely, the other I didn't. Apparently, I was in there because of the tantrums I was having at home, and to be honest life in St James's was more enjoyable than being at home. I recall the cook and I got along really well, she liked me and she would make sure I got extras for breakfast, namely more bacon and chopped tomatoes. I still like that combination to this day. I got on also with the nice sister, rather plumpish but with a great smile and she liked me too. I think I was on medication, and I also had to visit a doctor in St James's called Dr Crossley. He was a thoroughly likeable man and we got on very well together. I recall he lived in Stubbington and even invited me to his house for lunch with his family.

I have no idea how long I was there. I don't recall having any visitors, but generally speaking the people were nice and the food was good.

Eventually, I went home. I'm not sure whether my tantrums had improved or not, but the next thing I know is this woman knocks on the door and sees my mum. They then both ask to see me and to tell me I am going to London for the day next Saturday to see someone about my health. This lady collects me from home – she was lovely, kind, thoughtful and had a big smile. We board a train to London. I'd never been on a train before and when we arrived we got in a taxi and she took me to the Tower of London. Wow! I'd never seen anything like it and there were so many people there. It was just one huge treat and I loved every minute of it. Next she took me somewhere posh for lunch, I'd never been in a restaurant so she had to help me with the cutlery, etc.! This was all too much for me, I was beginning to experience happiness, I was thrilled with my day so far and I was in the company of a lovely lady.

From a very enjoyable lunch we went to an impressive-looking house not far from the Tower of London. We were shown into this office and a Catholic priest arrived, he appeared very friendly. I had no idea why I was there and as far as I can recall he never asked me about my tantrums or my time in St James's in Portsmouth. He asked general questions about my home life, family and school. I left there none the wiser!

Roughly two weeks after my visit to London, my mum sat me down in the kitchen and told me that I was a bright boy and that it would be in my best interests if I went to boarding school. I would need to buy a uniform and the school was a Catholic one in Ramsgate in Kent called St Augustine's Abbey.

This news broke my heart, I felt I was being punished for my tantrums but Mum kept assuring me that I was bright and the local council had offered to pay the fees. She said I was allowed to visit the school before leaving home and it was agreed that my sister Christina would take me.

In summary, I was terrified at the thought of leaving home. Although there were a lot of my mum's relatives coming and going, I can't say I wanted to leave. In spite of everything, I loved Mum and Dad and our home was comfortable. I'm not sure, with hindsight, that Mum ever enjoyed having children. Dad had very little say in anything, and just did as he was told. Whatever her motives were with me we will never know, but boarding school was the making of me and provided me with the emotional stability I needed and a reasonable education.

On arrival at the school we were met by the headmaster, a Benedictine monk called Fr Bernard Waldron. He was average height, rather stockily built and had piercing blue eyes. He appeared devoid of warmth, and I didn't take to him from the outset.

I believe I started there in September 1958. I was nine years old. Mum never came with me, she just said goodbye at Portsmouth railway station and I cried buckets. I was met by someone from the school at Waterloo and then we went to Victoria to catch the train to Ramsgate. There were other new boys on the train, so it helped to break the ice before arriving at the school.

There was a huge mahogany table in the foyer of the school. Every day the boys' post would be sorted and displayed on it. For weeks I approached the table before breakfast hoping desperately for some communication from home. But the daily letters I wrote got no reply, until I wrote to our next-door neighbour asking her to find out why my mum wasn't writing to me.

As a result of that there were a few letters and the odd parcel, but traffic was generally one way and I continued to be very homesick.

I settled in well at the school and I made friends. One boy, John Kerrigan, gave me a small transistor radio, which I used to listen to after lights were out in the dorm. I listened, as we all did, mainly to Radio Luxembourg and I discovered I liked Billy Fury and Roy Orbison. 'In Dreams' by Roy Orbison was the most unbelievable song I had ever heard, and I still play it regularly today on my walks.

There was, and still is, a deep melancholy about me. I like sad songs and I used to lie in bed listening to them trying to calculate how many years my mum and dad would be alive.

Most of my friends were into music, we managed to buy a Dansette record player. The only downside to it was that it was driven by a rubber band and once that wore out, you'd had it. So, we used to go into the town at weekends in Ramsgate searching for shops that would sell them. We loved the coffee shops because they would have jukeboxes and although we didn't have much money, we would listen to other people's selections. We used to watch *Juke Box Jury* on TV. Because I was always the bossy one amongst us, I arranged a take-off *Juke Box Jury* in our barn, where we would always hang around. We set up the desk with the panel on it, and made out we were celebrities as per the TV. Needless to say, I was the host, David Jacobs, spinning the tunes, and getting great delight in hitting the bell for a hit or that crunching sound if it was a miss!

Looking back, music played a big part in my life, either during the night at home when the parties were in full swing or at boarding school when we listened to the radio whenever we had spare time. It now feels as though it was a kind of therapy – little did I know at the time that several decades later I would become a Trustee for Nordoff Robbins Music Therapy and, for a while, their Chairman of Fundraising.

I was beginning to enjoy St Augustine's. I liked the priests, I became very religious although I would have gladly given up Mass at 5 a.m. in the morning, which was compulsory. The teachers were mainly monks apart from a handful of outsiders, and I guess my biggest complaint was that the monks ran the school as if it was a monastery, so it was somewhat over the top on religion.

It was a tough, strict regime, run by the headmaster, Fr Bernard, but it did teach me right from wrong and helped shape me as a person.

Life was surreal, we were surrounded by a beautiful church, within beautiful gardens leading semi-monastic lives.

I was friendly with a lot of boys, we looked after each other, we were polite and respectful too. There was no bullying, no stupid rituals, and little or no violence. I always wanted my children and grandchildren to have a similar experience.

I must mention my first trip home, which would have been the Christmas break. In assembly we all stood there whilst the headmaster read out our destinations for the holiday. He would read out: 'Johnson, Purley, Surrey; Kerrigan, Haslemere, Hants; Smith, Gerrards Cross, and then he would bellow out McLaughlin, POORTSMOOTH!!' in the most condescending manner!

I was relieved when we were all summoned to the main hall to hear our travel plans for our first Christmas break. Given that we didn't own a bike at home, let alone a car, I couldn't believe how many boys were being picked up by chauffeurs driving huge Bentleys and Rolls-Royces!

I was excited to be going home and I missed my mum so much. I shall never forget to this day, how I literally melted when from the top of the steps at Portsmouth railway station I saw her waiting for me at the bottom. We hugged and hugged and cried and cried.

I don't recall much about my break or Christmas – except that the house was full of my mum's family boozing, mostly at weekends – but I don't think Mum or Dad had a great deal of time for us.

My auntie used to visit us every Monday, bringing some of her children with her. I always looked forward to these visits as they used to bring copies of *The Dandy* and *The Beano* for me to read. Little did I know then that the publishers of these comics would become shareholders in HMV years later! I loved Superman and Batman comics, TV westerns such as *The Lone Ranger*. But I loved music the most, and I have my sister Christina to thank for that.

As far as school was concerned I was only ever good at Latin – the boys generally hated it, but for some reason it was the only subject I came top of the class in. We had an amazing Latin teacher who became a good friend, called Fr Dominic, a Friar Tuck-like figure from Spain with the most amazing smile. I loved him. Then I started getting to know another monk called Fr Stephen Holford, who also was to become a very good friend of mine in later life. He never actually taught me, but I used to see him after Mass, he had an amazing sense of humour and we just hit it off from the outset. He used to take me to see his aunt in Broadstairs for afternoon tea. He was an astonishing individual, loud, funny, witty and so, so kind. He was in the end my replacement father. We would spend time walking covering a multitude of subjects, but mainly politics and religion. I know for a fact that his friendship helped shape me as an individual, and he brought me so much happiness. Overall, these were somewhat wasted years academically, as I didn't like school very much and would be a handful for the teachers to manage in the classrooms.

Chapter 3

I can recall as if it were yesterday how excited I was to be going home for the summer holidays. I was on the train to Portsmouth and I could hear Billy Fury's new single called 'In Summer'. It's a happy, simple song but gave me enormous pleasure on the day.

Mum met me as usual at the bottom of the stairs at Portsmouth station, and we hugged and cried as we always did. I hadn't been home long when she said she needed to go to the doctor as her tummy was swollen and that she felt bloated most of the day. I did at one stage think she was pregnant. Life at home was quieter, not so many drinking bouts and I can remember Christina being around. Christina was married then, had three kids, and eventually went on to have four. All adorable children and I loved them to bits. Mum had been to the doctor's, and he said she had to go to hospital for tests, X-rays maybe. The next time she went to hospital I went with her, and as I waited in the waiting room for her, she came out and said everything was OK but she needed to go home and rest.

Christina used to come to us most days, cleaning and making lunch for us as Mum did what she was told and rested. The summer was lovely, I spent a lot of time in the garden in the mornings sitting under my favourite rose tree while

Mum was still asleep. I began to really like Billy Fury, Mum gave me money to buy some of his other singles I didn't have, like, 'Halfway to Paradise', 'I'll Never Find Another You', and 'Like I've Never Been Gone'.

As we moved into August, it became clear that Mum was struggling with the stairs and Christina decided to move her bed downstairs into the front room. In those days the front room was sacred, and only to be used for very special visitors like doctors or policemen. My dad carried on working and was always home at a reasonable time at night. He didn't spend much time with Mum and usually sat and watched TV.

I remember the policeman being shown in there one day and Frances and I were called in after him. We had been phoning 999, sending ambulances and police to various addresses as hoax calls from the phone box. When he accused us of this offence, I guess in my usual way, I answered him back, and next minute I was laying on the floor in awful pain after he punched me in the stomach. It was a good lesson to learn – I've never done it since!

Anyhow, Mum's bed was brought into the front room and she was very poorly. She could not get up to use the toilet, so she had to use a bedpan. During this time Mum and I became very close, and I nursed her through the day as best I could, getting her drinks and food. She loathed my dad's tea, as he used to stew the water, which she couldn't stand. She asked me to go to the kitchen and find the best china teapot we had and put it under her bed so Dad couldn't use it! She would wake early in the morning calling for me to make her a pot of tea rather than accept anything from Dad. Dad would go to work as usual and come home at dinner time. He would watch TV, often on his own. I don't think Mum and him were very close any more.

On Saturday 14 September 1963, Mum called me for her cup of tea, but while I was making it, she started screaming in pain. I called the doctor from the phone box. Under the circumstances, I thought it best to go and get Christina, as Dad wouldn't have been a great deal of help. I got the bus over to Froddington

Rd and told my sister what had happened, and she immediately put on her coat and told me to stay there and look after her lovely three children. This was at about 10 a.m. So, I looked after the kids, expecting her to be back by lunchtime, but she didn't show. I decided to take the children to my house at Brompton Rd and get them some lunch.

As I walked in the house, Christina said the doctor had been and gave Mum something for the pain and she was asleep. She then told me that she had known since Mum's last hospital visit that she was dying, and they had sent her home as there was nothing they could do for her. I subsequently found out that she had pancreatic cancer – she was only forty-six years old. I asked Christina whether Mum would one day get better, and she said no, she would probably die that day.

I can't quite explain my feelings – firstly that Christina kept this terrible burden to herself and secondly, knowing I couldn't. imagine my life without my mum being there. There were no tears. I had to go to the shop in Sultan Rd, to get some lunch for everyone. We all sat silently in the kitchen, my dad didn't know about the cancer either until that day, he looked very sad. Next thing, I heard this loud noise coming from the front room. Christina ran in there, wouldn't let me in, and when she came out, in floods of tears, she said Mum had died.

After that, it's all a bit hazy. I remember the doctor coming, Dr Sawyer, a nice man. Then Phoebe, a neighbour from up the street, a rough diamond if there ever was one, tattoos everywhere and looked like a bulldog! Apparently, she was the lady who attended to the dead in the road, whatever that meant, but she was in my mum's room for a while, while I was in the kitchen. The next callers were the undertakers, people I'd never seen before, carrying a large black sack. I sat in the kitchen with the door ajar, waiting to see what would happen next. A few minutes later, they emerge with my mum inside the sack, and it was then that I lost it. I realised she was gone forever and for an hour or so I couldn't stop crying.

Chapter 4

After Mum's body was removed by the undertakers, we all sat around in the kitchen. My dad and Christina were there and I believe my gran and my Auntie Babby were also there. That night, would you believe, they all decide to go to the pub, leaving me in the house on my own – this, hours after my mum had died? I must admit to being scared. I'd never encountered death and I had this terrible fear that if I opened the door to the front room, Mum might still be in there. Anyhow, there was fear and there was a smell, the smell of death that I've never been able to describe, but it's not pleasant. I missed my sister Frances, and although we would often fight, we were very close. Apparently, she was in hospital.

Mum's family started to arrive and the house was full. Christina asked me if I wanted to see Mum at the Chapel of Rest, which I immediately agreed to. I was led to a small, poorly lit room. Placed carefully in the middle was an open coffin with Mum lying peacefully inside. All the torment and pain from her illness over the past six months had disappeared. She was dressed immaculately in white and appeared to be at peace. My tears flowed without any inhibition as I realised I would never see her again.

My sister, Christina, dealt with the funeral arrangements. It was to be held at Corpus Christi Church in Gladys Avenue, North End. This was a Catholic church, and as I was an altar boy at the Catholic convent in Mile End, I was told I was going to be an altar boy at Mum's funeral.

Everyone started arriving at our home, even aunts and uncles I had only ever seen previously once or twice. My brother, Pat, and his girlfriend, Marion, also arrived.

The church was packed, and I followed the priest and the coffin to the altar and the service began. I admit to being a bag of nerves with my whole family watching me, and I seem to recall not carrying out my duties as an altar boy that well.

Mum was buried in Milton Cemetery, and throughout my life, when I am in Portsmouth, I often visit her grave.

Afterwards, we all went back to our house and then with a full Irish contingent the drinking began, followed by the singing. This went on for quite a while but then as everyone was leaving there was a lot of shouting and screaming coming from the middle room. I couldn't exactly tell what was happening, except someone said, your dad has been punched in the face. I couldn't believe it, on this day of all days, someone hits my dad! It turned out that it was Uncle Finbar who had too much to drink and objected to my dad asking him to leave. Dad went to hospital and I came to visit him next day, but just as I arrived, he was discharged. The shock of seeing him remains with me to this day, he had a lump on his forehead the size of a cricket ball, and I just broke down in tears. He was a lovely man, quiet, timid, but kind and gentle to all his children. He was genuinely upset in the church and at home afterwards. I think he loved her, even though she didn't love him.

But whatever, he didn't deserve to get thumped by her brother on the day of her funeral! He was a kind, shy and very simple man, brought up on a farm and disliked confrontation of any sort. One wonders after the funeral and the unprovoked attack on him, how he saw the future. My mum did everything for him, his whole world must have fallen apart. As for me, there was no counselling then, your mum had died, you had just better get on with life.

Chapter 5

We all stayed at our home, 20 Brompton Rd, after Mum had died. I was due back to boarding school in early September but because of Mum's declining health and subsequent death, I was allowed to stay at home a couple of weeks longer with the family. From memory, Christina kept a close eye on us all. Frances had also come home, and Tom and Enda were there too.

Dad went back to work on the building site, and we were all there for him when he got home in the evening. Apparently, he had never paid a bill in his life, and they just piled up in the kitchen until Christina arrived to attend to them. I recall him lifting the mattress in his bedroom and lifting up the floorboards too. Whatever he was looking for he clearly found – there was a lot of money tucked away in both places where I'm sure Mum had been squirrelling away for years.

In late October, I was told I had to go back to school in Ramsgate, and to be honest I didn't want to. I developed a fear that no one was going to look after Tom and Enda. Dad didn't have a clue about managing a family, paying the bills, shopping, and keeping the house clean. Christina had her own house to worry about and a husband plus three children. Frances was only fifteen and she was at school. Anyhow, I had to go back, and I have to say everyone was very sympathetic and kind to me on my return. In fact, my best friend, John, had been told while he was at school a few months earlier that his dad had died, and I can recall how devastated he was and how utterly useless I felt in trying to console him.

Life at school continued as normal it's fair to say, but apart from Latin I wasn't interested. I joined the choir, which I enjoyed, and I loved the Gregorian chant used in the Latin Mass. It's the most beautiful music and I'm convinced that it was my love of this that made me consider becoming a monk a few years later.

My relationship with Fr Stephen continued to grow, and I spent as much time as I could with him. Despite what has happened over the years in the Catholic Church, no one ever tried to abuse me or indeed any other boy that I know of.

Obviously, after losing Mum, I was very sad and down in the dumps most days and consumed with worry about my Tom and Enda. Fr Stephen and Fr Dominic both worked hard to keep my spirits up and constantly took me out for walks, or to Broadstairs for afternoon tea with Fr Stephen's aunt. They both said I was much older than my years and I felt that to be the case too, enjoying the company of older people to my schoolfriends.

There was little contact from home, but I did write back and ask if Dad or Christina could attend this special occasion at the school where all parents were invited. There was no reply, but a few days later I received a letter from a social worker in Portsmouth saying that she would be attending. How very strange, I'd never met this lady before, and my dad or sister had never mentioned her.

Anyhow, she turned out to be delightful, not only attending the official function, but also taking me out for a meal in a very posh restaurant in Ramsgate. I don't know her name, but she was lovely, we both got on so well, and it reminded me how few days in my life would have been as good as this one.

We were heading towards the month of December, and I continued to be homesick and still worried about Tom and Enda. My class was heavily involved in putting on a play for the school – 'The Importance of Being Earnest'. For me it was a shocking play, with the two main characters being very posh ladies who always had to shout! To this day, whenever I hear it's being performed somewhere, it never brings back good memories.

However, I did use this play to my advantage.

I had decided that my place was at home with my younger brother and sister and made up my mind to run away from school. I thought it through and realised that my best chance of escaping without being noticed was the evening when the school play was on. From memory, I only had a small part to play early on in the play so once I'd finished, I could escape. The main drawback was that I didn't have any money and I would just have to take my chances at Ramsgate station in getting on a train to Victoria without a ticket. The night arrived; the whole school was in the big assembly hall. The play began, I did my short bit, and then ran out the front gate and never stopped running until I got to the station. I did have a few pence on me and discovered for 2d I could buy a platform ticket that then would allow me access to a train. This idea worked brilliantly, I got on, but I have to say I was very nervous throughout the journey, should a guard come around asking to see tickets.

As it happened, I got away with it, and even managed to get from Victoria to Waterloo station without a ticket. I used the same ploy to get access to the Portsmouth train, buying a platform ticket and I was on my way. My family had no idea I was coming. It must have been getting late, say 9 p.m., when I left Waterloo. Another nervous journey but I saw Portsmouth station approaching and I still felt nervous but nevertheless elated that I would soon be home.

I got off the train and walked towards the Way Out sign – when suddenly I heard, 'Where's your ticket?' I thought oh no, I've been rumbled.

I said that I lost my ticket on the train. The ticket collector clearly didn't believe me (I was, and am still, not a very good liar), so he told me to follow him into this room. No sooner had I sat down when this huge policeman arrived, with 'British Transport Police' marked all over him. Same questions from him, same answers from me! He said I couldn't go home until I paid for my ticket. I had no money and repeatedly told them so. Eventually, they asked for my address, and took me home. He knocked on our front door and Dad, I think, was in bed, so too was everyone else. He opened the door, let us both in and left the room, coming back with the money in his hand to pay for my train ticket. I have to say, Dad had never been unkind to me, but I could tell once I was told to go to bed, he was not happy with me!

Chapter 6

After a family discussion it was agreed that I wasn't returning to Ramsgate. My concern was always for the wellbeing of Tom and Enda and therefore returning there was no longer an option. However, I was only fourteen, so I was told I had to go to school locally. I believe Christina made enquiries and I was sent back to the Catholic church school, St John's, where Frances and I had been for primary education.

Basically, my time at the new school was awful. The kids were very different to what I had been used to in Ramsgate. They were, shall I say, different, and they had no time for someone like me who had arrived from a boarding school. They constantly took the piss out of my accent – an accent I was unaware of – calling me posh and stuck up. The teachers weren't that much better, often resorting to sarcasm regarding my previous school and saying maybe they weren't good enough for me. Nothing could have been further from the truth! I tried hard to make friends, but didn't, and life at St John's from January 1964 was miserable.

The misery continued through to the spring term when I decided myself that I wasn't going any more. It took a while, but then letters started arriving from the council, threatening my dad with court if I didn't go back. Social workers knocked on the door, but Frances and Christina didn't answer them. And life at home was OK – I had my Billy Fury records to play along with some of Christina's, music by Eddie Cochran, Ricky Nelson, and Elvis.

We didn't see much of Christina as she had a family to manage, so basically it was Frances and me at home, with Tom and Enda at school. Dad started arriving home late from work, something he never did when Mum was alive, and he had often been drinking. It got to the stage that he stopped giving Frances enough money to buy the groceries and we had to beg the owner of the corner shop to let us have things on tick. To be honest, Frances and I didn't keep the house clean and tidy, we had just lost our way. We just lazed about, until one day there was a knock at the door, and it was a social worker called Miss Crisp. I can only reflect that a neighbour must have reported us and, looking back, rightly so. Miss Crisp wasn't impressed with the state of the house, neither Frances nor I were at school, and it's fair to say none of us, including the two kids, were eating properly. Things became so bad, that I had to go to the local convent and ask them for food. It's funny when you look back and recall coming home with bowls of food, mostly vegetables that we would have never eaten!

Unbeknownst to me, I was allowed to leave school at fifteen, which meant that once school broke up for summer in July, I could effectively leave school for good. Miss Crisp said that the council were not going to pursue any legal action as July was fast approaching. She asked lots of questions about Dad, Tom and Enda, and you could tell we were going to have more visits from her. Dad was drunk most nights; the kids were unhappy, and Frances and I were just existing in an awful environment. July arrived and I was free from school forever, it was one of the happiest days of my life.

That happiness didn't last long as Miss Crisp arrived with two men to announce that due to the conditions Tom and Enda were living in, they were being taken into care. I couldn't believe that this was happening, as whatever faults I had, I felt I did my utmost to care for them both and keep them safe. I was devastated, angry, very upset and I vowed that I would get them back.

In the meantime, I started to look for work, and eventually I got a job in a newsagent somewhere in Copnor. Prior to that, I had a newspaper round, working for WHSmith at the railway station. I remember getting paid £1 per week, which was a lot of money then, but the newspaper round was tough, with me having to cycle from one end of Portsmouth to the other. Nevertheless, the money was good, and I saved most of it up as I wanted to start up the Billy Fury Fan Club.

My new full-time job was hard work, rarely serving behind the counter, but mostly carrying out a lot of manual work for the two owners, who I didn't like very much. A few weeks after I started, they told me they didn't want me any more, something that upset me at first, but then, I wasn't enjoying it.

I would look for something else.

Chapter 7

Friends and family agreed that I liked music and pens! I would normally have a record on or a pen in hand.

I started to be obsessed with Billy Fury and on looking back maybe this was my music therapy, helping me to block out the reality of life, who knows? I used to subscribe to *Elvis* monthly magazine and was a member of his fan club. I used to look forward to this arriving at home every month, often as not I couldn't wait for it, I was that excited. The magazine wasn't very big, 6 x 4 maybe, but it was full of pictures and news about Elvis. There wasn't an equivalent for Billy Fury, so I decided I would start one! Why I believed I could, or was even qualified to do this, God only knows, but I did. I tried asking Billy Fury's manager, Larry Parnes, to help me, but he never replied. So, to cut a long story short, I had no inside news to relate to fans. I just used what I read in the *NME*, *Melody Maker* etc., organised some competitions, listed tour dates, and printed lyrics of many of his songs. It wasn't a patch on the glossy, sexy, *Elvis* magazine, as mine was on A4 – albeit coloured paper – but I was proud of it.

I've no idea how I managed to find someone to print the fanzine, but I did. In all, I was selling about 200 fanzines a month, charging two shillings. Fans paid by postal order, and I got regular letters telling me how much they enjoyed it.

I never heard from his management, got no letters telling me that I could not produce the fanzine or the lyrics. But in the end the cash I received was only enough to cover my expenses. I thoroughly enjoyed doing it though. I was doing something I liked, and something special that I was in control of.

Eventually, after twelve continuous issues of the fanzine, the time came when I felt that I would like to meet this Billy Fury guy. I found out through the music press that he was going to appear in Great Yarmouth in the summer of 1964 and I decided I was going to make the long trip from Portsmouth. I booked my seat for the two shows he was giving that night and telephoned the Rainbow Theatre to tell them that I was Billy's Fan Club Manager. I asked if it would be possible for me to meet him? After much to-ing and fro-ing, someone there said they would do everything they could to arrange a meeting and suggested I arrive an hour before the performance. It was a very long train journey, and the first performance was about 6 p.m. On the bill with him was the comedian and impressionist, Mike Yarwood, plus Rolf Harris and Brian Poole, who had already had some big hits. I since found out that it was only Mike Yarwood's first or second time in front of an audience. But lo and behold, I got there as requested, one hour before the show, and would you believe it, Billy Fury appeared in the foyer to meet me! I think I was speechless to begin with. He thanked me for running his fan club that he didn't know anything about, and he came armed with a few black and white photos that he signed for me. I told him I was there for both shows and he said, well why don't you come backstage between shows and meet everyone else?

The experience was wonderful, he was such a likeable guy, and I couldn't believe that little old me from Pompey had just had a private audience with him! Unfortunately, I didn't go backstage between shows because I realised that if I stayed for the second show, I would miss my train home.

I eventually got home at some very late hour and the next morning my sister Frances couldn't believe I'd made the trip and that I had met Billy Fury. To say I was chuffed with myself was an understatement.

Chapter 8

Miss Crisp, the social worker, called at our home to speak to Dad. Obviously, he was at work, but she told us that there would be a court hearing the following week to decide whether Tom and Enda would go into care full time or whether they could come home. She said that Dad would have to appear in court and if he wanted to keep his youngest children at home, he would have to persuade the magistrate that they would be well looked after and kept safe. The letter duly arrived the following week and he agreed to go to court. Frances and I said we were going with him.

I knew where the Magistrates' Court was, but I'd never been inside so it was all a bit of a shock, with people rushing around from one court to the next. We waited and waited, and eventually my dad was called. We followed him but we were told we weren't allowed in. Miss Crisp said she would tell us what went on and that we would just need to be patient. After about an hour everyone came out. I saw my dad first, followed by Miss Crisp. I said to Dad, 'Are they coming home, did you tell them we would look after them and keep them safe?' He said nothing, brushing past us, so I asked Miss Crisp what had happened. She said the magistrate had decided that Tom and Enda were to stay in care and would possibly go to foster homes. She said, 'Your Dad said very little and, on that basis, the magistrate had no choice but to come to that decision.' Miss Crisp confirmed that she saw it as the right decision, as Tom and Enda's wellbeing was paramount. First of all, I broke down in tears, in fact I was actually sobbing in the court. I had worried about them all the time when I was at school and remember, I'd been so worried about them I had run away from school so I could look after them. But that was to no avail, the magistrate had made the decision and there was nothing I could do about it.

My crying began to peter out, and then inside me all I could feel was anger, anger aimed at my dad for not putting up a fight to keep them. I went ballistic. I ran out of the courthouse looking for him. I could see him heading off down the road in the direction of Froddington Rd where Christina lived. Frances was trying to calm me down, but nothing was going to stop me venting my anger at him – he had let them down, he had let me down, in fact I felt he had let us all down. This was my dad, quiet as a mouse, obviously very shy and uneducated, and unable to say boo to a goose. Anyway, I let him have it, all the way to Froddington Rd, which must have been a good thirty minutes' walk. I was shouting at him, swearing at him, causing an almighty embarrassing scene in the process. But frankly, I couldn't care, I was mortified to think we had lost them without a fight.

These was the rantings of a fifteen-year-old boy, who loved his brother and sister, who'd just lost his mum. It was, I suppose, all too much for me.

Chapter 9

I was at home one night reading the Portsmouth *Evening News*, and noticed an advert for a sales assistant to work in the radio, TV and record department at Co-op House in Fratton Rd. I didn't know anything about radios or TVs, but I knew something about records, or put it another way, I was interested in them.

This was 1964 and I was fifteen, legally allowed to apply for the job. I don't remember much about the interview, except the manager, Mr Rose, was a very nice man and looked somewhat like Captain Mainwaring from *Dad's Army*! Somehow, I managed to get the job, on a weekly wage of £3, I think. Mr Rose said, 'You start Monday, and you should turn up smart as you will be serving customers on all three departments.'

They say luck plays a big part in your life; well, I have to agree. I had fallen on my feet getting that job at the Co-op, the other guys working with me, Terry Corben, Tony Kneller and Mick Auton were just so good to me. There was a huge service department behind the main counter and that was run by Barry Elkins. The Co-op itself was huge and one of the most successful department stores in the South of England. You could make friends easily from the other departments, you would go to lunch with some of them or have your tea break with them.

It was, I found in all circumstances, one big happy family, under one roof, all selling things to the public. Mr Rose was a great manager and spent an unbelievable amount of his time training me in salesmanship and educating me in all the new models of both radios and TVs that were just out, or about to come out. I did OK for the first few months selling mainly radios and TVs, and if I didn't know the answer to a question from a customer, I just made it up. I did find I had the gift of the gab, which used to get me out of difficult situations. By and large, I enjoyed it immensely. I loved working with all the guys, and they had all taken to me from day one and I was just so thrilled to be working with them. I was even told I could call Mr Rose 'Eric', and I could join them from time to time on promotional trips to London when new models were being introduced. Barry, the Service Manager, was a big part of the department and Eric used to treat him like a son.

I think Eric felt I was holding my own and gradually he allowed me to spend more time working with Terry Corben who managed the record department. I can recall The Moody Blues, Sony and Cher, The Rolling Stones, The Beatles, Frank Sinatra, amongst many other artists who were selling well around this time. By all accounts – apart from Weston Hart, a local chain selling what we were selling – the Co-op was highly respected by the record industry and was classed as the most important account in the South of England. One thing I do recall vividly was that I bought The Beatles' 'A Hard Day's Night' with my first pay packet. I had been in awe of them ever since I first heard 'Please Please Me' on the radio at school as I came down the staircase to the front lobby. The sound was amazing, I had heard nothing like it before.

I could tell early on I was more interested in working in the record department than with radio and TV. I began to become fascinated as to how the whole industry worked, the differences between one record company and another, why artists signed for one record company rather than another. I got on well with 'reps' as they were known, and there was this strange arrangement whereby you could buy The Beatles' releases and back catalogue from Decca Records, although they were signed to EMI. Selecta used to distribute Decca Records and I believe they were wholly owned by Decca.

While all this was fascinating, I could tell early on that the success of our record department depended on getting the stock under control. Admittedly these were not perishable goods we were selling, but overstocks could wipe out any profit you had made and generally the record companies would only allow you to return about 5% of what you ordered. So, the skill to be acquired was judging how many to order of a new release – in some cases, none at all – and then once the singles or albums began to sell, working out how many you reorder. Terry Corben, who basically managed the record department, allowed me to take risks, based normally on customer enquiries or demand. I think he enjoyed working more as a TV and radio salesman so that allowed me to learn the ropes quicker than I expected.

Socially, Eric would take us to the Co-operative Employees Club on a Friday night in Fratton Rd and afterwards we would go for a curry near the Kings Theatre in Southsea. I recall Eric eating these amazing hot vindaloos and sweating like a pig during and after the meal. Life for me in general around the mid-60s was great and I loved my job, and I loved working with Eric, Mick, Tony, Terry and Barry.

We were still living at Brompton Rd but I used to go to Christina's for lunch at Froddington Rd, which was about a ten-minute walk from the Co-op. I was still under eighteen so Miss Crisp also used to keep in touch with me. I liked her a lot, she was genuinely interested in all the family and she would arrange for me to visit Tom and Enda at weekends. They both seemed very happy where they were, and I suppose despite my outburst outside the court, the decision was the right one, as my father was never capable of looking after them.

Being at boarding school meant I never made any friends in Portsmouth, so although I was about seventeen, I didn't go out at weekends. However, life at the Co-op got even better as Eric employed two lads of a similar age to me as

'Saturday Boys'. One was Peter Renwick and the other one was James Wright. Eric gave me the job of training them in all aspects of the department, which I thoroughly enjoyed.

After a few weeks we met up one Saturday night in Southsea for a drink and it was clear early on that we were going to become good friends. At Ramsgate I had lots of friends, but my best friends were John Kerrigan and Charles Anstis. John was a similar age to me, and I believe he may have been in my form, but Charles was a few years older than me, and he eventually became Head Boy of the school. I cannot remember how we became friends but it was probably through music, and we were to remain great friends even after I ran away from school. He was full of fun I recall, good at most sports, which I wasn't, and I became very fond of him. Out of the blue a letter arrived from him at Brompton Rd saying he wanted to come and visit me, something I immediately said yes to and within a week or so he turned up. I think it was a Sunday morning. Charles was the life and soul of the party and loud, and very posh. He arrived early so I was the only one up. He suggested we went out somewhere for breakfast and I thought Southsea seafront might be a good idea. I was so excited to see him, he was, looking back, the older brother I never had, and we got on like a house on fire. I don't know where he lived, except that it was in London, but I began for the first time in my life to realise we may be living in a poor area compared with where he lived. His accent was certainly not a Portsmouth one and judging by the looks on people's faces in Southsea, he certainly stood out.

I was beginning to grow up slowly. I had a good job, I had made some good friends through the Co-op, and I had kept my friendships with Charles Anstis, Fr Stephen and Fr Dominic from Ramsgate. Eventually, though, Charles and I lost touch with one another and despite my efforts to find him, I met with little success, until one day I found the phone number of his brother, Stefan. I called him excitedly, only to hear that Charles had died just a few months before in his early sixties. Devastating news, a truly lovely man.

I was growing also in confidence in the record department, and eventually Eric asked me if I would join Terry Corben as a DJ on a Friday night at the Co-op Employees Club. I guess we're talking around 1967, it was an offer I couldn't refuse. During the day at work Terry and Eric were impressed with my judgement on stock and I even got a pay rise!

Now and then we used to get written enquiries from customers or complaints, both of which needed to be replied to. Eric would often give them to me to deal with. After I had written out the reply in longhand, I needed to get it typed on official Co-op headed paper. I asked Eric, where? I was pointed in the direction of the secretary of the Dry Goods Trade's Manager, who resided at the other end of the floor I was on. I knocked on her door, introduced myself and asked the secretary if she would type this letter for me. She was pretty and had a great big warm smile on her face, and over the next few weeks I began to see more of her, as Eric liked my responses to customers' letters. She was cheeky, and I have to admit I rather fancied her.

Deep down I was very shy, and I had no experience with the opposite sex. There was a girl that everyone fancied on our floor who I think was a bit of a tease, she was very sexy but as soon as you showed any interest in her she would disappear and go off talking to other blokes. No, my interest was with the secretary of the Dry Goods Trade's Manager – he was Tom Beech, and he was basically the big boss of the Co-op in Fratton Rd. His secretary was Sue Middlemist and very good at her job. She was a shorthand typist, something I never knew existed, and she was pretty impressive. To my delight she used to turn up at the Co-op Employees Club on a Friday night with her friend Jean Bonney, she was a nice girl too, and all three of us got on well.

To my surprise one Friday night this guy came up to me and Terry Corben after we had done our DJ session for the evening and asked us if we would like to do a similar job at the Mecca Ballroom in Arundel Street. Well, we were rather taken aback, we didn't think we were anything special, but we immediately said yes, and started there the following Monday night, doing three forty-five-minute spots when the local big band, Jack Hawkins, wasn't playing. I think we got about £2 each, which was pretty good money considering my weekly wage was then about £6.

Terry and I had come up with stage names, as the Mecca boss didn't think Brian McLaughlin and Terry Corben were dynamic enough for DJs. Eventually we agreed on Johnny Star for me and Tony Power for Terry! And I have to say Monday nights at the Mecca were full, over a thousand people dancing and drinking. They were fun nights and Terry and I used to play some good music, which we were told the paying customers liked. I've forgotten the name of the boss there, but we got on well. That eventually landed me in trouble with Terry.

We were behind the counter one day at the Co-op when Terry took a call. I could tell by his face he wasn't very happy and once he put the phone down, he said I was to call the manager at the Mecca, then stormed off. I called the boss. He said, 'I want you to do a Thursday night session as well as Mondays and I want you to do it on your own.' I said, 'What, without Terry?' He said, 'Yes, without Terry, and I'm going to pay you £10 per week.' I was flabbergasted and said I wanted to think about it, as Terry and I not only worked together, but we were good friends. This was very tricky for me. I wanted the job, but I didn't want to fall out with Terry.

When Terry came back he had a face like thunder on him, and asked how I managed to get the club to give me an extra night and to get him the sack? I explained that honestly I had nothing to do with it and that I wouldn't take the offer if it meant us falling out. But he said I should take it – he knew it wasn't my fault and said that it wouldn't affect our relationship. Although I was relieved, I could tell he was hurt, and hurt badly. Going forward he kept his word, we continued to get on well and eventually I could see he was very pleased for me, even to the extent of suggesting records I might want to play in one of my sessions.

Financially, the extra night at the Mecca made a huge difference to my weekly income, in fact the two nights' pay at the Mecca was nearly double as much as I was earning at the Co-op for five full days!

Both nights, I was told by the manager, were very successful and I was popular with the audience. In between my sessions I used to go to the pub across the road with a few other pals from the Mecca. The most I would have would be a couple of pints, but the downside of these nights were that they were late, and I still had work to get up for the next morning.

Sue, the boss's secretary, and her friend, Jean, started coming to the Mecca on both nights and although I would be working, we always managed to meet up afterwards and head for Southsea seafront and eat fish and chips. They were both good fun, but I was now getting home even later, which eventually got me into big trouble with my boss. I was turning up late for work after these late nights out, and although for a while Eric turned a blind eye, it reached the point whereby he called me into his office. Basically, he was very unhappy with me, he felt I had a future at the Co-op but this continuing lateness would no longer be tolerated. I had to improve my timekeeping or find another job. This was one of life's wake-up calls, and frankly I was shocked at the thought I would lose my job. It had the right effect, and I was never late again.

At home, Dad was arriving home later and later, and we were not getting enough housekeeping money from him. Christina decided that we were all going to move to her house, which we did for a few months. Dad, meanwhile, was spending Friday and Saturday evenings at the Irish Club in Fratton Rd, not far from there. Although he never said anything, we found out through a friend that he was seeing a lady who he supposedly met at the Irish Club. Her name was Sheila. We were all rather surprised as although Mum had been dead for over four years he had never seemed to be interested in any other women. Eventually we got to meet her at the Irish Club one Friday night. Frances, Christina and Brian McCreadie, Christina's husband, were all there. Sheila Hardy was her name, she was small, quite thin, and very unattractive, with thick glasses. She clearly took an instant dislike to all of us as she sat very close to Dad, holding his hand, and virtually ignoring us.

As for me, I was doing well at the Co-op, thoroughly enjoying learning about the record business and pleased too with how things were going at the Mecca. These nights were very memorable – we had the Jack Hawkins band playing and, in addition, one night per week they had a live act. I can recall the Small Faces, Geno Washington & the Ram Jam Band, and Amen Corner. Amen Corner was nothing short of a riot, the girls just screamed and screamed, and eventually stormed the stage. The band ran for their lives, and I know I was asked to help get these young girls off the stage, some of whom had clearly hurt themselves.

I also remember having a run-in with Eddie Floyd, famous for his hit single 'Knock on Wood'. I was due back on stage at 11 p.m. and Eddie wasn't getting off! I asked my manager what to do and he said get him off. The stage was circular, and by pressing a button, it moved clockwise, allowing another artist, or in my case a DJ, to do their set. So, I pressed the button. As Eddie was disappearing, he was shouting, 'Hey Mr DJ, you can't do this, Mr DJ, you can't do this, I'm Eddie Floyd!' Anyhow, it was all resolved, and I was just looking forward to going to the seafront for fish and chips with Sue and Jean.

Jean had a black Morris Minor and she always drove, because (a) it was her car, and (b) because Sue and I couldn't drive! We used to take turns in who sat in the front with Jean. It's fair to say that the three of us were getting along just fine. Sue was the good-looking one, she also was full of fun. Jean was lovely too, but quieter than Sue, I was very fond of both of them. We had developed a wonderful friendship and had so many laughs together.

One night we were on our way to my house after eating our fish and chips and I was in the front of the car with Jean. I jokingly said to Sue, if she kept taking the mickey out of me, I would end up joining her in the back! I had by now fallen for Sue and I was trying to work out how I could make a move without upsetting Jean. Clearly there was a lot of flirting going on between Sue and me. It wasn't the same between Jean and me, so I decided once we arrived outside my house, I would indeed join Sue in the back!

There was lots of laughter and banter but then it all went quiet as I kissed Sue. Fortunately, I was not rebuffed and to this day it was still one of the most daring things I have ever done, but with an outcome I was thrilled with. None of this lasted long, as both Sue and I had regard for Jean's feelings. We didn't have to wait long to find out what these were! She immediately turned the engine on and said, 'Goodnight Brian.' So I got out of the car as Jean tore away up Brompton Rd. But I was in heaven, completely in love!

Dad, Frances and I had decided to move back to Brompton Rd. Christina had too much on her hands at Froddington Rd, looking after her family. Frances would be looking after us now, and she did a really good job on little housekeeping money, although I paid my way.

I couldn't get Sue out of my mind. I was so happy and all I wanted to do was to see her again. As soon as I next arrived at work, I came up with an excuse to go and see her in her office, only to be told she hadn't turned up due to a family illness. I phoned her home several times over the weekend, but the phone was either engaged or just went on ringing. Eventually, I went to her house in Campbell Rd, and asked her mum if I could see her. She said yes I could, but not for long, as she was very upset. She came to the door and broke the news that her sister Diane had died due to an asthma attack. This was just dreadful news, and poor Sue was very upset. I felt unable to be of any real help to her. She said she would be in touch after the funeral, which would take place in a few days.

Meanwhile, my friends from the Co-op and I all had scooters, of varying degrees of roadworthiness. Peter Renwick, our Saturday boy, had a lovely almost brand-new Lambretta and he dressed like someone from a shop window.

He had this amazing brand-new parker and gloves, and he looked the business, in fact very dapper indeed! John and I had scooters too, but while his was fine in looks and roadworthiness, mine failed on both fronts. I hadn't paid a lot of money for it but, apart from the noise, it was working.

We all decided to plan a trip to Brighton one Sunday and agreed to set off early. It was a sunny day, we were all in good form and set off from Portsmouth along the A27. Everything was going well until we hit this stretch of dual carriageway near Littlehampton. As if from nowhere, a policeman on a motorbike pulled ahead of us, signalling with his arm for us to pull over – this we duly did. He asked several questions, why were we going to Brighton, etc. We had to show driving licences, which we all had. But clearly, he took a real interest in my bike which, as I said, didn't look great, and he started inspecting it closely. After a few minutes, he declared the bike unroadworthy and that he was going to report me, which would lead to a court appearance. He suggested we turn back and go home. We decided to ignore this advice and carry on to Brighton!

No sooner had we got to Arundel I got confused with the local road signs and ended up going down a one-way street the wrong way. To make matters worse, it was downhill and, all of a sudden, I realised my brakes weren't working and consequently at around 20 mph I collided with this building in front of me, which turned out to be the police station! My bike and I were on the floor, a policeman came outside and shouted, 'Turn that bloody thing off, and get inside here.' I was petrified, given our earlier dealings with the police at Littlehampton. He asked what had happened. I told him the brakes had failed. He said, 'That bike is not only worthless, it's bloody dangerous.' He then issued me with another document that would ultimately lead to another court appearance! The bike was to remain with him and would be scrapped. We decided therefore not to attempt Brighton and headed back to Portsmouth! The other guys found it all hilarious and couldn't stop laughing, and I suppose even I, in the end, could see the funny side of colliding with a police station, having just been previously booked at Littlehampton.

Having relayed this story to my boss Eric, he said he would lend me the money to buy a good second-hand Lambretta and I could pay him back in weekly instalments. This I agreed to, and I was thrilled to be able to go to the shop in New Rd and choose a decent bike. From owning an unroadworthy bike to this fabulous, fairly new Lambretta. I was suitably chuffed, and my friends were impressed. However, not long after owning it, disaster happened!

I was unusually late for work one Monday morning and I approached a set of traffic lights at Lake Rd as they began to change from green to amber. In a split second of madness, I decided to keep going. The next thing I know I was laying in the road with a lot of people around me. I'd hit a car but fortunately I was unhurt apart from a bruised arm and a few scratches. I was taken to hospital as a precaution and the police asked to see me for a statement. On top of making that daft decision not to stop on amber, I then proceeded to lie to the police saying that the lights were green when I went through, and the car driver was to blame. Eventually, I had to attend court as the car driver's insurance company believed him and was not prepared to pay for my written-off Lambretta. The magistrate listened to my version of events and decided, rightly, not to believe me.

Obviously, Eric was very disappointed with me and although I offered to carry on paying him back for his generous loan, he said he would write it off. That was the end of me and scooters, I was lucky to be alive given the madness of my trip to Brighton and my appalling decision not to stop at the lights.

Following the sad death of Sue's sister, we started to go out regularly as a couple. I'd fallen deeply in love with her and found each minute of the day without her difficult to come to terms with. She continued to come with me to the Mecca, although not with Jean any more. That relationship took some time to heal.

On 3 January 1968, Sue and I got engaged. It was a double celebration as it was also Sue's twenty-first birthday. I wasn't too sure what her mum and dad thought of me, but they were both kind and decent people. They lived in a big house in Campbell Rd, Southsea. It was wide and tree-lined, with very big three- and four-storey houses on both sides of the road. Their house was three storeys, her mum and dad lived on the ground floor, her nan and aunt lived on the first floor and Sue lived on the top floor. They appeared to be a normal, middle-class family. Sue had an older sister, Molly, who was married to Dave, and they lived nearby. Sue's dad was one of the nicest guys you could meet, ex-RAF, a huge Pompey Football Club supporter and worked locally in a factory. Her mum was also a big Pompey fan. She called the shots in the household, with Sue's dad opting for a quiet life. Sue and I would go out with friends during the week, drinking at our favourite pubs, the Monkton near North End and The Still & West in Old Portsmouth. She would be at my house in Brompton Rd some evenings too, and we would play records on my Marconiphone gramophone. She got on well with my dad and the rest of the family, and clearly they were happy for both of us.

I will always remember asking Sue's dad for his permission to marry his daughter. As soon as Sue said yes, I went and asked her mum. She said, 'You had better ask Bill, he deals with those kinds of things.' I was nervous all day. After dinner I made sure Sue and her mum were in another room. I went into the back room where Bill was watching television. I gingerly approached him and asked his permission to marry his daughter. He replied, 'Of course you can, now move out of the way of the television, I'm watching football.' So, with that all sorted, Sue and I agreed we would marry on 28 September that year. That would be one year on exactly from our kiss in the back of Jean's car.

At my home in Brompton Rd, life carried on much the same until Dad told us that he was moving out, and moving in with Sheila, his new girlfriend, who was shortly to become his second wife. She lived in a very nice part of Portsmouth,

Mayfield Rd, in North End. The house was spotlessly clean and contained lovely furniture and several antiques. Unfortunately, Sheila only wanted my dad and made it quite clear to us that we were not welcome. They married later that year and the wedding breakfast was held at the Queen's Hotel Southsea, the best hotel in the region. We were all invited, and our lasting memory of the occasion was Sheila bursting into song. It took everyone by surprise, we had no indication that she enjoyed singing – we certainly didn't enjoy it, it was painful!

After Dad moved out of Brompton Rd, so too did Frances and I. Frances was married to a guy called Chris, a thoroughly unlikeable individual. They rented an apartment in Southsea. Sue's mum agreed I could stay in Campbell Rd – in Sue's flat, but not in Sue's bed! Most people won't believe we never slept together until our wedding night, but it's the truth.

So, Brompton Rd, our home for many, many years, was empty and I had no idea what Dad intended to do about it. I used to call in there from time to time, but it wasn't getting cleaned so it wasn't any surprise to learn that Dad told the landlady he didn't require the property any more. However, what we didn't know is that Sheila handled the disposal of the furniture and the general contents without consulting anyone. This terrible decision led to the destroying of all our family photographs, correspondence and history going back nearly thirty years. Birth certificates, medical certificates – both were destroyed, as was our whole family history, by a stranger who had no understanding of our family or the memories associated with all the stuff she disposed of so carelessly. Was I surprised? No, my dad never handled anything well, and this was just another classic example of his incompetence. To this day, I have never forgiven them both for destroying our family memories, and it still hurts, over fifty years later.

The wedding date was still set for 28 September and we decided to get married in the Registry Office, as Sue's mum was against us getting married in the Catholic church, which I would have preferred. She had a bad childhood experience with Catholic nuns and it had left a bitter taste. Sue had no strong views either way, and I didn't want to cause any unpleasantness between us and Sue's mum. She had been good to us both and it was no big deal to give up the Catholic wedding.

I worked hard at my job and I was almost running the record department as Terry continued to spend more time on TV and radio selling. This hard work paid off as I was given a pay rise and was also allowed to collate all the orders from the other Co-op branches in Hampshire. The turnover involved wasn't huge, but it added to our status as a serious record retailer in Portsmouth.

Preparations for the wedding were well underway when Sue received the terrible news that her dad was suffering from lung cancer and only had six months to live. This was devastating news for her and her family having just lost Diane to an asthma attack. Bill didn't want any fuss and continued to go to work, he was in very good form considering.

My best friend from school, Charles Anstis, agreed to be my best man at our wedding. Sue liked him a lot, which was obviously important to me. Sue and I were very nervous as the day approached but for me, I was also excited. I was madly in love with Sue and couldn't wait for us to be married, living together, and starting a family. Her mum and dad allowed us to rent the top floor flat in Campbell Rd and as a wedding present bought us a fabulous new carpet for the lounge. The flat wasn't that big, but it was nicely decorated, and we were both looking forward to making our home there.

So, the big day arrived, and Sue and I were married at the Registry Office in Southsea, accompanied by several members of both families, including my brother Pat, who I still had little time for. Sue looked amazing, all in white with the biggest smile I have ever seen! The wedding breakfast was organised and paid for by Sue's mum and dad and they chose the Victory restaurant in Southsea. We had a private room upstairs. Everything appeared to be going well, there was no falling out between the various families, until Sue's mum came over to see me to say she was very disappointed that my stepmother

Sheila had chosen to eat on her own in the restaurant downstairs! I cannot remember whether she had already eaten with us but knowing Sheila she probably had! This was very rude, and Sue's mum was not only livid but very upset. This was somewhat typical of my family life, there was always an incident on big occasions, but to my complete surprise this time it did not involve my Irish relatives.

After this incident Sue and I were rather keen to get away, we were staying in London overnight and next day we were flying from Luton to Calella in Spain for our honeymoon. Neither of us had stayed in London before, we had not slept together, and we had never been on an aeroplane. The travel agent we used must have been good as they chose a lovely bed and breakfast for us near Victoria, and I still distinctly remember us eating at a little Italian restaurant nearby. We had a blissful evening, and the disappointment of Sheila's behaviour was now a distant memory. We were up bright and early and on our way to Luton.

The whole experience was wonderful, we arrived in Calella in hot sunshine, and were bussed to our hotel, which was large and very busy. I think it's now called a package holiday. All in all we had a lovely time, meeting a nice couple and enjoying Spain. We were both so happy together and so much in love.

Meanwhile, on returning to work, rumours began circulating that HMV were due to open in Commercial Rd in Portsmouth. For me they were the best. I had only once been to their store in Oxford Street. It was such an impressive operation, and their Dog and Trumpet logo to me was a brand as famous as Rolls-Royce.

You turn right out of Bond Street tube station and there you will see this huge emporium of records over three or four floors. The Co-op was a department store and did not specialise in one type of trade, they sold everything. Unlike HMV, which only sold records and was the best in Britain. Standing outside this hugely imposing shopfront, only displaying records rather than fridges or carpets, I was literally overwhelmed with joy just to be there. I wanted to work for them.

I sent off a letter to HMV in Oxford Street asking if there were any vacancies and I received a reply a few days later from Mr R. Boast, the General Manager. He invited me to attend an interview at the store in two days' time. Obviously, I was very nervous, as I had only been to a couple of interviews before, and I needed to be at my best for this one. The only preparation I did was to try and memorise the Top 10 in singles and my favourite artists.

I was shown into Mr Boast's office by a very pleasant young lady who was his secretary. He duly arrived, a rather large character with a black moustache and receding hair. Spoke rather fast and rather posh. He was pleasant enough and confirmed they would be opening in Portsmouth in November and asked me questions about my current employer, my experience and general interests. He did however strike me as someone not that close to music as he became rather evasive if you mentioned any artists in particular. I think he thought he threw me when he asked me to name the Top 6 in the correct order. I knew I didn't know the answer, but I also took a gamble that he didn't either, as he only had a blank sheet of paper in front of him. I decided to give him an answer that was pure guesswork on my part, and he said, 'Well done, you will be hearing from us.'

I left his office feeling rather pleased with myself but a week or so went by and I never heard anything from him. I explained to the local sales reps what happened and one of them said, why not join us tomorrow night at our drinks reception at the Pendragon Hotel in Southsea where you can meet the new manager of the HMV store?

I duly made it to the drinks reception courtesy of EMI Records and was introduced to the HMV manager, Chris Rimmer. EMI Records owned HMV shops so obviously they would be very keen to have a new store in Portsmouth showcasing even more of their records. Chris was an extremely pleasant guy and knew of me via Bob Boast. He told me that I hadn't heard back from him because the manager's position had already been given to him. I replied that I never applied for the manager's position, I would be just as happy being a sales assistant. By the end of the evening, Chris had offered me a sales assistant's position at £9 per week. I was already on £9 per week with the Co-op, so I was expecting to be earning more with HMV, and I was quite sure Sue would think the same too. I asked Chris if anything could be done to improve the wage and he said he would make enquiries. True to his word, he did come back to me and raised the offer to £11 per week, which I accepted. My start date was to be 11 November.

I spoke at length about this with Sue obviously, but once the deed was done and I had to resign from the Co-op I began to have second thoughts. I was a very cautious individual and lacked any form of confidence in myself. I kept saying to her, what if that happens, what if they do this, what if they go bust, etc., etc. Fortunately, Sue had more faith in me than I did and eventually she convinced me that HMV was where I would be happy, selling records exclusively and not having to worry about selling TVs and radios in between.

I felt bad about resigning; Eric, Terry, Mick and the gang were so good to me. I felt I belonged to a huge family as I got to know many people in the store from the various other departments. Eric was disappointed but understood why I would want to work for a specialist record retailer rather than the Co-op. He did try to match the HMV offer of £11 per week, but even then, I knew it wasn't about the money. There was something hugely exciting working for the best in the business, an opportunity basically too good to turn down.

I began my job as planned on 11 November and Chris introduced me to Tina, another sales assistant. The store actually opened for business on the 9th and Chris reported that although sales were OK, there was nevertheless a lot of people browsing. It was a long narrow store in a good location on Commercial Rd next door to an umbrella store, Salisburys, one side and a shoe shop, Clarks, on the other side. It was bright, with browsers on the left-hand wall from back to front and freestanding browsers in the remaining space either side of the gangway. I was impressed immediately with the neon HMV sign outside the store and the professional graphics inside. Graphics at the Co-op were normally made by the Works Dept, and it showed! There was a small counter at the back on the left-hand wall, an office with a rear entrance and, on the right-hand wall, a listening booth.

Clearly, the more I worked with Chris, my manager, I realised how little I actually knew about music. Our range at the Co-op, it turns out, was pretty limited compared with HMV and that was largely down to Chris's knowledge and experience. He was a very likeable individual, very quiet and very shy. You wondered why he became store manager as he didn't strike me as the sort of person who would be happy with authority. However, what he lacked in management skills, he made up for with his encyclopaedic knowledge of music. As each day went by, we responded to our customers enquiries by expanding the range and our customers returned again and again. While the Co-op stocked mainly pop music, HMV had an outstanding selection of jazz and blues, country, classical, films and shows; it was, in my opinion, a proper record store based on the values of the huge HMV store in London, which dates back to 1921.

Chapter 10

On 21 July 1921 Sir Edward Elgar, the celebrated British composer and conductor, officially opened a new record store in London's Oxford Street. It was, quite possibly, the world's first ever instore personal appearance. More significantly, the launch also signalled a transforming moment in popular culture. HMV's massive new store was the first to catch the burgeoning demand for recorded music, opening the way for an extraordinary revolution in consumer shopping trends and public aspirations.

Although HMV's original Oxford Street store has since relocated to a larger site across the road, its legacy as the 'world's most famous record store' lives on. In particular, it set the template for record retailing as we know it, anticipating many of the superstore trends that have become part of today's high street. In its early years HMV stocked not only gramophones and radios, but also popular recordings from music hall stars of the day. It additionally carried classical works and a full range of sheet music by the artists signed to the Gramophone Company, which owned the store and used it as a showcase for its products. The Gramophone Company, of course, was later to become the renowned EMI Records.

HMV pre-empted many retail trends; the store was a lavish entertainment experience in itself, boasting a luxury interior of wood panelling and oil paintings, fine carpets and comfortable seating areas that were more in keeping with a country home. The exterior featured fantastic window displays that highlighted new releases and major events, while the façade was embellished by 'the most striking illuminated electric motion sign yet seen in London'. The front-of-store logo – 50-ft wide by 30-ft high – featured the huge outline of a man placing a record on the revolving turntable of an 'His Master's Voice' gramophone. The sign came complete with musical notes lighting up around the turntable, and included the names of leading artists like Caruso, Gigli, Melba and Heifetz, which were highlighted by red arrows two at a time.

All this was highly innovatory at the time, and was a key factor in helping to lay the foundation of HMV's rich heritage. No other record retailer can claim such a significant role in shaping the way that access to music has progressed from the concert hall to the home.

Mark Barraud was a Victorian painter, who was employed by the Prince's Theatre, Bristol as a scenic artist. In 1884 he brought home a puppy – part fox terrier, part Jack Russell – for his children. They called the dog Nipper and it lived happily with the family for three years. Unfortunately, Barraud died unexpectedly, and the family was split up, with the five young children being sent to schools and convents as orphans.

There was, however, no provision for the family pet until Nipper attached himself to Francis Barraud (1856–1924), one of Mark's younger brothers. Francis, a talented artist, took the dog to the Liverpool home of yet another of the Barraud brothers who had recently acquired a brand-new invention, a 'talking machine' called the phonograph. Nipper's engrossed response to the record player was to become the inspiration for one of the world's most enduring and recognised trademarks.

'It is difficult to say how the idea came to me beyond the fact that it suddenly occurred to me that to have my dog listening to the phonograph, with an intelligent and rather puzzled expression, and call it "His Master's Voice" would make an excellent subject,' Barraud later recalled. 'We had a phonograph and I often noticed how puzzled he was to make out where the voice came from. It was certainly the happiest thought I ever had.'

Barraud visited the Gramophone Company – newly formed in 1897 – to borrow one of their brass horns for the painting. The painting initially featured a phonograph, but one year later (1898) this was subsequently painted out and replaced by a gramophone after the company paid the sum of £100 to acquire the painting and the copyright. Nipper made his first appearance illustrating an advertising supplement in January 1900.

In the following years, the Dog and Trumpet painting was used on everything from needle boxes to promotional novelties. By 1910 the Gramophone Company had also registered the words 'His Master's Voice' as a trademark, to be subsequently used as the name of a record label and, of course, the company's first shop. Today, only the initials are commonly used – the HMV chain owes its name to the inspiration of a Victorian painter and his dog.

* * *

In the 1920s and 30s, HMV in Oxford Street became one of London's landmark stores. Its interior was fabulously designed in the prevailing art deco style, the clean lines of its architecture emphasised by the elegant simplicity of the store's furnishings and signage. HMV was the epitome of aspirational living, a monument to modern taste.

During this time, the store sold only HMV goods which, by the 30s, included records of such burgeoning American styles as jazz, swing and dance band music. Everything, however, was destroyed in a blaze that swept the building on Boxing Day, 1937. It took 250 firemen to bring it under control, by which time the entire building was gutted: It was London's biggest fire since the Crystal Palace had been destroyed, nearly a century before. The company took temporary premises at 104 Bond Street until, on 8 May 1939, HMV's Oxford Street store was officially reopened for business by the celebrated conductor, Sir Thomas Beecham. Four months later it was hit by another minor obstacle: the start of World War II.

For the next six years HMV Oxford Street stocked patriotic music and 'forces sweethearts' records, at the same time defiantly displaying 'Business as Usual' signs in shop windows that incorporated hinged panels and hoardings designed for the blackout and air-raid precautions. The store was, in fact, designated an official air-raid shelter by Westminster Council.

The parent EMI company's factory in Hayes, Middlesex, was turned over to munitions manufacture, and shellac – the raw material for 78-rpm records – was in short supply. The HMV store therefore also became a major collection point for the public to bring in old records to be recycled: An initiative that allowed the music industry to continue even despite the wartime hardships.

* * *

From the company's earliest days, EMI had franchised HMV's products exclusively to one record and electrical store in every major town around Britain. This system was abandoned in the mid-50s, however, when Sir Joseph Lockwood became EMI's Managing Director. He made HMV's records and electrical goods available to all dealers – thereby paving the way for HMV to stock rival products and opening the door to real high street competition.

The move came just in time for the rock 'n' roll explosion that was at the centre of an emerging youth culture. Indeed, one meeting at the HMV Oxford

Street store – on 8 February 1962 – played a decisive role in helping to shape the very direction of popular music.

The store's manager Bob Boast, who conducted my initial interview, had become friendly with a Liverpool entrepreneur called Brian Epstein who visited HMV with a demo tape of a band he was managing. In those days the store had a small cutting room for transferring music from tape to 78-rpm discs. Epstein had been trying to get a deal for his band – The Beatles – but had been rejected by Decca, EMI and other companies, he now needed more demo discs to continue in his search for a contract.

HMV's disc cutter, Jim Foy, was immediately impressed by what he heard and called Sid Coleman, the General Manager of music publishers, Ardmore & Beechwood, who had offices in the building. Coleman proved equally enthusiastic and on realising that Epstein was seeking a recording deal rather than a publishing contract, called a contact at EMI's small Parlophone label – George Martin. A meeting was arranged and within a few months, in June 1962, The Beatles – freshly signed to Parlophone – arrived at EMI's famous Abbey Rd studios to record a new single 'Please Please Me'. The 60s revolution in pop music was about to begin.

Over the next seven years there was a massive upswing in business as the music industry found itself at the epicentre of a huge cultural shift. It was to prove, in particular, a decade when albums, rather than singles, were to become the primary vehicle for selling music: UK production of LPs escalated from 17 million units in 1960 to 66 million ten years later, nearly a fourfold increase. It was a period of maximum confidence and, for the first time, HMV grasped the opportunity to expand from its Oxford Street headquarters. By the end of the decade, there were fifteen new stores throughout London; the modern face of HMV was beginning to emerge.

* * *

When I joined HMV in November 1968, there were nine stores including HMV Oxford Street. The other eight stores were predominately acquired by buying small rival chains that owed EMI Records money. These included the chain Rimington Van Wyck, and Saville Pianos. From the Saville's chain, Mike Donaghue (Ilford) and Brian Strong (Wood Green) were appointed Area Managers along with Godfrey Channon from Enfield. Head Office sent weekly sales figures for the chain and it was always great to see that under Chris's leadership Portsmouth was usually the best performing store, apart from 363 Oxford Street. By the end of the decade HMV had fifteen stores, mainly in the London area. They were all mostly small units and often in secondary locations. Looking at the weekly sales figures one could easily tell that the chain was not performing well and this led to Chris telling me that Bob Boast, the General Manager, and Brian Strong, the Area Manager, would be paying us a visit soon to discuss the future. This did not bode well despite the fact that HMV Portsmouth continued to perform exceptionally well. Bob and Brian duly arrived a few days later and spent most of the morning with Chris.

To cut a long story short, Bob informed Chris that the chain was in difficulties and was losing money. Cost-cutting measures would be introduced immediately, which meant that one member of staff was to be made redundant from each store, immaterial of whether they were performing well or not based on last in, first out principle. This meant there would only be two of us working in the store and at this stage I wasn't sure who would have to go, me or Tina. Fortunately for me, it turned out that Tina joined shortly after me, which meant she had to go. On top of this ridiculous decision, Bob Boast told Chris we were to start selling greeting cards within a few weeks due to the higher margins that could be achieved. As a consequence, he told us that the complete left-hand wall of browsers for albums would have to go and be replaced with greeting card display stands. Chris and I were in total shock, we were purely a record store being asked to give up a third of our space to records and replace it with greeting cards. It was the most ridiculous plan I had ever heard. It was, if implemented, destined to ruin our store and put us into a loss-making situation along with all the others.

Fortunately, the greeting card plan was scrapped but Chris and I had to run the shop with just the two of us, which we found out was not an easy task.

A new General Manager called Trevor Timmers was appointed and Ken Whitmarsh was promoted to manager of the flagship store in Oxford Street. Mr Timmers made little impact in the short time he was with us and after a few months he was replaced by a guy called Dave Wilde who was to have a lasting and significant impact on me and the future of HMV. Dave came to visit us at Portsmouth and told us what a remarkable job we were doing. The shop was the second-most profitable store and most importantly, Dave was most impressed with the range that was on offer to our customers. HMV had a policy of allowing its store managers to develop and promote its range to suit the local community, and as I was to find out many years later, this was a unique skill and not everyone could acquire it!

Dave joined from Debenhams whereby he was in charge of their fairly small record departments. I liked him the minute I set eyes on him, he was humble, and was a record man through and through. For HMV to prosper as a chain going forward it had to continue spreading the values and history of the famous store in Oxford Street, and I knew very quickly that Dave was the man to ensure this would happen.

I had enormous respect for Chris Rimmer, he had broadened my knowledge of music, he had taught me what would sell and what wouldn't sell in Portsmouth, and now we had a leader, Dave Wilde, that was going to put HMV on the map as a national chain.

My decision to leave the Co-op had been vindicated!

Chapter 11

Life was getting better for me. I had a new job in a company that specialised in music, it owned the famous Dog and Trumpet painting and it had the worlds' famous record store, His Master's Voice, in Oxford Street. On top of this, I had met the girl of my dreams, attractive, pretty and full of fun. She had even married me!

Between us, we put in a lot of work to make our flat in Campbell Rd cosy. It wasn't huge, but it was our home. After all those years at Brompton Rd with all its troubles, I now had a place of my own that I shared with someone who loved me. Life even got better still, because not long after we got married Sue told me she was pregnant. It was the most amazing news and we were both absolutely thrilled. Financially we had two salaries plus my wages from the Mecca Ballroom, so we were confident we could manage when Sue would have to give up work. We had a reasonable social life – we would visit Sue's sister and brother-in-law, Molly and Dave, and we would spend time too with my family, Christine, Brian and their children. Tom and Enda were being well looked after in the home in Cosham and Sue and I would see them on a regular basis taking them for days out. Frances had moved to Swindon and married Chris, much against my better wishes, I did not like that man.

I enjoyed living at Campbell Rd. We saw a great deal of Sue's family and her mum said she would buy us a second-hand car if we agreed to take Sue's dad to work in the mornings, ensuring he wouldn't catch cold while walking. We decided on a lovely red Hillman Minx, which transformed our lives, and we had no hesitation in taking Sue's dad to work. Sue's mum was a fairly opinionated woman and began taking great interest in who visited us throughout the week and at weekends. We began getting used to her saying, 'Why have you invited them round? I don't like them!' We would gingerly reply that they were lovely people and they were visiting us not her.

It was the first sign that although we loved our flat, we didn't have the privacy we needed and that eventually, if we could afford it, we would want to move to our own house. Sue was beginning to show her pregnancy and regularly attended her doctor's appointments as well as antenatal visits to the hospital. We both had absolute faith in her doctor, Dr Castle, but Sue was worried about the treatment she was receiving at the hospital. They clearly weren't very tolerant when she asked questions, dismissing them as nothing to worry about even when on her notes they would write things that did worry her. Sue became very apprehensive about having our baby at St Mary's and her mum and nan both shared this apprehension. Wonderfully, they agreed that Sue could have our baby privately at the Eddystone Nursing Home in Southsea where, incidentally, Sue was born. Her lovely nan covered the costs.

Our baby was due in the last week of August. Sue was well throughout her pregnancy. The nearer the date came, the more nervous I became. You think, will I make a good father, will Sue be OK giving birth, will the baby be OK? As we approached the last week of the month, nothing much was happening so I used to take Sue out over bumpy roads in the hope it might trigger a reaction from the baby! No such luck, but on the morning of 27 August 1969, Sue began having contractions. She wasn't sure, but we both felt that I should ring Matron at the Eddystone. Matron agreed that this pain could well be contractions starting and told me to bring her in. This I duly did, and I recall being extremely anxious and a nervous wreck. Sue was calm as usual, we kissed goodbye, and Matron said she would call me if there was any news to report. I remember vividly that it was a Wednesday and the shop closed for a half day at 1 p.m.

I have to say my nerves continued all morning, and as we were approaching closing time, I decided to phone the nursing home. Little did I know what sort of reception I was to receive from Matron on answering the phone!

I said, 'Hello Matron, this is Brian McLaughlin, have you any news on my wife?' Her response was, 'Mr McLaughlin, I am in the middle of delivering your baby, will you kindly bugger off and let me get on with it!'

With that she put down the phone. I was now even more anxious, praying that everything was going to go well for Sue and the baby. I locked up the store, got in my car, unwound my window and stuck my head out so I could check I wasn't going to reverse into the car behind me. However, as I wound the window up, I forgot to move my head inside and the window caught my lip as it closed. Needless to say, I was in agony, and I could feel the lip swelling up. I just thought, what a complete idiot Brian, but it did underline how nervous I was! I went home to Campbell Rd and Sue's mum made me some lunch. Not long after that, Matron called to say that I had become a father to a beautiful baby girl. Both mum and baby were doing well, and she said you might want to know that the baby was born a couple of minutes after your phone call! Clearly, I was absolutely delighted. Matron said I could call in later and see them.

It's difficult to describe in words your emotions when you see your wife just after she's given birth. Sue looked even more beautiful, sitting up in bed with her usual big smile on her face. And alongside her was a small cot, which was housing the most adorable little girl, who we called Louisa Jane. I was so proud of my wife, and I was so happy I could have jumped for joy on the spot. Baby was over 8 lb and Matron said she was in good health and had an amazing pair of lungs on her. That's all I wanted to hear!

I managed to tell the whole family that great news and I couldn't wait to go back to the nursing home the next day to bring both my girls home. I arrived early and Sue was ready, baby in arms to go home. I still have the photo of them with Matron near my car prior to going home. It was without doubt, the happiest moment of my life.

Sue's mum and dad were thrilled to see Sue and Louisa looking so well. This was not their first grandchild. They had four others. Richard and Robert from Diane and Keith, and Debbie and Darren from Molly and David.

Unfortunately, not long after Diane died, her husband Keith got up one morning in Campbell Rd, packed some suitcases, put the two boys in the car, and drove off. Sue's mum and dad, plus the rest of the family never heard from him again. To this day, Sue believes there was a fallout between her mum and Keith, something her mum always denied. But it meant the arrival of baby Louisa was a huge tonic for all the family and she was much loved by them and my own family too.

I soon found out that becoming a father was not all plain sailing. I was prepared for feeding during the night, which I was happy to do as and when required. But I didn't bargain for Louisa screaming from the moment I got home at night until I woke in the morning. At first, we just believed we were unlucky, and we just had to get on with it. But in the end, we took her to the doctor who diagnosed her with colic, something a lot of babies get through bottle-feeding. The medicine helped a great deal, but with little experience between us for bringing up a young baby, we had no routine for Louisa, meaning that she found it difficult to settle and often was awake in the middle of the night, when we weren't!

Apart from these downsides, we were both in awe of her. It was just wonderful watching her grow and develop, but above all to see her smile at six weeks old was just a joy to behold. Sue was proving to be both an excellent wife and mother, still managing to work a few hours at the Co-op in Fratton Rd, putting food on the table and looking after our lovely home. We couldn't have been happier as a couple with our life, I loved my new family, I had a great job working for a company I respected and admired. What possibly could go wrong?!

Well . . . There were management changes at the Mecca where I was a DJ on Monday and Thursdays. My boss was very supportive, and a decent individual. However, I came in on the Monday night to find out he had been sacked and a new guy was taking over.

It's funny in life, but immediately I didn't like the look of this guy, and I suspect the feeling was mutual. The goings-on in the Mecca hierarchy were no concern of mine, and although I would miss my previous boss, I had a job to do and had to get on with it. For the first couple of weeks nothing changed – I did the same hours, the customers seemed pleased with each show I did, so I had no reason to worry about the future. Anyhow, after my show on a Thursday, a couple of weeks later, the new boss asked to see me. He looked rather scary and stared at me a while before enquiring who gave me permission to leave the building between shows. Furthermore, who gave me permission to go to the pub across the road and consume alcohol on duty? I replied that I had always done this under the previous management and continued to do so under his management for the past three to four weeks. He angrily replied, 'You're out, I'm not having my staff in the pub across the road during working hours.' I said, 'But Mr–' He just said, 'Get out, you're sacked.'

I was absolutely astonished, I had hardly seen the man since he became my new boss, and when I did he never expressed an opinion on anything I was doing. I was in a state of total shock and wondered how I was going to break the news to Sue, who had lost most of her weekly wage since giving birth to Louisa. Financially it was a terrible blow, the pay from Mecca was basically about the same as we lost from Sue's salary and I just didn't know, with a new baby to feed and clothe, how we were going to manage.

HMV Portsmouth continued to be successful and Chris Rimmer and I were getting along fine. Because of my loss of earnings at the Mecca, Chris used to allow Sue to work in the shop on a needs-must basis, the extra cash coming in very handy in difficult times. With this and Sue's parents agreeing not to charge us as much rent we were above water but only just.

From a relatively early age I was interested in politics. Mainly, I suppose, because Mum and Dad were both Labour people, not activists, but staunch. I can recall one evening when they went out for a drink together, they had barely left the house when I ran down the road after them to tell them that Hugh Gaitskell, the Labour leader, had died.

I was a Harold Wilson fan and can remember him squeezing into Downing Street in 1964 and winning a landslide victory in 1966. He had plenty of charisma and always managed to win hands down in the Commons during prime minister's question time. Britain was not a happy country in the late 60s, lots of strikes, lots of rows in the Labour cabinet and within the party. In June 1970, Harold Wilson called a General Election and I wanted to help him get re-elected. They had Frank Judd, the Labour candidate's offices opposite my old house in Brompton Rd. I went to see them and offered my help on polling day, collecting people from their houses and taking them to the polls to register their vote for Labour. Edward Heath was leader of the opposition, a rather boring individual compared to Harold Wilson, and most people expected him to lose. I was fortunate to see Wilson in Queens Street, Portsea, during the election. The square was packed with people and it was a warm evening with some of the crowd heckling the prime minister about his relationship with George Brown, the foreign secretary. George had finally resigned after threatening to many times. He was unfortunately very fond of a drink.

Come polling day, the weather was good, the polls still pointed to a Labour victory and I worked really hard knocking on people's doors and getting them out to vote. I got home to Campbell Rd quite exhausted after a long day and as usual parked the car in the drive at the front of the house. Within five minutes of arriving Sue's mum appeared shouting and bawling at me. She was not happy that the car she bought us was covered in posters saying Vote for Frank Judd! Sue's mum and nan were both staunch Tories and they couldn't believe that there was a car in the drive covered in Labour posters! Sue's mum began to remind Sue that not only had she married a Roman Catholic, she also married a Labour supporter. The only compensation for them was that the Tories won unexpectedly and Heath became prime minister. But Frank Judd retained his seat in Portsmouth West. I felt all my efforts were not in vain, but it was some time before Sue's mum and nan spoke to me again!

Friends of ours were talking about buying their own home and that maybe we should do the same. It was something Sue and I dreamed about, but we didn't have the 20% deposit that was required to obtain a mortgage. My wages had improved at HMV, but we still had no savings, so buying our own home would have to wait. We discussed this with Sue's mum and dad over dinner one night and to our amazement, they said they would arrange a loan of up to £500 and we would repay them the interest on a monthly basis. This was wonderful news, and we couldn't wait to go out house-hunting for our new home.

Building societies weren't that helpful, their conditions and repayment schedules were quite tough given our earnings. Someone suggested we contact the local council, as apparently they did mortgages. We organised a meeting, the guy we saw couldn't have been more helpful and in fact their terms allowed us to borrow slightly more. We could just about afford houses up to £3,000 and we settled on one in Talbot Rd. A nice terraced house and we submitted our application to the council. The manager of the loan department called us in and said he had reviewed our application but felt we were a couple with some potential and therefore he was prepared to advance some more money allowing us to trade up to an even better house. He was like our guardian angel – we found a better one in St Pirans Avenue in Copnor and we were thrilled. Once all the legals were sorted we moved in within about two months with our young baby. We could not have been happier.

At work, business was good. The HMV store was very popular in Portsmouth, mainly due to Chris's product knowledge and his deep understanding of the local market. The strange thing about him though was that he often stayed very late in the evenings and then arrived late in the mornings. It was often therefore difficult for me to do the banking once I arrived, if I was on my own, and had to keep an eye on the store. Head Office had a guy called Harry Shave, he was like an auditor. He would turn up at your store unannounced, and boy, you were in big trouble if the banking wasn't deposited at the bank or the figures entered in the daily report were wrong. Chris got himself into all sorts of scrapes with Harry, often the banking wasn't done when Harry arrived, and often as not Chris used to get me to keep him talking so he could go into the office, take the banking from the safe and dash out of the store heading straight for the bank. Harry was meticulous, ruthless and nothing got past him. What though eventually let him down was familiarity. He got to like Chris and me, and we liked him. Once this happened, we got away with murder.

Around 1971, HMV continued to expand under Dave Wilde's leadership. We'd recently opened in Birmingham, Brighton, Manchester, Newcastle, Wolverhampton and very soon Bristol. It was a very exciting time, I had a good job, lovely wife and a gorgeous daughter. At the time I had no real ambition other than to continue working hard and supporting my family.

Chris Rimmer was promoted to manager of this new store in Bristol and I was told Dave Wilde was considering me amongst others, to replace him as manager of Portsmouth. I had never been more excited in my life. I had learnt so much from Chris. He had, in a few very short years, turned me from a cocky little know-all, who incidentally, knew very little, into a professional shop manager with immense product knowledge. On top of this I had a huge capacity for hard work and I would work twenty-four hours a day if necessary to get the job done. I just hoped that Dave Wilde recognised these skills and appointed me as manager.

Two weeks later he did just that and I was absolutely thrilled. So pleased for me obviously, but so thrilled for Sue as well. I set about my new role with endless energy and determination. I was allowed to hire new staff, an Assistant Manager and a sales assistant. I found two very good people, Mike Gulvin and Roger Whatcott. Together we drove sales up, exceeded budgets and made Dave Wilde a very happy man.

Unfortunately, that December 1971, Sue's dad died of lung cancer. Initially he was told he had only six months to live, but through sheer luck, endless determination and a lot of love and care, he had proved the doctors wrong and lived for a further six years.

Louisa was still very young, but she adored 'Billy' as she used to call him. The whole family was heartbroken, he was one of the nicest human beings you could ever want to meet and he would leave a huge void in all our lives.

I could not have been prouder when I got a call from Head Office to say that Dave Wilde was visiting my store in a few days' time. This would be the first time anyone in authority would talk to me as previously all contact at a senior level was with Chris. I had the shop looking wonderful for his visit, all three of us were very excited! He arrived just before lunch and asked me if I would like to join him. Could I recommend somewhere locally? I didn't know anywhere nearby but suggested we went to an Italian restaurant in Elm Grove, Southsea. Although I was nervous, Dave was really easy-going, keen to put you at ease, and from that lunch I could tell that Dave and I would hit it off and were likely to be friends for a long time. He was thoroughly impressed with the sales figures, very complimentary about me and my staff and he wanted to share with me that next door was available and that we were going to double the size of the store. I couldn't believe it! What amazing news, we could expand so many of our ranges, the demand was there, and we were going to be hugely successful following this move.

Having met Bob Boast for my initial interview, it was refreshing that Dave was nothing like him. Bob, I would say, was very corporate, very old school, but Dave was quiet, very humble but had just bags of common sense. He was a real jazz fanatic, I never enjoyed jazz so there was little to talk about there.

He did say the refit would be done within six months and that he would send Jim Fraser, the new Finance and Administration Manager to see me to discuss the budget for the enlarged store. Apart from Dave, Harry Shave and Jim Fraser, we had a supervisor, Mike Donaghue, who would be there to ensure standards were achieved as per Dave's instructions and to help any of us should we need it. Mike was a nice guy too. He came into HMV via one of the acquisitions and was previously a store manager. Jim came to see me and, like Dave, we hit it off immediately. He was bald, quite short, had a problem with one of his legs that meant he limped, but he had a great sense of humour and provided me with so much help prior to the opening of the new enlarged store.

On time, June 1972, the store duly opened and it was a huge success from day one. The chain itself was expanding but I still don't believe it was that profitable. Chris was doing well in Bristol. It wasn't a big store but its weekly takings were enormous. Bristol, like so many other big cities, was crying out for an HMV store, the key though was in such a low-margin industry, how do you make money? Margins at the time were about 24–25%, not enough to cover fixed costs such as rent and rates. Staff costs, albeit a variable cost, were such that you just had to have a basic amount in order to trade successfully. Changes were continually taking place within our parent company, EMI Records, and in November 1973 a new Managing Director, Gerry Oord, was appointed. This meant that our boss, Dave Wilde, would report to him, but so often with these

EMI people they weren't interested in HMV, so he delegated the task to one of his senior directors, Alan Kaupe. No sooner had they taken charge we were all told that from January HMV Shops Ltd would become EMI Record and Tape Centres, one of the most appalling decisions ever made.

HMV managers were always invited to the EMI Records annual conferences. In 1972 they held it at the Grand Hotel, Eastbourne. It was a mad drunken couple of days, and I had great fun with Chris Rimmer, Dave Wilde and Jim Peal. Jim had just been named Northern Retail Area Manager and was to become a lifelong friend. Truth be known, we were all cynical of these EMI guys, most of them believing the sales hype from the senior sales and marketing teams. Gerry Oord made a speech. He was from Holland, and his English was not very good. Our view was that after renaming HMV stores, EMI Record and Tape Centres, he was bound to fail. How can you destroy all that brand heritage overnight because you as the CEO are committed to promoting anything that EMI Records control under the EMI umbrella? Fortunately, common sense did prevail with the Oxford Street store; this was to remain HMV.

In the spring of 1973, Sue told me the wonderful news that she was expecting another baby. This was just amazing news, and I couldn't have been happier.

During 1973 more stores opened and I heard that Plymouth would be opening towards the end of the year. I was keen to get promotion and to manage a bigger store and leaving Portsmouth was something that didn't bother either Sue or me. Dave was receptive when I mentioned it to him, and he suggested that Sue and I go and spend a few days there to see whether we would like it. This we did, and I have to say I was overjoyed about living in Plymouth. It seemed fairly backward compared to Portsmouth, but I still wanted to manage a new and bigger store. We waited until Dave was ready to make his decision and in the end he said he felt I should wait until next year when something even bigger and better maybe coming along. I have to say both Sue and I were somewhat disappointed, we were finding family life difficult to manage in Portsmouth and longed to be on our own.

Within HMV, managers were upset that the name of their store had been changed to EMI, which incidentally did very little to improve the relationships between the two companies. True to his word, Dave Wilde came to see me in 1973 to offer me the manager's position of the new Leeds store that was due to open in 1974. Leeds was a long way away from Portsmouth and it was up North, somewhere I hadn't been before. Despite my early hesitancy I said I would talk to Sue and get back to him. Sue as always was just brilliant, she said it's a big step up for you, it's a much bigger store, it's new and it will trade over two floors. 'You have to go for it!' I was concerned she would miss her mum and her sister, but she said we must make our own decisions, which will inevitably shape our future. I knew this was a big ask for her, but her view was always, I will support you wherever you go, and she always did.

I let Dave know our decision and he said we should look forward to our baby's birth, which was imminent, enjoy Christmas, and then he would take me up to Leeds and show me around.

On 9 December we became proud parents of a baby boy whom we called James William. Like Louisa he had ginger hair, coming from my mum and Sue's dad. He was born in St Mary's Hospital. Everything went smoothly and Sue and I were over the moon. James didn't suffer the colic problems that Louisa did, and this meant that we got a lot more sleep in those crucial first few months! Just like Louisa, we adored him.

Chapter 12

In the early part of 1974, as promised, Dave took me up to Leeds. I shared the car journey with my new boss, Jim Peal, who was responsible for the new Leeds store. Jim and I got on very well, and when we were with Dave we never stopped laughing. We all had a very similar, juvenile sense of humour and it was something to cherish between us. Prior to our car journey, Dave and I stayed in a hotel at Solihull near where Jim lived, and we went to his house for drinks and I was introduced to his wife Margaret, and their family. Jim had been part of Saville Pianos, which HMV had taken over in the 60s and was the manager of Enfield. He was promoted to manager of the Brighton store, which didn't do very well. Jim, to this day, still blames this on the owner of the shopping centre who failed to install a lift to the beach. It's become a bit of HMV folklore.

Leeds was an eye-opener for me. Its city centre was fairly run down and many of the buildings were in disrepair. Even the hotel we stayed in was awful, but as per normal, Dave, Jim and I were always able to see the funny side of it. The new store was in Trinity Street and was next door to the back entrance of Marks & Spencer. On the face of it, it looked a good position and it had a decent-size frontage. My only concern was that the shopfront design was awful, shaped like a TV screen.

Clearly that Leeds trip was not only successful from a business point of view, it was to cement and help build on a close relationship between Dave, Jim and I for a long time afterwards.

Preparations were underway to get the store open and Sue and I spent a few days in the area with the sole purpose of finding a new home. Dave was keen that we included Harrogate on the list of towns to visit and after spending just one morning there we had no hesitation in deciding that was where we wanted to live. Property was significantly cheaper in the North compared to the South and we were able to find a lovely three-bedroom semi-detached house on the outskirts of Harrogate, a place called Starbeck. It was a little village with a railway station, shops, pubs and a few cafés. The house was in Fairways Avenue, number 9, and it wasn't far from a level crossing that we would use a great deal during our time there.

Sue was happy, as I was, with Harrogate, it was a beautiful town dominated by the Stray, wonderful gardens that brought so much pleasure to everyone. We left there feeling we had made the right decision and very soon a new chapter in our life was about to unfold. We went back to Portsmouth, very excited and immediately put our house in St Pirans Avenue up for sale. We had enjoyed our time there, we were both very happy and the neighbours became very good friends.

The legals were progressing on both transactions and in July we said all our farewells, packed the car up and headed for the M1 to Harrogate. We weren't disappointed on arrival, neighbours from either side and across the road knocked on our door to welcome us, an amazing friendly welcome that we would not have received down South. We sorted out Louisa's school in Starbeck and found a child minder to look after James so Sue could go to work. I was involved in preparing the new store for opening and helping to close the old one. Jim Peal was a regular and helpful visitor and that meant there were many late nights next door at the Whitelock's pub.

The store was near ready for opening. Under Dave Wilde there was a new store design that included a strange terrazzo floor on the ground floor. Since Dave had taken over, he improved and indeed revolutionised a number of the trading practices within the chain, including introducing self-service. For instance, in most record shops the disc and the sleeve were separated; the record itself was held behind the counter with only the sleeve on display in the racks. The idea behind this (that was known as 'masterbagging') was simply to prevent theft. The flaw in the system was that people used to steal the sleeves and a lot of sales of particular LPs could be lost over a long period of time unless you did a regular monthly check, which in itself was hard work and very time-consuming. So, in HMV Leeds and most of the other new stores masterbagging became a thing of the past and self-service, with all its financial risks, was here to stay.

Our peculiar store detective, Dot Stennet, was not a great fan of this change but she was instructed by Dave to support him and make the new system work. Another of the advantages of self-service was that there was no need for large, long counters to file the records behind. That meant more retail space was available in each store, which in turn, improved the selection for the customer.

Having opened the new store with its ambitious first-year budget, sales were poor and so too was footfall around the area. Remember we were situated next door to Marks & Spencer, but it was their rear entrance rather than their front entrance. Trinity Street was new and apart from HMV and Marks & Spencer there wasn't a great deal else there for the public until you walked towards the tail end of a disappointing covered retail area. With the rent being very high, reflecting the store's position and the sales being very low, HMV Leeds was a loss-making store, which was not good for my reputation.

Dave and Jim visited regularly. In fairness to them they challenged me on all my thinking, my management practices, my stocking policies and the quality of the staff. I tried many of their suggestions, some made a difference, but overall, nothing that we did seemed to make any significant changes or improvement to the sales figures. But as a company we were growing and we had opened some good stores up and down the country.

Dave used to invite managers to London regularly for meetings whereby we could all share best practices and generally support each other. Competition was tough, Virgin had opened in Tottenham Court Rd and were beginning to open up new stores. Fortunately for us, Virgin was never run using the same retail best practices or retail standards we aspired to, a godsend, that was to ensure that HMV eventually became the most successful record retailer in the world.

At that time WHSmith were the market leaders, they had devoted huge amounts of space to music and I heard that some of their bigger stores in Birmingham and Manchester were taking enormous sums of money. Woolworths, with 800 stores, was another serious competitor.

Retail price maintenance, which controlled prices by law, had been abolished by Edward Heath before he became prime minister, and this led to the start of discounting generally in retail, but gradually was being introduced by WHSmith and Woolworths. The independent sector was strong and it too was pricing keenly, something HMV refused to do because, to quote Dave Wilde, 'It devalues the product.' We used to discuss these issues at our regular meetings with Dave and we never came up with any solutions.

Ken Whitmarsh, the General Manager of Oxford Street, would always, after our meeting, invite some of us into his office on the third floor of the store. Ken was also a very likeable guy: great, dry sense of humour, and unfortunately another jazz fanatic! His hospitality was well known throughout the visiting managers and used to be the highlight of our visit. He had an extremely well-stocked drinks cabinet and many bottles of vodka were consumed. Following the store closure at 6 p.m. we would all head to the pub across the road and stay there until we collapsed into the taxi taking us back to our hotel.

The mid to late 70s provided HMV with the opportunity to continue its UK expansion, but mainly in the Midlands and the North. While 363 Oxford Street had a significant market share in the South through this one iconic store, the problem for HMV in the South was a chain called Our Price. Owned by two popular entrepreneurs, Mike Isaac and Gary Nesbitt, they cleverly built a chain of small stores around the London area using very successful advertising on Capital Radio to promote their brand. With the increasing popularity of the cassette, they were able to offer an attractive range taking up much less retail space. Eight-track cartridges, being much bigger, were more of a problem for them but then, as a format, sales were not very exciting generally. Unlike HMV, all stores were virtually the same. Very distinct red Our Price logo on their shopfront, an annoying, easy-to-recall jingle on Capital Radio, a controlled range, albeit a limited one due to space constraints. It was easier to recruit managers and staff as product knowledge was not essential at Our Price, and it was well known that staff weren't at the higher end of pay in the retail sector.

Even with HMV's commitment to rolling out stores in the Midlands and the North, which emulated the values and practices of the HMV store in Oxford Street, somehow things were not working for them. Competition was a big problem: WHSmith, Our Price, Woolworths, Virgin and the strong independent sector. Pricing, as I mentioned earlier, was a big factor but also unlike WHSmith, Woolworths and Our Price there was no national marketing campaign, no promotions and no true brand identity.

Of course, HMV did have successful stores. Manchester for example was very successful and profitable. It was managed by Peter Waddington, a very smart, very likeable and very music-driven individual. The store had a tiny window on the ground floor with the sales floor up a flight of stairs. Despite the unorthodox layout, Peter and his team built a great business and the store was famous throughout the North of England. Peter was popular with other store managers and was openly looked up to. He tended to be very much his own man, rarely agreeing to follow Head Office directives. This didn't seem to matter to Dave Wilde as long as the store delivered the goods!

Gerry Oord, the Dutch EMI Records CEO, failed to deliver the increase in market share that he had promised the great and the good. He was replaced by Leslie Hill, the man famous for signing The Sex Pistols in 1976. Leslie would, like his predecessors, assume control of HMV, which led to lots of trouble for my dear friend Dave Wilde. As for me, I continued to run the Leeds store but there was no improvement in the sales and, if anything, one wouldn't have been surprised if I had been sacked. I realised that Leeds was a much bigger challenge than Portsmouth, it was a much larger store and had a great deal more competition. Discounting was a major issue and that was not under my control. I felt the store was bland and had a supermarket look to it, rather than a cutting-edge, sexy record store. I was at a low ebb, but as I discovered in my life, luck plays a big part.

Would you believe, Dave came to see me and said that with the increasing number of stores they needed an extra Area Manager – and he would like to offer it to me. I was absolutely astonished and accepted his offer immediately. Sue was equally surprised but pleased for me as she knew I had strong views on how things were being managed at HMV, and this promotion would give me the opportunity to make a much larger contribution. Apart from the welcome increase in salary, we were also to receive a company car. Our old car was on its last legs anyway, so this was fantastic news. We were told we could only choose a Ford Cortina Estate as Area Managers had to carry stationery and other administrative items for their stores in the back of their cars. To keep costs down, Area Managers would distribute stationery items to their stores via their Cortina Estates. I always found this to be a complete waste of my time as my focus was always on how we could improve sales. But I can still remember the thrill of being handed the keys and driving it home to Harrogate. Sue and I had grins on our faces the width of England.

My area consisted of ten stores, from Leeds/Bradford and as far north as Edinburgh/Glasgow. This was going to be a tough challenge for me as I was not used to managing remotely. When you're a store manager, all your staff are under one roof and decisions can be acted upon instantly. In addition to this I was still responsible for the Leeds store, its losses were lowering the profitability for the whole area.

We all knew Dave was under pressure. Mike Donaghue in the South and Jim Peal in the Midlands along with me in the North wanted to do everything we could to help him. Looking back, it's probably fair to say that Dave wasn't a very good leader or businessman. Had expansion not happened, I feel Dave would have coped running a smaller entity that was less corporate and where family values were of more importance in the business. Most of my stores were overstocked, bearing in mind that unlike Our Price, managers in HMV chose their own product range. A good number of them got this right, applying Chris Rimmer's skills of buying for your local market. However, when they got it wrong, it could not only cost you dearly in lost sales, but large overstocks would also drag you down too.

I found myself interested in analysing the figures that our Finance Department gave us to help us manage our area. I'm not sure if anyone ever looked at these before but most of what I saw did not make good reading. There was no consistency. For example, similar size stores would have different staffing levels, yet sales figures were similar. Similar size stores would also have wildly varying levels of stock, yet again with similar sales figures. Often when you spent time going through the browsers in a store, there would be huge variation in ranges. Some stores would have massive jazz sections – perhaps because they knew Dave liked jazz. Managers would often promote their own musical tastes by having extended ranges of music that never sold. This was not just a problem in the North, it was, as I was to discover later on, a huge problem everywhere. Despite all this, I saw my role as the guy who could support the manager and his staff to attain their sales, stock and profit budgets.

Jim Fraser, along with Dave, introduced a very generous bonus scheme if store managers and assistant managers performed well. My visits were designed to ensure company policies were followed. Dave supplied us all with a ten-point list of the important standards that had to be achieved, and Dave being Dave, in between each point he had an entry saying: 'Don't forget the music'! I'm afraid this was easy to do, and he knew that only too well in the ever-increasing corporate world he was living in. I was tough and very demanding; I will admit this and it's probably not everyone's cup of tea. I had no formal business training but, instinctively I guess, I believed that if it was made clear to someone what was expected of them in exchange for their monthly salary, the onus was on them to deliver. This view I never altered or amended in all my years in HMV and even today, as I am writing this, I would not change one word of it. I had high expectations of everyone, I didn't bawl or shout at people, I was more than happy to walk the floor with the manager, discuss the various things I liked or didn't like and then we would review everything in his office.

I was always keen to meet every member of staff, as an important part of my job was to develop people for future management, both within my area and throughout the company. During our review, I would take the manager through the up-to-date financial information and get his views as to why things were going well – or not, as often the case would be. The point of the review was, if possible, to reach an understanding of the issues facing the store and draw up an action plan that the manager would then share with his staff. Some things, like the competition, were outside of our control, especially if it involved discounting. But once we had visited all the competition together, we may have spotted a weakness, for example in a particular range, and adjusted and improved ours accordingly. Managers would look for help and guidance from me regarding the performance of their staff and I saw this as an extremely important part of my role. The good managers could spot the people with potential and provide them with extra responsibility, but others unfortunately failed to spot underperformers, which would often as not lead to the manager's downfall and ultimately damage the profitability of the store itself.

Dave was pleased with me from the outset. He was particularly impressed with the mileage I was achieving, and this praise spurred me on. He felt it might be a good idea if we visited a few stores together, something I truly welcomed, as it meant I could spend valuable time with him discussing what I thought was some of the key issues facing the region and the company.

We started off in Manchester; Peter Waddington and Dave got on well, and they had a great deal of respect for each other. I had already explained to Dave that I didn't have favourites and that I treated everyone the same. In addition, the agreed standards and practices were to be applied by me throughout the area, immaterial of store size, sales, or profitability. In other words, a consistent approach I believed would bring better results and more respect from our store managers. So, our joint visit to Manchester would be a good test.

Peter, however, did not welcome my appointment as Area Manager, presumably because I was not prepared to treat him any differently to other managers. He was a law unto himself, and my monthly visits were not necessary in his eyes, and as a result there was regular conflict between us. Funnily enough, I had enormous respect for Peter, his product knowledge was second to none, he shamed us all with his incredible passion for music and his great understanding of the Manchester customer.

But when we arrived at the store, Dave, and I, we received a frosty response. I asked Dave if I could show him how I do a store visit and for him not to comment on this until we were in private later in the day. This he agreed to.

We went for a tour of the store, I pointed out areas that could be improved, praising Peter if he had introduced something new that was very successful. Finally, we headed for the office for a financial review and general discussion about his and the store's performance. Peter took the opportunity with Dave in attendance to display his lack of support for me and my methods. It was icy and I was interested in how Dave would handle this, given their well-known previous relationship. To my complete surprise, Dave lost his temper with Peter, telling him he had to conform or else. 'If I hear Brian has any more trouble with you, I will be back and kick your ass all the way up Market Street.' Wow, I was astonished, so too was Peter, I don't think he had ever seen that side of Dave before, and it shocked him.

Well, it had the required effect, Peter did conform, our relationship improved greatly too, and more importantly Dave endorsed my management approach to the area, which was so necessary if I was to succeed.

Looking at my portfolio of stores, this was always going to prove difficult. Take Stockton and Middlesbrough for example. Both stores were in secondary locations, in areas that were clearly run down and in need of investment. The Middlesbrough store was an appalling store, made of wood, and you always got the feeling that one dropped match would see the whole place go up in flames. Also, the manager was not particularly good and nor were his sales.

Stockton was even worse. This was a fairly new store with the TV shopfront design and the Italian flooring. Like all similar stores it lacked atmosphere, fun, and was more suited to selling groceries than music. The town itself had massive unemployment, and judging from my visits there, most of the 'customers' just hung out in our store, and more often as not you were likely to get a huge mouthful of abuse if you attempted to throw them out. The manager appeared to tolerate this, something that I wouldn't. Again, like a lot of towns HMV were in, the local WHSmith was better located, and the indie store had more atmosphere and lower prices.

The management of stock was a major problem for the region and for all I knew, for the company. There were no controls in place, and no budgets so it was difficult to get managers to change their behaviours. Basically, they had blank cheques to fill in on a daily basis and very little thought was given to the fact that this was HMV's cash that was being spent and a lot of it was wasted.

The record companies used to sell new releases into our stores in large quantities due to the lack of skill on our managers' part, but they would only give us a 5% returns allowance which, given the scale of the problem, was insufficient.

In those days the store managers had quite a degree of power and it was firmly understood and established within HMV, that the store manager chose his range, and it became my goal to try and change this. My concern was: why should we allow someone who works for us as a store manager indulge themselves personally by stocking and promoting a range they happened to enjoy?

My stance was not helped by the fact that, as I said, Dave Wilde was a passionate jazz fan and on store visits only offered feedback to a store manager on the makeup of his jazz range. What unfortunately escaped him was the fact that nationally jazz sales were about half that of classical, around about 5%.

So, the company was facing some tough issues, quality of store management, layout and design, marketing and buying, store locations and last but not least pricing. Quite rightly, Dave believed in HMV as a true specialist record retailer led by the values and standards of our flagship store, 363 Oxford Street. The problem though was that HMV Oxford Street had the space over three floors to be the amazing specialist retailer that it was. But when the chain outside of Oxford Street is trading over an average of say 2,000 square feet, you cannot emulate those values without diluting everything. That was the nub of the problem along with the level of autonomy a store manager had.

Jim Peal, Mike Donaghue and I would debate these issues, often amongst ourselves and often with Dave. We talked, but nothing improved, and nothing got resolved.

At Head Office in Dean St, Dave was feeling the pressure from EMI and the new Chairman Leslie Hill. As his predecessor had done, Leslie Hill, when he took over, appointed another EMI Records director to manage HMV. This time the job went to the Finance Director, James Tyrrell, the man who signed the cheque to fire The Sex Pistols. Unlike all the other EMI board directors, James was different. Alan Kaupe for example and Ken East, both important guys, showed little interest in HMV. They thought it was doing fine because the success of the Oxford Street store continued to disguise the problems in the chain nationwide. James, however, told Dave from the outset that he was going to be hands-on.

Dave Wilde, after his first meeting with James, told me he was to be the ruination of HMV as we knew it and that he, Dave, would probably either be sacked or he would resign. For people like Jim, Mike, and me, with families and mortgages this was very worrying news. Despite all Dave's shortcomings, we loved him dearly and had enormous respect for him. It was clear to us that this new guy was going to make his presence felt very soon. And at their first meeting James said that he would like to spend time visiting the stores with each respective Area Manager.

Dave telephoned me to ensure I was available for a couple of days to escort James around some stores. I asked Dave what James was like as a person and he said 'First of all he's a toff, in fact he's more than a toff, and he's a chinless wonder. You can't get a word in edgeways; he asks question after question and he believes he knows the answers to all our problems. He's going to be a bloody dinosaur.'

I met James in HMV Leeds, and our plan was to go on from there to Stockton and Newcastle. He spent ages just wandering around the Leeds store, but he also spent ages visiting the competition. He did ask a lot of questions and I had no problem with that because you could see from his whole approach that he was taking his new role seriously. I described him to Sue on the phone later that night as a breath of fresh air. .

He could come across though as an eccentric individual, but the more time you spent with him, you knew this was part of his makeup. We stayed in a local hotel in Leeds and dined at the only decent restaurant, an Italian that he liked.

I noticed, he got louder after a few glasses of wine, and I just felt that James and alcohol were not great partners. I suppose the reason I took to him so soon was his probing questions, why we do this, why we do that? Why are the stores so dull and lacking in excitement? Who came up with the new dreadful store design and especially that Italian terrazzo flooring? Why do I enjoy being in an independent store more than an HMV store? Why are we so expensive compared to the competition? Why are so many stores in the wrong place? Why is HMV Leeds losing so much money? These are just a few of the questions he threw at me during dinner and in the car in between store visits. Unlike anyone else, he made me think and, in my opinion, he was right about so many issues that, until he arrived, we had never faced up to.

Obviously, Jim and Mike had the same treatment when they spent time with him and between us we agreed that this guy is not going away, and all we could see was trouble ahead between him, Dave and probably Ken Whitmarsh, the GM of 363 Oxford Street. Dave spoke to me following my trip with James and I was honest with him. I realise Dave did not want me to say either I liked him or that I agreed with him, but I did. Dave was not happy.

Dave told me that James wanted to attend our managers' conference in Leicester that was being held in a couple of weeks' time. He said it would be a disaster and that we had to try and persuade him not to address the managers with his crazy questions and ideas. That, I thought, was going to be difficult to stop, as he had already told me he was going to speak.

The Leicester hotel was the Post House, and apart from store managers there were others from Head Office, including Jim Fraser, our Finance Director, and Ken Whitmarsh from Oxford Street. Dave had drawn up an agenda that covered: up-and-coming new releases for us to discuss, some operational issues, some finance topics, but there was nothing to do with the future and how we as a company are going to address it. It was all pretty low-key stuff until James got up to speak.

It was an amazing speech. He covered everything that we discussed in Leeds, and he didn't care that Dave didn't agree with a word of it. He was on his feet for a good hour, and you could see from the looks on the managers' faces, that a great deal of what he said made sense. He didn't like what he saw, dull, boring uninteresting stores, trying to sell a fun and exciting product. Poor layouts, poor designs, poor window displays. No buying policies and no answer to the threat of Our Price and the discounting that was becoming more prevalent. Rents were often too high – he mentioned Leeds specifically – and margins were too low. He finished up by saying either we fix it, address, and face up to these issues or we go bust. It's up to all of us to ensure that this great brand never goes under due to our incompetence and lack of vision. He spoke for so long we were late for dinner, but clearly his speech was the only thing people were talking about. Dave and Ken were furious with him, but Jim Fraser our Finance Director thought he did well, and this was not well received by Dave.

Late at night in Dave's room, the key people met without James. Dave said what he did, what he said, was outrageous and that he would ruin the company, not us. Jimmy Fraser didn't agree, and this time Ken Whitmarsh turned on Jimmy, charging him with sucking up to James because they are both employees of EMI Records. In fact, he was wrong because Jimmy had joined HMV, but Dave and Ken never trusted this likeable ex-EMI man. As for us, it was sad to see Dave so depressed, we all adored him, but we stressed, without taking sides, that Dave needed to be careful, and Ken as well. They should at least listen to what James had to say rather than just dismissing it. Dave and Ken were having none of it. The man is mad they said, and if necessary, Dave said he would talk to EMI about replacing him. Little did we know that the Leicester Post House Conference would end up changing the future of HMV forever . . .

Chapter 13

It was clear that EMI were not interested in Dave's concerns about James as they announced that James Tyrrell, Finance Director, EMI Records, had been promoted to Managing Director of HMV, or EMI Records and Tapes Centres, as they were currently called. I took the call from Dave, and he was beside himself, he had no other job to go to and frankly, he didn't want to leave HMV.

Despite all our warnings Dave set out not to cooperate with James and eventually the new boss was forced to act. He called Dave and Ken Whitmarsh to his office, explained that he was effectively taking day-to-day control of the business and that they would both be offered new positions. Dave was offered Ken's job as General Manager of Oxford Street, and Ken was offered the new position of Business Development Manager based in Dean Street, our Head Office. They both accepted their new roles and were also told that Ian Gray from the finance department was being promoted to Marketing Director, reporting directly to James. Both Dave and Ken were disgusted with all the news and Dave telephoned me and I guess both Mike and Jim too. He was utterly scathing about James; said he would ruin what we had all built up between us. James, he said, was not a record man; he was a numbers man and a toff! Once again, I tried to explain to Dave that he wasn't in a great position. The company was barely making any money, the competition was growing, and EMI had taken the view that James has to come up with the results. I suggested that he tried to work with James because EMI were not going to reverse their decision. I said give him a chance, he has ideas, some of them I admit are crazy, but equally, some of them could work.

For example, James was keen on replacing the bland terrazzo flooring that Dave installed. He was also keen on improving our window displays, employing a Marketing Manager and generally lifting the profile of the company. I had no problem with any of this, but Dave did, believing nothing was wrong so why try and fix it? Dave accused me of sucking up to James and asked me where my loyalty lay. I completely disagreed with him, stating that I had enormous respect for Dave, both on a personal level and a professional level.

Meanwhile, James was now fully in charge of the business and established himself in Dave's old office in Dean Street. Ken also had an office there and kept his head down, getting to grips with his new role, whatever that might have been! He employed a Personnel Officer called Pamela Edwards, but she immediately managed to clash with Dave and then eventually with everyone else. What did get Dave's approval was James's decision to turn all the stores back to 'HMV' again, something we all totally supported. I don't think the stores were aware of the power struggle going on. It was still a very small company and managers tended to build relationships within their regions.

At home, Sue and I were thoroughly enjoying living in Harrogate. Both James and Louisa were happy at school, and Sue's mum moved up to join us. It was the making of her, normally a quiet introverted person began a new life and enjoyed every minute of it. She even got a job at the Odeon Cinema and went on to make lifelong friends as a result. We too made friends easily, with Brenda a few doors down from us, Miss French next door, and Doreen and Ken across the road. We used to drink in the Conservative Club in town and the Working

Man's Club in Starbeck. Everywhere we went people were friendly and loved both of our children too.

When we first moved to Starbeck we had noticed a house just off the main road, on Bogs Lane. We both stopped to look at it. It was a lovely Neo-Georgian property with gardens all around. Obviously back in 1976 we couldn't afford a house like this. As my salary increased over the years, both with the promotion to Area Manager and subsequent annual increases, we were in a good position financially and were on the lookout for a bigger property. To our amazement our dream house in Bogs Lane was up for sale and after doing our sums, we felt we could afford the monthly mortgage payments and so we made an offer. Our offer was accepted and in the early spring of 1979 we moved in. We were absolutely thrilled, a bigger house, much larger gardens and we were still in the village of Starbeck. Admittedly, Sue and the children didn't see much of me as I was on the motorways most of the time. Even on the day we were supposed to move in, I couldn't be there, leaving Sue to oversee the removal people and begin the unpacking.

Given the problems HMV was facing internally with Dave and James, plus the competition and discounting issues, I wasn't making a great deal of progress on sales and profits. Costs were much more under control and some redundancies were unavoidable in some overstaffed stores. The most interesting development though, which I take little credit for, was an idea that Peter Pearson, the manager of Leeds, came up with. At the back of the store there was a counter that due to low sales was often unmanned and closed. Peter, trying desperately to hit his budgets, decided to designate that part of the store to selling singles. Our single sales were poor and Peter believed we could steal business from WHSmith, Virgin and the independents by creating a separate and dynamic area for them. I remember he covered the back wall full of 7-inch records in their different and wonderfully colourful sleeves. He had a couple of staff who loved their music but also had a massive interest in building up a unique 'singles shop', a shop within a shop. When I first saw it, I was thrilled, it was well stocked with browsers surrounding the counter. Sales slowly began to rise. What Peter (unknowingly maybe) had done was to introduce a specialist area of music to the store which separated us from the competition. He also introduced energy into the store, as singles were often fun and featured heavily on the radio and on *Top of the Pops*. I congratulated Peter on this innovation.

The 'singles shop' idea was well received in several of my stores and particularly in HMV Newcastle by the newly appointed Chris Taylor. Chris was an enthusiastic, hardworking lad, who I was sure was going to have a major impact on the store. He too was a 'singles nut' as we called them, amazingly knowledgeable and enthusiastic. Customers in Newcastle liked their music but loved their singles and again it had the effect of bringing more people into the stores, creating fun and a lively atmosphere which, as James Tyrrell had pointed out, our stores lacked. James liked the 'singles store' idea, he also asked for improved lighting to go in the windows. Flashing, colourful lighting it had to be, to draw people's attention. Of course, Dave thought that all of it was a waste of time and told James so. Managers were impressed with James, albeit he was loud and very posh, they believed he made them think and they knew his heart was in the right place.

Security in HMV generally was poor, especially as so many of the stores were trading as self-service stores now. We appointed a Head of Security, a man from Enfield called George Stone and it was his job to introduce measures to reduce shoplifting and staff theft. George contracted a new company that would send people in pretending to be customers, make a purchase and report whether the assistant had registered the sale and placed the money in the till. I was alerted by George that there were irregularities in the Manchester store and they needed to be investigated.

Meanwhile unbeknown to us regional managers, Dave had purchased the entire stock of a small, almost unheard-of company called CRD. They specialised mainly in jazz and blues, and frankly outside of the Oxford Street store we didn't sell much jazz and blues. Dave had the job lot delivered to the empty first floor in the Nottingham store and all three regional managers were summoned by Dave to help him assess what he had bought and arrange distribution to the stores. I was due in court following the arrest that was made in the Manchester store for the staff theft, but no, I was told by Dave that the CRD stock took priority, and my presence was required. We spent several days sorting out what was thousands of obscure records. Certain managers were even invited to pick what they wanted, one manager whom we called Symphony Sid arrived and said he would buy it by the yard. Well, we just fell about, how bad is it that he could say such a thing without even checking what he was buying? He was not going to last I thought! The whole process was backbreaking, extremely boring, a complete waste of senior people's time, but to my amazement all the stock sold thanks to the commitment of Jim Peal.

With James in the driving seat, I began to impress upon him how serious discounting was becoming amongst our competition. Dave said it would devalue the product, as if the LP knew how much it should be sold for!

As I was told by senior record industry figures, WHSmith and Our Price were selling the bulk of the Top 50 albums and cassettes in huge volumes – I believe at that time Top 50 albums and cassettes accounted for over 30% of sales. In HMV it accounted for about 5%.

James said that he agreed with me that we needed to compete, but the problem was that EMI Records owned HMV shops and if the shops were to discount, EMI's customers, i.e., our competition, would feel EMI were condoning and encouraging discounting in HMV stores to their detriment. James and I had witnessed this sort of thing at first hand when we opened the new HMV Liverpool store and the owner of the local department store who sold records, came into our store, piled up a huge number of our albums on the counter, saying 'You can invoice me for these, they're out of stock at the EMI warehouse.' Everyone knew that EMI and HMV were two separate entities, and no favours were given to HMV as a result.

It was just pure fun for our competitors to stir things up because as the old saying goes, 'If you throw enough mud against the wall, eventually some of it will stick.' James nevertheless critically believed that there was no future for HMV if we didn't offer our customers value for money and operate in a fun environment. He called me a few days later to say that if we could put a financial case together as to why it was so important for us to discount, he would take the paper to the next EMI board meeting and seek permission for just one store to discount on a trial basis. He said he would write the paper with Jim Fraser, our FD, and I should give thought to which store we chose. Clearly, and immediately, I thought it's going to one of my stores and it's going to be Leeds! This was my biggest problem, both as a manager and now as a regional manager and I was determined to get the store right and made profitable. James called again to say he had written the paper and he felt we had a strong case to go before the board of EMI and get the permission we need. He said the meeting was in two days' time and he wanted me there to explain in my own words why we must discount. I was absolutely petrified of attending such a meeting. I had never been to a board meeting of any description before and immediately I knew I would make a mess of it. James wouldn't hear another word. 'You're going and you will convince them, I'm certain of it.'

Well, I wasn't, but this was a huge turning point in the company's history and if we failed, there would be no HMV and no job for me and hundreds of my colleagues. We headed over to Manchester Square in London where the board meeting was being held. Both James and I were suited and booted, I was feeling sick and sweating profusely! We were shown into a waiting area and then into this peculiar circular room where the meeting was being held. The directors I thought were all there, the important one certainly was, the MD, Leslie

Hill. We all sat there quietly, no one was speaking and I'm looking at James as if to say what the hell are we waiting for? The next second a lady appears as the door of the circular room opens and she says, 'Gentlemen, be upstanding for L. G. Wood.' Well, I couldn't believe it, I thought he had retired. But no, he was the Chairman of the Board and that made me even more nervous. He was the most senior and most well-respected figure in the music industry and had been for years. I had to pinch myself – Brian, you are in the same room as L. G. Wood, and you are going to have to persuade him to let you upset all his customers by allowing HMV Leeds to discount. He glared around the room, stared at me and said to James, 'Well, we haven't got all day, what are you and your friend here for?' James introduced me, and then asked me to explain why we must discount and become competitive in HMV Leeds.

After a shaky, nervous start, waiting for my tongue to eventually come back up to my throat, I briefly outlined the problem that was backed up by the figures in the paper before them. Wood looked at Leslie Hill and said, 'There will be uproar amongst our other dealers, how will you cope with this? Won't this have a real negative effect on our relationships with people that we've built up, over many, many years?'

Fortunately, I believe James had already got to Leslie and pressed his case firmly. Leslie didn't want to see James fail in his first post as a Managing Director, and so he said to Wood, 'Len, I think we have no choice. It's the way of the world now, resale price maintenance has been abolished, it's not just the record industry that will be discounting, it's going to be happening across retail generally. If we don't allow this trial, there is no future for our retail chain and the costs of closure to EMI Records will be colossal.'

L. G. went very quiet and then said, 'OK, go ahead, but in this one store only you hear?' James, very smartly said, 'If it works, sir, our trial, can we extend it to the rest of the chain?' He replied, 'No you can't, you can jolly well come back here with your results and I will then decide on any further extension.'

I was absolutely elated, so too was James, we had taken the first step to restructuring HMV and put it on course to become a serious player in record retailing. We told Dave, who wasn't very interested, but Jim and Mike both saw it as a massive decision that would help their stores as well if the trial was successful.

I announced to Peter Pearson that HMV Leeds had been chosen for the discounting trial. He too was thrilled, we had a great range in this store, albeit it was off-pitch, but the singles shop was doing well and more people as a result would buy their albums or cassettes from us. However apart from our expensive chart prices there was just too many people in Leeds who did not know we existed. Our dilemma was that if we reduced the price of chart titles and failed to increase the volume, we would be earning even lower margins than we currently were, and financially the trial would be seen as a total failure. James was aware of this too and decided we needed some additional outside help.

After a couple of weeks, he told me he had engaged a company called Yellowhammer, a PR company whose job it was to put HMV Leeds on the map. James introduced me to them. We worked night and day with them to come up with new graphics for the window and instore. We needed new price stickers, which were large and bold to put on the chart titles. We needed a separate area at the front of the store, like a huge wall to display our new discounted chart range. We achieved all of this and more. I was still concerned that even using the local newspaper was not going to be powerful enough to reach the thousands of new customers we needed. This continued to be my main worry until the following Sunday I was reading the *Sunday Times'* colour supplement, and I read an article about a guy who specialised in putting on celebrity store appearances. He found the artists, managed the artists and got them to turn up whenever and wherever a customer needed them. I thought to myself, this has got to be the answer – we needed a celebrity to draw the crowds to the store in Leeds and let them see our range, our singles shop, and our cheaper chart titles.

I called the MD of this company up the next day. We spoke for a while and then he agreed to meet me in Leeds the next day. He liked what we were doing and said, on the day of your launch, which was a Saturday, I will have Ed 'Stewpot' Stewart, the Radio 1 DJ, available for you. I thought that was marvellous, Ed Stewart had an enormous radio following, millions in fact, and he would be perfect, although, quite rightly, our managers and staff would feel he wasn't a good fit for a specialist record chain like HMV. My view at the time was that at this stage we just needed to get bodies into the store and get us on the map. I asked the MD to give me a quote and once I'd received this, I could ask James to sign it off. James loved the proposal, so too did Yellowhammer and although Ed was going to cost us around £2,000 the view was that it would be worth it.

The date for the launch was set, I'd briefed our manager and staff on how the day would pan out. Yellowhammer would organise everything and the windows and instore display areas would be professionally dressed the day before. We hadn't agreed a time yet for Ed Stewart, but I didn't believe that would be a problem as the MD said he was available all day. Yellowhammer preferred a 10.30 a.m. launch with all the whistles and bells, and I agreed to this. On speaking to the MD, the bombshell was dropped, Ed Stewart was on radio live on a Saturday morning, so he wouldn't be in until about noon! I thought how the hell did I forget that? But I did, and we all had to adjust our time to suit him. We leafletted the whole city with news of Stewpot's appearance, we had adverts in the station, in the newspapers and every bus stop in Leeds. We were all thoroughly excited, my wife, Sue and children, James and Louisa were to join us. It was going to be the most important day in my life professionally. I was desperate for us all to succeed after putting in months of sheer hard work.

During the day the crowds outside our store were amazing – we had, in truth, created a carnival atmosphere. We had pretty girls giving away balloons to the children and promotional leaflets to the adults. The area around Marks & Spencer was packed – people trying to access the beginning of the small shopping precinct adjacent were not happy. Inside the store sales were building, and not just on our discounted chart titles. The 'singles shop' was getting more and more popular, especially on a Saturday morning, we were in danger of creating a high-class problem for ourselves in crowd management!

Our team, Head Office, Yellowhammer, the store staff and everyone connected with the event were really excited and looking forward to Ed Stewart's arrival. I spoke to John and he confirmed that Ed had left the BBC studios in London and was driving himself to Leeds. He duly arrived on time at 2 p.m., it was wonderful. The Trinity Street precinct where the store was located is a pedestrianised area, but as a special favour to us, they allowed him to drive through the precinct to the store. It was magnificent! Ed was driving a fantastic Rolls-Royce, which glided through and came to a halt outside the shop. The crowds by now were huge and we had police and our local security guards in place to allow him a safe path into the store.

He was a brilliant showman, shaking everyone's hand, signing autographs before cutting the ribbon signifying the start of lower chart prices at HMV Leeds. Even this minor duty he carried out with style, fun and much laughter. Everyone loved him, hundreds if not thousands queued up to get his autograph at the back of the store.

James and I were thrilled with the outcome, it was a lot of hard work, but we were convinced that our efforts had put the HMV store in Leeds on the map and that was what we set out to achieve. Sales of chart titles went through the roof compared to a normal Saturday and if that continued, we were on our way to making a profit in the store for the first time. Dave was there but kept a very low profile and hardly spoke to me all day. Very sad, because he's a good man. My view, shared by others, was that Dave's time was running out.

It had! I got a call in the November of 1979 from James to say that both Dave Wilde and Ken Whitmarsh had been dismissed. All three regional managers would therefore report to him with immediate effect. He said he had run out of patience with both of them and that he had no choice but to let them go. While I was sad, I was not surprised. I and many others had told them that this would happen if they didn't begin to cooperate with him. I spoke to Jim and Mike Donaghue who were of the same opinion, and they too saw this coming.

I spoke to both Ken and Dave on the phone and they were in shock. Why, I have no idea, but they were. They both said he was a lunatic, and it was best if we all left, because there wouldn't be a company worth working for under him.

The whole business was shocked, indeed so was the industry. Dave and Ken were popular figures amongst the record companies, but even they must have seen this coming.

James came up to Harrogate a few weeks later and stayed overnight in the pretty village of Knaresborough. He invited me out to dinner and over a rather good bottle of red wine he asked if I would move to London to become his Operations Manager. I would be in charge of all day-to-day running of the business and Mike Donoghue in the South and Jim Peal in the Midlands would report to me. I was totally surprised at this offer; I knew James would have to appoint someone to this role, but I never thought it would be me! My initial reaction was am I up to such a big promotion, am I likely to gain the respect of Mike and Jim and all the store managers in the South and the Midlands? James had no doubts, he pointed to the successful relaunch of the Leeds store, the reduction in costs and stock levels in my area and the improvement in profitability. I would need to be in my new job immediately, I would report directly to James and be based in our offices in Dean Street.

Looking back, it was an amazing journey from the Co-op in 1964 to Operations Manager at HMV in 1980. I still believed HMV had the right people, the passion for music and the best brand to become No. 1. James had enormous energy that rubbed off on all of us. It was an exciting time, but there was still a lot of hard work to be done.

Chapter 14

While I feared failing, as I always do whenever I take on anything new, deep inside I was elated and chuffed with myself that my hard work had been recognised. Working for James I knew was not going to be easy, he was a finance man, and not a retailer and he would often shoot from the hip, sometimes with disastrous consequences. I did feel that now I was going to oversee all the stores I could make an impact, I had a great deal to learn, but with James's support the company had a real chance of becoming a serious player in the music industry.

I left the restaurant that night telling James that I would love to take the job, but I needed to talk to Sue. The timing of this move was not great, we had only just moved into our dream house, which we had all fallen in love with. I went home, poured Sue a drink and told her what had happened over dinner. Typical Sue, she said 'You must take it, you and James are a good combination, and it will work.' I was thrilled, but not surprised, she always believed in me, and said she goes where I go.

The problem now was having to tell her mum, who was happy in Harrogate and had, as previously mentioned, for the first time in her life, begun to make friends. In addition to this, Sue looked at house prices within the London area and they were very scary. There weren't any three/four-bedroom houses available within our budget. My pay rise from James plus the potential bonus was good, but most of the increase would go on the increased mortgage we needed to get just a reasonable house. I discussed the problem with James, who said he had little room for manoeuvre, but nevertheless gave me a further increase of a few hundred pounds. He advised us to move further out of London, maybe to the area he lived in, where house prices are going to be lower. James lived in Upper Basildon, near Reading, and the train journey from Reading to London was only twenty-five minutes.

We put the house in Harrogate on the market and I moved down to London, staying in hotels near Shaftesbury Avenue and Leicester Square. I would stay in London until Friday and then travel to Harrogate. I did this for a few months, which was painful without seeing Sue and the kids every day, but eventually the house sold, and Sue came down to London so we could find a house in the Reading area. We spent a few days touring around the various villages, but virtually everywhere we liked was too expensive. We didn't like Reading even with its fast train service, so it would have to be an affordable village within driving distance of a railway station. Eventually we bought a house in the village of Woodcote, which was about a ten-minute drive to Pangbourne from where I could get the train to London.

Frankly, I didn't like Woodcote, it was very high up from Pangbourne, there was little life to speak of and the house was not a patch on the one we had just sold in Harrogate. Apparently, the schools were good, which was very important to us and again with Pangbourne only ten minutes away it would be ideal for Sue to do her shopping.

Prior to us moving in, my dear friend Alan Zoltie offered to rent me a flat he owned in Abbey Rd, St John's Wood. James agreed and for a few weeks I lived there and was much happier than living in hotels in central London.

Our completion date for Woodcote was 1 January 1980, and with that being so close to Christmas, I suggested to Sue that we all spend it at the flat in Abbey Rd before moving on to Woodcote. We brought Sue's mum as well, and we had a marvellous Christmas there, Louisa and Sue still talk about it today.

Sadly, Sue's mum decided she wouldn't stay in Harrogate on her own and would want to move as near to us as possible. Unfortunately, she couldn't afford Woodcote, and after a lot of soul-searching, she decided to move back to Portsmouth where she had another daughter and grandchildren.

The day we left Starbeck was truly a sad day. The kids were in Christmas carol services, and as we were packing our personal items plus our cat Bubbles into the car the tears began to fall. In fact, I'm not sure the kids stopped crying until we reached London. On top of that, the cat soiled itself in her basket, the smell was just unbelievable!

We moved in as planned on 1 January 1980 and it was cold and gloomy. In fact, my memories of Woodcote all these years later was that it was like that all the time. I was driving to the station in the dark and driving home in the dark. The train journey if it worked was fifty minutes, but often it was much longer than that.

I guess with having to leave Bogs Lane, and our social life there – where, apart from the Conservative Club and the Starbeck Workingman's Club, we had on our doorstep the Yorkshire Dales, Fountains Abbey and countless racecourses that we all thoroughly enjoyed – I was somewhat depressed. I was leaving the house at 6.30 a.m. and not getting home most nights until 10 p.m., it was therefore no surprise when Sue asked me what the hell is all this for and what the hell is going on? She was miserable too, but she was fortunate to have made friends with our neighbours Sandy and Judy, who have remained close friends with her for forty-two years. All I could tell her was that it would get better. She rightly asked me when, for she was facing the embarrassment of going into town with a friend from school, frightened that the friend may suggest stopping off for a coffee when Sue didn't have enough money in her purse. The pay rise went on the increased mortgage and then we had to find the season ticket for the train, leaving us, after buying food etc., no disposable income at all.

Sue, I'm sure, was beginning to wonder how long either of us could live like this. She said I looked terrible, and if I carried on doing this travelling along with the long working days, I would be ill. I admit I was very miserable, but as the lighter evenings began to appear things didn't seem as bad and I hoped we would get through it.

At work I was fortunate enough to have a secretary called Jane Smart. Jane was a lovely, bright, cheerful girl and I don't mind admitting I would have gone under if it wasn't for her. She was amazing, a harder worker you couldn't find, bright as a button, and would often still be in the office after I left.

Our workload was just enormous. Basically, we had to start the operational practices from scratch. While it would take several more years to address the inconsistencies in our range throughout the chain, we began to make a start on introducing best practice across everything we did, no regional variations, no opt-outs. We had to put down a framework, spell out our values and seek continuous improvement in everything that we did. I made a few changes at the start regarding my key people. First I asked Jim Peal if he would accept the post of Buying Manager that was soon to be advertised. The reason I asked Jim to consider this was that he had for a few years been buying job lots of discontinued stock for us at keen prices, and it was clear to me from the success he was having, his skills were more suitable for buying than retail operations. Jim had a great affinity and love of music, and he had a canny eye for a bargain and saw opportunities that others, like myself, didn't!

For example, the night Elvis Presley died, Jim had managed to buy up all the remaining stocks across the country of his albums, stored them in his bunker at

Coventry and distributed them to the chain. That was typical Jim, and we made a small fortune as a result.

It's also fair to say that I'm not sure that Jim was totally sure about me in this new role, as I began making wholesale changes to the business practices he had supported previously.

Nevertheless, he made a huge success of it, going on to become a very important Senior Manager in our Store Development division who was to spearhead our ambitious expansion. He supported me through and through and we remain great friends to this day.

Ian Gray, the Finance and Administration Manager, had recently been promoted to Marketing Director. He had, though, worked for James at EMI in a finance capacity and James saw great potential in Ian in a commercial role. Jim would work for Ian, and I assured him that both would get along well, and they did.

I promoted Chris Rimmer, my ex-boss, to manage the newly created Southwest region, Sean Coleman from the Coventry store to run the North and Steve Rossi from Plymouth to run the Midlands.

Jane Smart and I began tackling the enormous task of introducing best practices and work began on compiling a significant manual. We also had no Personnel Officer as Pamela Edwards had left, so all the people issues had to be dealt with, and so too did the remuneration issues. We couldn't afford a Personnel Officer, so I paid an external company an annual fee to allow our managers to access by telephone professional personnel advice.

Following the success of the relaunch of our Leeds store, James telephoned Leslie Hill at EMI Records for permission to discount across the chain. Leslie, after consulting L. G. Wood, came back and said they would only agree to a further six stores. We took that decision as favourable, because we were certain that these six further stores would react in the same way Leeds had. We contacted Yellowhammer our now full-time marketing agency and we rolled out the Ed Stewart promotion to a further six stores. The results were excellent and this led to EMI agreeing to allow us to compete and discount along with the rest of the industry.

Looking back, I think it's fair to say that even then, with the permission to compete granted, I am certain none of us had any idea what the formula was for positioning HMV to become market leader. The whole thing apart from Oxford Street was a mess, poorly located stores, poor shop management, no stock controls, no consistent standards and ultimately no profit. The task before us was enormous, HMV Oxford Street was profitable, very few other stores were, and the UK was now in recession.

While I was working with my new team to introduce consistent standards James had taken day-to-day control of HMV Oxford Street. We were not sure this was a great idea, he wasn't a retailer, and he didn't know much about music. We therefore assumed he'd taken on this day-to-day control of our most important store to accelerate his knowledge of HMV and more importantly, the record industry itself.

As I mentioned earlier, margins were very low in record retailing and that was a serious strategic threat to the business that we wanted to grow.

James saw margin improvement as his number one priority. He was a charming man and although very different to most of us in the record industry, he was well liked and through his uniqueness, could often get away with murder. His office was large, and he had access to food through the staff canteen. So, he decided to woo the record companies by inviting them to lunch in his office, wining and dining them in order to get bigger margins. He had a certain degree of success but as I knew later, getting a margin increase from a record company was like getting blood out of a stone. He charmed the pants off them basically; he was very popular and if he thought he might fail with any particular individual he would often find out what particular wine they liked, or food they liked. One Managing Director apparently liked to watch porn, so James organised for a TV and a VHS player to be available in his office during their lunch!

I hadn't known that many senior record company people until then as I was up North, but James introduced me to people like Dave Harmer from RCA, Bob Lewis from CBS, Jimmy Hanks from EMI. I liked them and got on well with them.

Also, high up on James's agenda was a total refurbishment of the Oxford Street store, which was going to cost hundreds of thousands of pounds. He was in the process of putting together his justification for such a huge spend when the news broke that EMI Ltd would merge with Thorn Electricals. No one had seen this coming and immediately we were all fearful of what this would mean for us. The new company was to be called Thorn–EMI.

Thorn owned several successful retail and TV/radio brands such as Ferguson, Radio Rentals, DER, Kenwood, and Rumbelows.

It was a sad day for many of us to see EMI lose its independence, having signed The Beatles and making extraordinary profits as a result. The problem with the EMI board was that it had no idea what to do with this newfound wealth and so decided to invest in 'entertainment' ventures. They owned nightclubs, the Blackpool Tower and, would you believe, Thames Television. They also went on to expand into films, setting up EMI Films.

EMI was once an industrial research company and Godfrey Hounsfield, a researcher at EMI back in the 1950s, did some pioneering work on computers, helping to build the first all-transistor computer. Unfortunately, the division he worked in wasn't profitable and was sold in 1962, just at the time the company signed The Beatles. The Beatles' profits paved the way to retain Godfrey at EMI and allow him time to conduct independent research to see what he might come up with. He went on to invent the CT brain scanner and then shared the 1979 Nobel Prize for Medicine. This was the first machine produced to apply this new technology to the diagnosis of brain lesions. Profits flowed from this innovation until EMI failed to get clearance to market and sell the scanner in the US.

Profits going forward were heavily skewed to this huge market in the US, which alas never materialised.

Bernie Delfont was hired to run all the entertainment investments, and the EMI Chairman, Sir Joseph Lockwood, stood down to make way for Sir John Reid. Soon after his appointment the merger with Thorn was announced. Sir Richard Cave, the Thorn Chairman would continue in that role and Sir John Reid would become Chief Executive.

This was worrying for us at HMV and James decided to make some changes at senior management level. He promoted me to Operations Director, and he promoted Bernard Kelly to Finance Director, following Jim Fraser's retirement. Jimmy was one of the nicest people I have ever met. His wife Eva was equally as nice, and they had a long and happy life together. Jimmy was an old-fashioned accountant, bright as a button with a wonderful sense of humour and a love of gin and tonic. We spent many days and nights on the road together and it's fair to say we never stopped laughing and never stopped drinking. We became very close and when things got very political over Dave Wilde, Jimmy was always there to give me the advice I needed and so prevented me from tripping myself up. Life was never the same after he left HMV, but Sue and I were fortunate to see him and Eva over a period of many years until their death. Both lovely people, and we still miss them.

So, our new board consisted of James, Ian Gray, marketing, Bernard, finance, and me in operations. James was frantically trying to get news as to who he would be reporting to, and what division of Thorn–EMI we would be part of!

He didn't have to wait too long as he was told that our new bosses wanted to visit us at Dean Street on the Thursday after the merger was announced. We all attended as instructed and we were introduced to David Neale, Deputy Chairman of Thorn–EMI, and David Johnston, CEO of Rumbelows. They asked James to make a presentation to them outlining the history of the business and our strategy going forward. As one would expect, the meeting was very formal and once James had completed his presentation, Neale said they were carrying out a number of these meetings to try and decide whether we remained under the umbrella of EMI Music or a subsidiary of Rumbelows.

Once they left, James led the board into a discussion regarding the two options and we believed we may as a company fare much better under a retail umbrella rather than return to EMI Records, which never appeared to have a lot of interest in us. However, this was not our decision to make, and we would have to wait to hear from David Neale. As luck would have it, Ian Gray and I attended the NARM (National Association of Record Merchandisers) Conference in Los Angeles. This is an annual event mainly for record companies and retailers in the US to meet up and discuss the issues facing their industry. It wasn't an exclusive US gathering and record retailers from around the world were encouraged to attend. Because we were still technically a subsidiary of EMI Records, Ian and I were introduced to various senior EMI executives, one of whom invited us to dinner at his house the following evening. He lived in a mansion in Beverly Hills, the likes of which you only see in the movies or on television. It was staggering inside, completely over the top, but nevertheless it was a good opportunity for Ian and me to discuss the future of HMV with the CEO of EMI Records worldwide, a guy called Bhaskar Menon.

Over dinner we were asked our opinion as to where HMV should report into in this merger with Thorn and we responded by asking him for some indication that if we remained under EMI would we get the financial investment we required to build our business. Bhaskar was not so sure and felt that EMI Records was a manufacturer and not a retailer, and that our future might be better secured if we reported into a retail sector in Thorn. On our return to the UK, we briefed James and the rest of the board on our trip and James said he agreed, and would arrange to see David Neale to get the ball rolling.

It was therefore decided that HMV would report to Thorn–EMI Retail and that would include Rumbelows. David Johnston, as MD of Rumbelows, would chair the new division and that James and the HMV board would report directly to him.

In the meantime, I had a great deal on my plate. Working with the regional managers, I toured the country visiting every store and with the Midlands and the Southern region, most of those shops I had not been to before.

I was very straight, honest and direct with all the managers I spoke to. My aim was to get everyone singing from the same hymn sheet in the shortest possible time and those guys who were clearly not up to the job were dismissed or demoted. The business failed, in my opinion, to recognise that we were carrying too many people and holding back the careers of people below manager level. This was something I wanted to rectify quickly, which I did. The new talent that was coming through the ranks were motivated, enthusiastic, and keen to make a huge contribution to the national debate we were having as well as addressing the issues in their own store. One guy I recall was the catalyst for change, and that guy was Keith Johnson. I appointed him to run the HMV concession in the Top Shop store in Norwich. Keith was a great character, full of life, great company to be with, but above all, he just loved music. He was infectious, and set about improving the range in Norwich, but above all, unlike many of our managers at the time, he knew what his customers wanted, and he went about making sure that we had it, and then spreading the word to other stores. Like me, he also liked a drink!

We were beginning to see the future, which involved incredibly empowered managers, who knew as much about music as their customers, and were able to pre-empt their needs. This had to be done in a fun environment, with helpful, knowledgeable staff. And I believed this was the only way as a chain we would ever gain credibility with our customers and present HMV to them as their first-choice record store. Norwich sales were catching the eye of several people and in particular my boss.

James continued with his dual role as Managing Director and General Manager of Oxford Street. Quite rightly, he had identified that the store was due for a revamp and that it would cost a great deal of money. He began working with the various floor managers to get their input, but it's fair to say that the store was beginning to look very tired, and our management weren't that enthusiastic about having James there or having a major refit. The key though was to get the plans prepared and the financial case in place to present to David Johnston at one of our future board meetings. And our first board meeting with David in charge was interesting to say the least.

He arrived half an hour early and wandered around the floor we occupied in Dean Street, going in and out of people's empty offices, as they were yet to arrive for work. On starting the meeting dead on 9 a.m., David went through the usual pleasantries and then launched into this attack on us all, picking up a carrier bag and emptying the contents of it onto the boardroom table. The contents were biros, about forty of them, and he said these were collected by him from various offices, and indicated to him a culture of waste, which allowed our people to have far more pens on their desks than they needed.

I was accused of, during my store visits, being too focused on the minutiae (much of which I believed was important). But emptying a carrier bag of forty pens onto the table was in my opinion not the right way to start off chairing an important board meeting. James looked utterly horrified and I knew this management style of David's was not going to go down well with James. Working his way through the agenda, David only appeared to be interested in my report.

He was running at least 200 Rumbelows stores on a very much hands-on basis, so I knew I was going to come under quite a lot of scrutiny. He tended to bark at you, and just throw provocative statements up in the air without any facts or evidence to back them up. He was very intimidating, especially to me, and I knew that he was going to continue like this until I produced some better results. We were not doing well at this time, but frankly neither was Rumbelows.

Often, we would hold our board meetings at Rumbelows' head office at Waltham Cross and that's where I got to know their Personnel Director, Bill

Legg. Bill was a decent guy, very supportive of what I was trying to do and told me that I had to keep going and to keep my spirits up. This was always going to be difficult when the store that continued to weigh me down, HMV Leeds, was encountering more problems as the manager, Peter Pearson, had left. I'd given his replacement a lot of thought and decided upon Keith Johnson, the exceptional Norwich manager. I distinctly recall dashing from a board meeting to Norwich one afternoon to have dinner with Keith and offer him the job. I always felt enthused in Keith's company and having dinner in the vibrant city of Norwich was the icing on the cake. Fortunately, Keith accepted and his appointment as store manager in Leeds started off a new and important chapter in our history.

David Johnston had made the decision, quite rightly in my opinion, that James could not continue in his dual role of GM of Oxford Street and the MD of the chain. JT (as we now referred to him) wasn't thrilled about this but nevertheless accepted it and decided to search for his successor. Of course, JT consulted me and I suggested Chris Rimmer, my old boss at Portsmouth and now my Midlands Regional Manager. JT felt for some reason that this appointment should be from someone outside of HMV, a retailer of music, yes, but not from HMV. I personally had not heard or was aware of any outstanding managers from our competitors, but JT said he had a guy recommended to him who was already running a successful store in the UK. JT and I had a very robust disagreement on a number of issues but this Oxford Street vacancy was to be our biggest and most damaging one in our otherwise excellent relationship. He insisted on the whole board interviewing the new man, despite the fact that once JT stood down as GM, the new GM would report to me. I believed strongly that this guy did not have the necessary experience to run a store of this size and importance and I felt if he was appointed, I would have to resign. JT was acutely aware of this, and I knew he didn't want to lose me, but we are both stubborn individuals and neither of us was giving any ground!

JT went behind my back and asked the guy to London to be interviewed by the whole board once he and I had seen him first. During our interview, JT was so desperate to get his guy over the line that he was spoon-feeding him the answers to the questions he was asking!

Although the new guy was a very likeable and charming individual he did not, as I have already mentioned, have the presence, the experience, or the competence to hold down a job of this size. He looked extremely uncomfortable throughout the interview and looked terrified when it was my turn to ask him a question. I sensed though that JT himself noticed the shortfalls in his answers yet nevertheless continued in a jolly, and I must say, very informal manner for a senior job interview. Then he gave us the nod that it was time for us to bring in Ian Gray and Bernard Kelly to join the process, but also astonished me by asking his secretary to bring in lunch! I could not believe it. He was doing everything he possibly could to make our applicant less nervous in the hope that he might impress the board and I would have to resign.

As I predicted, Ian and Bernard gave him an easy ride, bowling him short balls that he knocked for six! Once it was all over, JT asked for our views and clearly, I had lost. They felt he had potential and that it was time to bring in fresh blood to the company as indeed JT, Ian and Bernard were fine examples of this new policy. Sensing my utter defeat, I appealed to Ian and Bernard saying that this appointment is an operational appointment, and that the Operations Director should have the final say. To JT's utter disgust, they reluctantly agreed, sensing that if I was defeated on an issue of such importance to me, I would have to go. JT responded immediately, believing the process was robust, professionally managed and that we had all collectively made the right decision to allow the Operations Director to appoint his senior people, who ultimately he would be accountable for. I can tell you, I was so relieved at this decision, if we had got it wrong it would possibly have meant the end of HMV, as our flagship store continued to keep us all afloat.

Chris Rimmer, my Regional Manager for the Midlands, was duly appointed General Manager of HMV Oxford Street. Although he was a terribly quiet and shy individual, there was no one better in the UK to take on this role and by doing so set a fine and wonderful example to the rest of the chain.

Including Chris Taylor at Newcastle, Keith Johnson at Leeds and Keith Armstrong at Derby, I was slowly identifying guys of similar enthusiasm and love of music. I could also sense that once we got the OK to extend chart discounting to six more stores, the dam would burst, and discounting would become the norm in HMV.

That proved to be the case, the six stores proved to be successful and just one phone call from JT to Leslie Hill, the EMI Records CEO, resulted in the green light. While this was helping us, and the 'singles shop' too, we still had a terrible imbalance across the chain between space and range.

Managers were still authorised to choose their own range in the space they had in each store. There were no tills that recorded individual sales, nor were there any computers to give you a daily print-out of sales by genre. It was a complete mess and few if any other industries would have allowed such a practice to exist. The problem was that we were trying to replicate HMV Oxford Street, which was 12,000 square feet into a chain of stores measuring anything from 800 square feet to 2,000 square feet. The challenge for me was how to get the ratio of space to range right without technology. Rock music for example, as Chris Rimmer had already proved in Portsmouth and Bristol, was becoming the dominant genre yet, often because of managers' lack of commercial nous, or because of their interest in a particular type of music, this massive change was not being reflected in the stores. Without technology, all I could do was ask questions, why have you sold so few of this title like other shops are selling? Why have you given over so much space to jazz or blues?

Under the old masterbag system, when the sleeve and the record were separated, the record went into what we called a masterbag, and apart from the title and the artist, normally written on the right, you would also use a date stamp to record the day it arrived in the store and how many copies were purchased.

This was really the store manager's only means of having a stock control system. As regional manager, I then had the ability to go through the browsers, pick a title that I didn't think should be there and ask the manager to show me the masterbag to check when it arrived and how many copies were ordered. If one copy was dated as arriving on say 1 January, and I asked to see the masterbag on say 7 June, if that record was not sold or reordered from 1 January, I could question why it was bought, and why similar titles like it were also bought. This process took up a great deal of time but would at least continue to give us an insight into the manager's ability and into space/stock/sales ratio. It was though a long, drawn-out process, and it definitely had its drawbacks. But it did allow managers a degree of autonomy, but in this revolution we were part of, it clearly was massively advantageous when a number of individual managers got it right, and then we could share this skill with other managers.

I don't intend to bore the reader with the internal debate about stock control when the chain went fully self-service and the masterbag system became no longer necessary. But after huge disagreements across the chain, we all decided on a filing card system that contained all the masterbag information, except that instead of it being stored behind the counter taking up valuable sales space it was put into a small box in A–Z order. It was a replacement system, perfectly OK and very successful, however if you forgot to write out a card for a particular new release, it never got reordered once it was sold.

For me, it was critical for our success to get this space/range/ratio improved – it held the key to our future. At this point, there was little science applied, everything we did was by the seat of our pants and if we got it right, sales and profits would improve significantly. Eventually I came up with a 'quick and dirty' solution. I asked each store manager to list on paper all the various genres that his store stocked, i.e., jazz, pop/rock, easy listening, classical, etc. Each time a sale was made the genre category got a tick confirming the sale. So, at the end of the week, you could have a piece of paper looking something like this:

Rock	55%
Easy Listening	10%
Jazz/Blues	5%
Country	5%
Classical	10%
Pop	15%
Total	**100%**

We then asked the managers to draw up a paper that broke down their range as a percentage of their space, for instance:

Rock	35%
Classical	20%
Pop	5%
Jazz/Blues	15%
Country	5%
Easy Listening	20%
Total	**100%**

This is very simplistic and only one example of the experiment we entered into – across the chain we were getting fairly similar results, indicating the imbalance of rock and pop music sales to the range we were carrying. Some of this could be explained by the fact that our flagship store in Oxford Street was heavily biased towards easy listening, jazz and classical, and that this was influencing managers and assistant managers within the chain. After a few months and sufficient data, I asked my regional managers to correct the imbalances within their stores and end up with a sales/stock mix that maximised the space allocated to the specific genres. This instruction also applied to Oxford Street, where the rock/pop range was on the first floor. Can you believe that? The range of music in most demand was not on the ground floor!

The next area we had to tackle was stock levels.

Basically, there were few controls in place for our store managers, and you could, in theory, order as much as you liked from the record companies and HMV would pay for it. Regional managers, on their visits, were dealing with the consequences of the stock/sales mix campaign that had just finished, which produced a great deal of unwanted stock. Visually, overstocks were there to see in any store you visited, and it was up to the regional managers to check this and educate the manager accordingly. This system or approach was not working, and although I was not an accountant, even I could see that we had a massive problem of overstocks building up almost unchecked throughout the chain and swallowing up huge amounts of working capital. It became an obsession for me and I decided to act.

I used common sense basically. Crudely, I based my new stock control measures on my monthly pay. I was paid X by my employers, known as income, and I was allowed to buy things with that income, called expenses. I believe, Mrs Thatcher as prime minister was derided by people by applying a similar policy to running the country. In essence, operations and finance sat down and put together a sales forecast for each store, covering say six months. It could never be 100% accurate but it would be close based on previous sales data. Attached to this monthly sales forecast would be a stockholding forecast and the rule was, essentially, your sales and stock numbers needed to be the same. You couldn't buy more than you took in sales. I called this 'Purchase Controls' and introduced them sometime in 1981.

I'm not sure I got a great deal of support from all the regional managers, and I was met with a deluge of opposition from the store managers and the record industry. I was aware that these measures were quite draconian, but we couldn't carry on the way we were. The system was a recipe for wasting hundreds of thousands of pounds each year, and clearly, just as HMV were the losers, our inefficiency ensured that the record companies were the winners. So, the protests from all the senior record company executives were very loud and JT was inundated with phone calls and letters from them expressing their anger and disbelief that we could implement such measures. Furthermore, they told us that constraining our managers in this way would hurt us severely as a company through lost sales, and our competitors were already laughing at us. I made no apology for trying to do my job, and part of my job was to ensure I did not waste the company's money on unsold stock.

I can look back on this policy with a great sense of achievement as once we had got over the initial resistance, this policy in years to come provided HMV with a substantial negative working capital position that allowed us to expand the chain and grow our profits year after year.

My good friend Eric Nicoli, former Chairman of EMI Music, my Chairman too at HMV. He saved both HMV and Waterstones from financial collapse and referred to me as his hairy-arsed retail friend!

The late Sir Colin Southgate, Chairman of Thorn EMI, our owners. He was my guardian angel from above – he protected me and supported me for many years.

My good pals Bob Lewis, the driving force behind BARD, and John Kennedy, former Chairman of Universal Music.

My Dad, Patrick, with his new wife Sheila.

My brother Pat and my sister Christina, with our Mum around 1943.

At my brother's wedding in my school uniform, 1964.

Great memories, great times.

Dave Wilde, General Manager of HMV. He promoted me to regional manager and laid the foundations for HMV's expansion outside of London. A kind, decent man, he taught me so much about life.

Billboard

INTERNATIONAL

Industry Turns Out To Honor HMV COO McLaughlin

The front page of Billboard, reporting on my Music Industry Trust Award in 2001. The editor Adam White supported both me and HMV for many years.

The one and only Gary Farrow from Sony Music. Gary introduced me to Richard Keys and the HMV Football Extravaganza came into being as a result, raising millions for our music charity.

Geoff Shreeves, with his wife Diane, Alan Curbishley and his wife Carol, with Richard Keys. Geoff, Alan and Richard helped us raise over £8m for the Nordoff Robbins charity through their support for the Legend of Football dinner.

Karen Little and Emma Allen, known as Brian's Angels. Karen organised the early HMV Football dinners, and Emma was my long-suffering PA. Tremendous people.

Sue, with James Tyrrell and Jim Peal, my dearest friends. James became the first Managing Director at HMV in 1979. An accountant by trade, he became the man who set up HMV to become the most profitable music retailer in the world. Jim was my boss whilst I was at HMV Leeds, and he went on to spearhead our expansion in the 1990s.

Another great celebration at Don Giovanni, but this time, featuring my latest grandson Max.

The iconic HMV store at 363 Oxford Street, opened by Sir Edward Elgar in 1921. My first visit convinced me that I wanted to work for them.

Keith Johnson, manager and regional manager whose love of music and understanding of our customers changed the face of HMV.

The late Sir George Martin unveiling the blue plaque with Nipper at our flagship store, 363 Oxford Street, following its closure.

Our wedding day: 28 September 1968.

With my Chairman, Stuart McAllister, and one of my earlier bosses, Mike Donaghue. Both have sadly passed away now.

Another family celebration at our favourite restaurant in Goring, Don Giovanni at the Leatherne Bottel. Back row: my son-in-law Ben, Sue, my son James, his wife Donna, my daughter Louisa and her husband John. Front row: my daughter Katie and my grandchildren Amy, James and Samuel.

And now we are 4. My sister, Frances, brother Tom, and youngest sister Enda. Sadly, Patrick and Christina passed away within a year of each other.

My great friends John Clark, Chris Rimmer, Jim Peal and Steve Knott. Their combined skill and talent ensured that HMV would never be a small, mediocre company.

Catching up with old friends from the music industry – Jeff Beard, Jimmy Mulvoy and Paul Conroy.

A rare photo of my siblings and me all together. Tom, Christina, Frances, Enda and Patrick.

Family and friends in Barbados, celebrating my daughter Katie's 30th birthday.

Sue and I celebrated our 54th wedding anniversary in Barbados.

My wonderful son-in-law, John Nicoll, taken from us so young with a rare form of cancer, Sarcoma.

My best friend, Shaun McNamee, at the Henley Regatta. He sadly passed away, having succumbed to pancreatic cancer.

Raising my Music Industry Trust Award in the direction of all the HMV Managers.

Paul Burger, Chairman of Sony Music, a good friend and supporter of HMV.

My darling wife, Sue, in Barbados.

My great pal and owner of Pinnacle Records, Steve Prebble.

Steve Knott, my Operations Director and Mike Lymath, my HR Director – outstanding executives and good friends.

Pauline Etkin, CEO, Nordoff Robbins with Harry and Sandra Redknapp at the Legends of Football Dinner.

The late great Maurice Oberstein with Paul Russell, Chairman, Sony Music.

Billy Fury, my boyhood hero.

Chapter 15

Thorn–EMI were proving to be very supportive in the early days and this meant we could move forward with the Oxford Street refurbishment and the opening of another major store, which was to be in Manchester. JT was convinced that apart from our strategic operational and marketing initiatives, a huge statement was needed to demonstrate to our suppliers and competitors that we were getting our act together and intent on becoming market leaders in the UK. Refurbishing Oxford Street was critical to achieving this, and the news that we were going to open a big store in Manchester was enough, putting our money where our mouth was!

A fabulous site became available opposite the old store in Market Street, although we would have liked more space on the ground floor. It had a wide shopfront, and it was considered then one of the best sites in Manchester. David Johnston, our Chairman, was terribly enthusiastic about the investment and felt that between us, the HMV board was competent at tackling the issues we were facing.

Looking back, the issues were formidable, yet we were ambitious, hungry and very determined to become number one in record retailing.

Ian Gray, our new Marketing Director, worked well with our advertising agency Yellowhammer and we were beginning to have a major presence in the *NME* and *Melody Maker*, the two music papers that were hugely influential with our customers.

The opening of the Manchester store was a huge sign to the music industry that we were going to become a serious player in music retailing.

It was probably a career-making decision for JT, and he was going to make sure it was a big success. We gave considerable thought as to whether Peter Waddington should manage the new store, especially as the old store was so respected locally, but on balance JT and I decided that Peter and the new disciplines we were introducing were not compatible. I had enormous respect for Peter, and you couldn't meet a nicer and funnier guy if you tried. We wished him well, and he went off to own and manage a very successful koi carp business.

Peter didn't take the decision well and we never saw or spoke to each other until the opening of our hundredth store in Fort Dunlop, Birmingham, many years later. That night after all the speeches, Peter and I stood at the bar for hours reminiscing and laughing about the good old days. I always liked and respected Peter, I also learnt a lot from him too. Looking back, I'm thrilled we spent that time together because although he didn't agree with much of what I did during his time, it gave me great pleasure to know that he had great respect for what I eventually achieved. Sadly, he passed away in 2020, but I will always remember him with great affection and so too will many others from HMV.

We appointed Graham Walker as the new manager, often seen as a safe pair of hands, with his quiet, yet understated demeanour. Graham was clearly the right choice, and JT was delighted with him.

On the day of the store opening, JT opened it in style, even persuading the mayor to travel down Market Street with him in a horse-drawn carriage. He was in his element, Market Street was packed to the rafters, we had several artists there signing autographs, and a huge turnout from the record companies. It was a fabulous day, JT clearly was going to not only save this chain, but also make us number one. He was amazing, giving nonstop press interviews, addressing the staff, and even serving customers from behind the till. This was his day, and he deserved all the accolades that were bestowed upon him afterwards. Our Chairman, David Johnston, was there and he too was pleased, and impressed by James. JT was clearly a showman, but deep down I believe his greatest strength was his ability to think things through strategically. He was, I feel, in a hurry and may have contributed to his eventual downfall.

But the opening of the new Manchester store proved to be a successful investment, it was exceeding budget and we could have decided to open similar-size stores in the big cities where we had poor representation. Alternatively, as JT favoured, was for us to acquire Virgin from Richard Branson. I'm not sure the board were with him on this, but it would have provided us with the level of clout we needed to get the record companies to improve our margins. For all the good work my team and I had achieved, profits were non-existent except in Oxford Street. Poorly sited stores and lack of trading space were huge contributors to this, but the gross margins we were earning were very low at around the 25–26% mark. JT had had various discussions with Branson and by all accounts he was interested in selling. He too was suffering from the same problem as us and saw, like JT, that the two chains joined together could unlock the key to profits. This was clearly JT's baby, and nothing we said was going to change his mind. For him it was clearly acquire Virgin or we go under. There was a board meeting due, and he told us he was going to raise it with David Johnston, the Chairman.

One couldn't predict David's response, because we didn't have a strategic plan that the acquisition of Virgin was part of. Furthermore, I was struggling with his harsh and unfair management of me at board meetings, despite the fact that I had given this job my all, at the expense of my family and my own personal wellbeing. He was aggressive, direct, and bullying towards me. I wouldn't have minded, but he often struggled to understand why things were as they were, and why I couldn't change them or improve them. So, I was not looking forward to this board meeting, especially as I was sure he would reject the Virgin proposal.

Once we had got through the normal agenda, JT set out his strategic plan for the business and that included buying Virgin. David listened with great interest, asking was it a merger or a takeover. Who would be the CEO if it was a merger, and similar intelligent questions. JT did not like David, I'm afraid. They were from two different walks of life, chalk and cheese would be a fair description. We discussed the plan at length, David acknowledging the need for us to have scale in order to build up our margins and profits, but he was unsure whether Thorn–EMI would agree. He decided therefore that he would arrange a further meeting the following week and would invite his boss, David Neale, the Deputy Chairman of Thorn–EMI, to chair the meeting and give a decision. JT was not hopeful and frankly Ian, Bernard and I would prefer it if they turned him down. We favoured organic expansion without the huge debt we would have to carry following the acquisition.

At our specially convened meeting, with David Neale in the chair, JT again set out his strategic plan, which included asking Thorn–EMI for several million pounds to purchase Virgin. It was a long boardroom table with David sat at one end, and JT sat opposite him down the other. JT was in great form, passing papers around the table in support of his plan, standing up, pacing the room, then sitting down, reaching for some graphs that clearly proved what a great investment this would be for Thorn–EMI and how HMV would, overnight, become market leaders in music retailing. Neale, as previously described, was a cold individual and said very little throughout the presentation. Suddenly, he interrupted JT, and asked how much profit this 'business of yours' intends to make this year. JT looked somewhat surprised, what did that have to do with a strategic planning meeting? JT said almost that and carried on. Neale said, 'You've not answered my question, Mr Tyrrell. How much money will you make this year?' Clearly annoyed with this line of questioning, JT dug into his briefcase and pulled out a green folder, opened it and said, 'If we have a good Christmas, we hope to make about £53,000.'

'£53,000' said David Neale, '£53,000? You must be fucking joking. Are you in your right mind Mr Tyrrell? You've got the audacity to take up my valuable time, asking me to approve an investment that will cost Thorn–EMI millions of pounds, without any guarantee of success, and you are telling me that all you're going to make this year is £53,000?'

'Well,' he went on, picking up the strategic plan document. 'You insult me, how dare you, and you stick this document where it deserves to be stuck.' And with that, he threw it at some speed down the table heading in JT's direction. The atmosphere was electric, even David Johnston, who likes a scrap, was shocked! With that Neale got up, his face red and about to explode, stormed out of the room. No one saw it coming. Neale had remained silent throughout but gave no indication he was going to go ballistic! David Johnston left the room saying nothing. We looked at JT and knew this was the end of him.

It was a terrible blow for him and over the next couple of weeks he wasn't himself and we began arguing over changes he wanted to make to the second floor at Oxford Street. Unbeknown to me, he had lunch with Penguin, the book publishers, and he got it into his head (rather like Bob Boast and his greeting card nightmare) that we should trial selling paperback books on the second floor of Oxford Street. Chris Rimmer and I were keen to extend the space for cassettes, which were growing as a share of the market, and I was absolutely dumbfounded as to why a record store, a famous record store, would want to sell paperback books. Like Bob Boast, JT was only interested in the margins you could earn from books, around 45% as opposed to 25% on music. He called me into his office and literally ordered me to get in touch with the Sales Director at Penguin to arrange a visit to Oxford Street so that we could finalise a deal. I flatly refused and told him he had taken leave of his senses. Whether he liked it or not, we were in the record business first and foremost, not the 'profit at any price' business.

Our job, I told him, was to work our way through the minefield we were in, called record retailing, and try and find a way through it. It was senseless to go down this route, whatever the margins were. We would end up not only confusing the customer, but our staff and suppliers too. He clearly wasn't interested and told me to carry out his instructions. I said I wouldn't, and in any case we should both head to Paddington station or we would miss our train home. JT lived in Upper Basildon and got the train to Paddington at Pangbourne, the station where I joined the train too. We used to often travel together, there and back if we were going into London. Anyhow, he said, 'Yes, we need to go to Paddington.' We darted out of Dean Street to the bus stop as we usually did, but on this occasion, he got in front of me, rushed upstairs and sat next to a stranger! I thought, sod him! When we got off, he brushed past me, heading into the station and he sped up the platform and got on the train. Clearly, he didn't want to sit with me, so I joined another carriage and sat on my own! The same thing happened when we arrived at Pangbourne. He got off, walked straight past me, saying, 'Good night, Mr McLaughlin!'

I didn't see him the next day as I was out and visiting stores, but I did see him the day after. He called me into his office and said he had reflected on our discussion on Monday night and felt my argument had sufficiently swayed him to reverse his decision on selling paperback books in Oxford Street. He felt though that only he understood the severity of the situation we were in and that unless some strategic alliance was made with Virgin, HMV would go under. I explained to him that under the surface, lots of changes were being made as to how we operated and marketed ourselves as a company.

We had a recession to deal with, and huge competitor issues with Our Price having a monopoly in London, Virgin continuing to expand, and the record companies continuing to prop up the largely inefficient independent sector that was causing us a lot of damage.

I was working flat out to improve the quality of our staff and store managers. Purchase controls were introduced, freeing up working capital to allow us to expand and re-site the stores we had in secondary locations. We were competing now on price for chart titles, we were in the middle of a major realignment of the stock/space mix in all our stores, and we were refurbishing our flagship store in Oxford Street.

If he was patient, I told him, we could eventually turn a lot of this hard work into sales and from that, increased profits. I told him also though, that it would take time and that our competitors would continue to take us on, but eventually my team and I were confident we could succeed. He didn't look convinced, but he agreed that we had no choice.

I set up a series of monthly meetings with my team, having asked Mike Donaghue to become Head of Central Services, and replacing him as Southern RM with Stuart Hartley, previously in Oxford Street. These Operations Meetings were critical to the business as it gave me the opportunity to ensure we were leaving no stone unturned in our drive to instil consistent operational practices, brutal cost controls and increase sales in all formats – singles, albums and cassettes. I worked very closely with Bernard Kelly our Finance Director and his team to ensure they produced all the information we needed each month, on a store-by-store basis. The quality of their work was excellent, and it allowed me in a relentless fashion to drill down by region, and by store, into any statistic the business was recording. I use the word relentless, mainly because in later years many of the team told me that's what I was. I knew no other way, because we were all fighting for a brand and a company we loved. I was not prepared to be nice or sensitive to people's feelings when so much was at stake. I coined a phrase that eventually stuck – 'continuous improvement'. They must have got bored with hearing that, but I believe it became a part of our DNA and remained within the business until the day I left.

Despite all our efforts to improve our performance and translate that into profits, David Johnston the Chairman, telephoned JT and told him that further cost reductions were required by Thorn–EMI and needed implementing immediately.

This was a terrific blow to us all, and although we appreciated the almost break-even situation we were forecasting for the year end, we honestly believed the forecast had been accepted at Thorn–EMI level, but obviously not. We were instructed to move Head Office from Dean Street in Soho, to Banner Street in the East End, where we held our central supplies of admin and stationery. Banner Street was a large building with a cheap rent and could possibly house our staff from Dean Street. But compared with the buzz and vibrancy of Dean Street, Banner Street was very dull with few stores and nothing memorable about the environment. Furthermore, we were told that the annual pay award due in April was to be deferred until July. JT was very depressed about the situation and vowed that he wouldn't work from Banner Street. We decided on a positive response to David's instructions but bought ourselves some time on the move to Banner Street by asking his permission to set up a steering committee to manage the move and ensure, logistically, that what he was asking for could actually be put into practice. Behind this of course was our desire to put off this awful move for a few months in the hope that sales and profits may pick up in the meantime.

To keep JT's spirits up the refurbishment of the Oxford Street store was nearly finished and he was looking forward once again to put his showman's hat on to get maximum exposure at the launch. The store was looking fantastic and after many arguments we persuaded the floor managers to accept our proposals for the new layout of the range, including the very sensitive moving of the rock/pop floor to the ground floor, and the opening of a TV/video area on the first floor. Chris Rimmer and I opposed JT on his need to sell hardware on the first floor, but we felt we had to let him go ahead with it, to prove it wouldn't work. JT organised a big party in the store, and David Johnston and David Neale were guests of honour. There was a huge turnout from the record industry, to witness another substantial investment on our part to retail their music in a professional manner in one of the most sought-after stores in the UK.

Once we were open to the public, the sales uplift we were looking for wasn't there and Chris Rimmer and I felt that more managerial changes may be necessary until we got it right. JT and I were on a collision course again, shortly after the reopening of the store. VHS video machines were popular, we were even selling them in Oxford Street. Video rental shops were popping up everywhere and JT wanted a slice of this market. My team and I were not keen as this was not a retail product, it was a rental product that we would never own. The economic model wasn't good and to make any real money a popular VHS tape would have to be rented many, many times over to make a small profit. JT was always looking to sell and promote something new, whereas I constantly explained to him that there wasn't anything wrong with that, but we so far weren't succeeding or maximising the potential of what we were currently selling. We can't just discard our heritage, our values, to jump on yet another bandwagon. To cut a long story short, I agreed to a video rental trial in six shops and that was enough to keep the peace for the time being!

Shortly after this, we went to HMV Brighton together where we were relaunching the store and we were fortunate to have the very popular Boy George do a personal appearance. The store was packed, it was a fun day, and JT and I had lots of laughs about our disagreements, both of us knowing that they were because we were both so passionate about the business. All in all, it was a very successful day and truth be known we all drank too much champagne.

That afternoon I was driving to Ramsgate to stay at the Monastery, St Augustine's Abbey with my dearest friend, Fr Stephen Holford. It was not a wise decision after drinking all that champagne, and I found myself on a motorway heading for Ramsgate, literally falling asleep at the wheel. Other motorists were sounding their horns as I weaved in and out of the lanes, until eventually I woke and couldn't believe how close I was to killing other people as well as myself. It was the scariest moment I ever encountered, and I quickly looked out for a service station to stop and calm my nerves. I parked the car probably around 6 p.m. and then slept until about 8 p.m. I was due in Ramsgate at 8 p.m.! There were no mobile phones in those days and the telephones at the service station weren't working. So, I rejoined the motorway, knowing that I was seriously late, something I hate being, and yet I still had at least another hour to go before I would arrive in Ramsgate. Fr Stephen was very kind and understanding, suggested I had a snack and went straight to bed. I went to see him for some advice, he was the nearest person I had to a real father and I loved him.

I told him my life was not a happy one. I was letting Sue and the children down by getting home late every night. I was moody at weekends, and I spent much of my time at work fighting JT, David Johnston and our Marketing Director, Ian Gray. In addition to this I had to train and develop a team of regional managers, store managers, and find the key to making money for Thorn–EMI to protect our futures. Fr Stephen admitted that he wasn't a businessman and so could not advise me in matters of this nature. What he did say though was that he felt after everything that had happened to me in my life, my terrible childhood, losing Mum at fourteen, and then not having a real father to give me leadership, I now had real purpose in life, a wonderful family and an important job. He could see that I had an enormous passion for HMV whenever we got on to the subject and felt that while Sue and the children may suffer in the short term, he was confident that I was showing him the level of determination that was needed to make a success of myself and

HMV. There was, he felt, a mountain to climb, but urged me to stick with it, and understand that there would be even more setbacks going forward before the dream was achieved. We spent some time talking about the church, politics, and St Augustine's Abbey. It was a remarkable and thoroughly enjoyable weekend and when I look back, offloading my concerns and fears to him clearly helped me as an individual and as an employee.

On the Monday, I went to the office in Dean Street as normal and prepared for our management meeting with the board. Thirty minutes before this JT asked to see me. He looked very anxious, and I could tell it wasn't good news he was going to tell me. He began explaining that he saw a great future for this company, it had an iconic, famous brand and there was a huge determination on everyone's part to see it become the market leader in record retailing. However, he honestly felt that ever since David Neale from Thorn–EMI turned down his proposal to buy Virgin, he could not see us achieving our goal for many, many years, and that he felt he wanted to manage a big company soon or failing that hold a very senior position in a company that was ambitious and already hugely successful. I could tell that this was a very difficult decision for JT to make, as he had fallen in love with HMV and its people. He went on to say that with huge regret he was resigning his position as MD of HMV and joining the Abbey National Building Society as their Finance Director from next month. I was not surprised to hear this, but I was nevertheless very sad, as I would miss him and so too would the company.

There was no denying that he was an amazing human being. From starting with a finance background, he had galvanised a very sleepy organisation into waking up and realising its potential. I was about to ask him who was taking over from him, when he dropped the bombshell that it was going to be Ian Gray, our Marketing Director. For a very short second, I thought it might be me, but even I was realistic and knew that I wasn't ready for this huge responsibility just yet. However, my mouth must have dropped to the floor – it was the worst news I had heard in years and I knew immediately because of my deteriorating relationship with Ian, that I was likely to be out of a job. It was so bad between us that we were barely on speaking terms. As a guy, Ian was fine, but we didn't agree about the way the company was being marketed.

JT said that Ian would do an excellent job, he was a very bright young man and that I need to encourage the whole business to get behind him. I was very upset with this news; I joined the management meeting as I recall and sat through it barely saying a word. Ian saw me afterwards and I congratulated him on his promotion, but that's as far as I could go. My team were devastated once I told them the news and they too believed I would lose my job.

Life went on as normal for the last month of JT's tenure as MD, except that Sue and I were seriously concerned for our future. HMV meant everything to both of us, we were clearly devastated and life as we knew it was never going to be the same again.

We gave JT a wonderful send-off, he clearly was very moved with all the wonderful tributes that were made to him, both from HMV employees, but also from the music industry. He was so well liked, everyone would miss him, but no one would miss him as much as me. If I'm being honest, JT didn't really understand the specialist nature of our offer to the public. I'm not sure he even really needed to. What he did understand though was that income has to exceed expenditure, and for that to happen you have to have a business model that works. Sadly, our business model was work in progress and to this day, I'm still very sad that JT wasn't with us on the journey he set us on and to see the results that were eventually achieved.

Chapter 16

I got a call at home from Ian Gray on the Saturday after JT left asking me out to lunch on Monday. I immediately said yes, in a very surprising way, as I thought if he's going to sack me, why waste your money on a lunch? Anyhow, I was optimistic and duly turned up at this very pleasant French restaurant in Cambridge Circus. Ian was very jolly, as he can be, and made me feel at ease, ordering a rather nice bottle of red wine. He admitted that his appointment would not be well received by me and that this lunch was to thrash things out and see if there was a way in which the two of us could work together. This was not the Ian I knew, I thought, he was very relaxed, very warm towards me and very much enjoying the red wine! So much so that another bottle was ordered and we continued to talk through how things might work out. We covered in some detail the obvious reasons for our disagreement and we both agreed that we didn't try hard enough to resolve them amicably. We rather instead kept finding more reasons why our two departments were falling short and continued to apportion the blame. But then, suddenly, Ian said, 'Brian, I have the utmost respect for you and what you are trying to achieve, and I want us to work together going forward, bringing the success to this company, that we all seek. The work to date you have done on stock control for example, is nothing short of amazing. No one asked you to get the stockholding figures down, you did this instinctively as a retailer, and it has improved our working capital requirement immensely.

'Let's then agree,' he said, 'to allow each of us to get on with their jobs, without interference and criticism. I promise you Brian,' he went on, 'to let you run the stores on a day-to-day basis, as long as you allow me to manage the business strategically, so that everyone then meets their agreed goals. Those agreed goals would include a huge input from you, as I value your experience and your retailing skills.'

I was really knocked back by this and said that I thought we may not be able to find a way in which we could work together. 'But if this is the offer and you are serious, I accept, and you will have my 100% support.'

It was a very successful lunch overall as Ian and I were able to confront a lot of our issues between us, but also because I saw a different Ian Gray that day. An Ian Gray that maybe was going to enjoy being MD, much more than he ever did being Marketing Director. I was elated and a bit pissed too! I called Sue as soon as I got back to the office and like me, she was thrilled. I called all my team and there was a huge sense of relief I could detect amongst them, as many of them wondered – if I was sacked, how many of them would survive?

So ended a hugely successful day for me and my family. I hoped it would be equally successful for HMV too.

True to his word, Ian allowed me complete freedom to run the stores on a day-to-day basis. Out of respect for him, I kept him abreast of all the major decisions, and often as not, would consult him in advance to double check my thought processes and accept his advice.

My problem though wasn't Ian, it was the Chairman, David Johnston. Unfortunately, he continued to bully me and intimidate me at board meetings, and I began to wonder how much more of this I could endure. I was doing my job well, I was making huge progress, yet David was never satisfied and would continue to question and criticise much of what I was doing. In the end I decided to see Bill Legg, the Rumbelows' Personnel Director and seek his advice. I liked Bill a lot, he was a huge supporter of mine and in the early days of the Thorn takeover, he provided me with a lot of advice and understanding.

I arranged to see Bill and explained the problem I was having with David. He was surprised, as he only ever heard good reports about me from him and suggested I take it up with David on a one-to-one basis, explaining the stress and anxiety you were going through. He assured me that the outcome would be a positive one and that David did not want to lose me. So, I took Bill's advice and arranged to go and see David at his office in Waltham Cross. It was miles from anywhere in my eyes, I was so spoilt working in the West End and in particular Soho. It was always vibrant, busy, noisy and alive whereas Waltham Cross was anything but!

David could be nice, and if you caught him on the right day, he could display a cheerful disposition. I was in luck this day, but maybe Bill Legg had tipped him off about my problem. He was very chatty, very complimentary about my achievements to date, and in fact he used the words – what I had achieved over the past year would have broken many an executive, you are to be congratulated!

Wow, I thought, how can I now tell him he is making me very unhappy and very anxious when I'm with him? Anyhow he asked the question, why did I want to see him, and rightly or wrongly, I decided in a split second to tell him. He looked totally surprised as I gave him example after example, where I felt he had behaved unfairly towards me, and throughout my tale of woe, he never once interrupted me. When I finished, he came over to me, and said, 'Brian, I'm really sorry to hear this, you are one of the few people in business that I respect, and I offer you my sincere apology.' He went on to say that what I had achieved over the previous two years would take most executives a lifetime to achieve.

Sometimes, he explained, at these board meetings he became a different person, often not listening to people's replies, and was in danger of becoming disliked for his management style. He admitted that he was tough, but there was no excuse for the treatment he was dishing out to me and said things will improve, you have no need to worry.

I told Sue, and like me, she was very relieved, as it was influencing us both and adding to our feeling of general insecurity in life. I had no qualifications, no O-levels, just a few years as a record retailer. I believed the job market for me was limited, I only wanted to work in music, and apart from HMV I had no desire to work for any of my competitors. Having convinced myself of this, I was continually insecure, and continually worried about the mortgage and my ability to look after my family. This feeling never left me for many, many years and it was a feeling I could have done without.

However, a few months after I saw David, Bill Legg called me and asked me out for a drink in Soho. I thought this was a bit strange, but nevertheless agreed to meet him. Basically, he confirmed that my meeting with David went well, and that David had no idea he was behaving so badly towards me. In addition, he asked about where I saw myself in a few months'/years' time, doing the same job or a different job, either with HMV, or within Thorn–EMI? I had never given that any thought, never planned my career, as many people I know do. So, where I've ended up has been pure chance and a lot of good luck.

I asked, 'Why all these questions?' He said there were going to be changes within Thorn–EMI soon that would affect HMV and Rumbelows and that I should maybe look to my future outside of HMV. Asked to explain that, he said he couldn't add to what he had said, but just to give it some thought. I had no idea they were looking to move me to another part of Thorn–EMI, it was not something I had thought about, or something that I wanted.

Bill called me a couple of weeks later and asked for my response. I told him honestly, that while I was flattered to have been considered for what turned out be a very senior role within Rumbelows, I felt my job at HMV was only half finished, and that the company and its people were in my blood. I therefore declined his kind offer.

Ian Gray and I continued to get on well and he asked me to come and see him to discuss a potential dispute with CBS Records. He explained that like JT had said, we needed to improve our gross margins if we were ever to be successful as a retailer.

Lack of clout, which JT saw improving by buying Virgin, was a major weakness. Our Price continued to dominate the London area, with a tightly controlled business model that was cleverly marketed via Capital Radio. We were still managing our secondary sites around London, which were not bought for strategic reasons – often as not they were acquired by EMI because the owner owed them too much money.

Nevertheless, Ian had to convince the record companies that we were a business to invest in for the future and that the better the terms they offered us, the better our relationship would be, and the more presence their repertoire would have in our stores.

Bernard Kelly, our Finance Director, sadly resigned and was replaced by Mike Jones. I liked Bernard, we both got on well and he was very supportive of what my team and I were trying to achieve. He would be missed. He was very bright, and very commercial. Managers had respect for him and trusted his judgement.

The threat of us all having to move to Banner Street was eventually lifted when Ian submitted a paper to the board pointing out that overall, there were very little savings to be achieved, and if anything, the one-off cost to cover the move could prove very expensive. We were all relieved when David Johnston agreed with Ian and gave him permission to find extra space within the Soho area. Rents were becoming more reasonable and there were a lot of empty offices around at that time. Eventually in July 1984 we moved from Royalty House in Dean Street to Film House in Wardour Street. These were our original offices in Wardour Street under Dave Wilde, so it was great to be going back.

There was a general feeling of optimism in the business and Ian told me that the way things were going we could possibly achieve £1 million in profit for the first time! He was honest in as much as he said there were a few accounting windfalls that would be included in this target, but nevertheless it was a great number for the business to chase, and what a morale booster it would be if we actually made it!

Ian was working with the advertising agency, Yellowhammer, to come up with a solution that would help transform the atmosphere in the stores and give us a bit of a cutting-edge with our core market. There was enormous enthusiasm within the company and quite rightly Ian said that we should launch our new profit target with our instore marketing initiative at a managers' conference.

We held this at Heathrow Airport, and it was a tremendous success. Yellowhammer unveiled what is now known as the 'Amoeba' wallpaper, which was in fact wallpaper and was to be applied to all walls throughout the chain. The new look, together with the profit target, gave everyone a huge boost and one had the feeling that after a very hard slog, we might be seeing some light at the end of the tunnel. Managers couldn't wait to get back to their stores to start 'wallpapering' and what one manager discovered, probably Keith Johnson in Leeds, was that if you painted the white ceilings black and if you replaced the white spotlights on the ceilings with coloured ones, it complemented the new wallpaper and provided the very cool and cutting-edge atmosphere that we were trying to achieve. Window displays were hugely improved too. Coloured, moving lights were added, and managers were instructed to turn the instore music up loud. The result of all these measures was that we were beginning to lose our bright sterile look that I believed made us look more like Woolworths or WHSmith than the trendy, fashionable chain of specialist record stores I believed us to be.

Our recruitment practices were improving too, we only hired staff who had the same love and passion for music that our customers did. We trained our staff to be polite, and never offer a view or comment on what people wanted to buy. We were trying to capture the lion's share of that key eighteen-to-twenty-five market without alienating regular buyers who may have felt intimidated by our stores. Further changes to the board took place in 1983, with Ian Gray appointing Ian Duffell from Sony to be our new Commercial Director. The timing of this appointment was key, as Philips was about to unveil the compact disc, and knowing us we would want to be out of the traps fast and steal a lead on our competitors.

In Ian Duffell's first few months he worked very closely with all our suppliers to discuss the huge changes that were going to have to happen to accommodate this new and exciting product. Display and merchandising, along with pricing and marketing all had to be resolved before the industry was ready to launch. The display and merchandising of the CD posed a major challenge as the album browsers were designed for twelve-inch albums and not 5′x5′ compact discs, or CDs as they commonly became known. Our current browsers would have to be adapted to take the smaller disc and this would involve a considerable amount of cost.

The US record retail industry was not prepared to make this investment and therefore asked the suppliers to design a new package. Unfortunately for the UK market the packaging solution they came up with was not compatible with our vision of how this new and exciting record should be displayed. The US packaging was nicknamed the 'long box' as it was designed to hold the CD in a tall box, primarily to fit their existing album browsers. The UK record retail industry rejected this design and set about working with the suppliers to get an agreement that the CD would be marketed in the UK in its original packaging. Little did we all know at this time, but this decision, along with the customers' appetite for new technology, would kick-start a growth period in the record industry that would last for over twenty-five years.

At our monthly property meeting, Thorn High Street Properties, our sister company, mentioned to us that a huge space in Oxford Street could be coming available within the next few months. At that time, we were not looking for additional space in Oxford Street, as we were trading very well at 363. But we were also offered the opportunity to become one of the headline retailers in a new, sexy shopping centre in Leicester Square, called the Trocadero. Chris Rimmer and I were interested in these new possibilities, but we weren't able at that time to put forward a compelling case for either. After the property meeting, Ian Gray asked me to come and see him in his office. He looked rather nervous, something he rarely is, and told me outright that he had accepted an offer to become the new CEO of Rumbelows. David Johnston was being promoted to head up a new retail division called Thorn–EMI Retail and Rumbelows and HMV would report into him. I gathered from his face that I was not going to be offered the opportunity to become MD of HMV, and he confirmed this by telling me that Ian Duffell, our new Commercial Director, was to get the job.

When JT left, I felt it was too early for me to become the MD, but with Ian leaving three years later, I felt as though I was ready, and therefore felt very disappointed. In fairness to everyone involved in this decision, I didn't look or behave like a typical MD of a company should. I wasn't a snazzy dresser, I didn't go to university, and I lacked confidence in myself. An MD had to look, talk, and behave like one, and frankly I didn't. Even my friend at Rumbelows, Bill Legg, told me that, and said, 'That's life, Brian.'

Ian Duffell and I got along well, he was a decent enough guy, very genial and had an excellent sense of humour. Despite our earlier differences, Ian Gray and I were a successful team, and we began to like each other. He had an incredible brain and I benefited enormously from his strategic thinking and his enthusiasm. HMV and I owe him a great deal.

Nevertheless, Sue was also disappointed when I told her the news, but we agreed it wasn't a job we were seeking but felt this was possibly the time when I was ready for it. In amongst this news, was a bigger reorganisation within Thorn–EMI itself, with a new company set up called Thorn–EMI Home Electronics. This new company was to be led by a guy from Volvo called Jim Maxmin, and he brought with him Stuart McAllister as HR Director and Stuart Morgan as Business Development Director. David Johnston, the new head of Thorn–EMI Retail, would report directly to Maxmin. Sir Richard Cave, the Chairman of Thorn–EMI, was standing down and he was being replaced by a guy called Peter Laister. Upon taking up his new position, he decided that there needed to be some synergy between all the various brands they owned and as such they decided to give Maxmin a huge empire to manage, which included Rumbelows, Kenwood, HMV, Ferguson, DER and Radio Rentals. Not long after he had been appointed, the key senior people from all of these brands were invited to a conference where we would all see and hear Laister for the first time.

As I recall, the morning was made up of speeches to be given by Laister, Maxmin, and McAllister, followed by lunch, and an afternoon summary. The morning was so boring, listening at length to the world of DER, Radio Rentals and Kenwood Food Mixers! However, it got worse! We were ushered into the luncheon room with table plans, and I discovered looking at my table, I knew no one at all. I was to be surrounded by all these radio and TV guys. But it then got even worse. As we sat down, Laister appeared and addressed the room. He said this was an extremely exciting period for the group and the opportunities for Thorn–EMI going forward were great. However, we are a diverse group, apart from the radio and TV brands, Kenwood, HMV, the group also owned EMI Music, and a missile business! He went on to say that leaving aside EMI Music, our job over lunch was to get acquainted with our fellow companies and spend our time identifying how we as a group could come up with one defining strategy that would maximise the synergies that clearly existed between us.

I'm not sure about everyone else's reaction, but I immediately felt that if you and your new board don't have a strategy, why should we devise one for you, this was not in our remit! Anyhow, we spent the next ninety minutes around my table, trying to work out how DER, Radio Rentals, Kenwood, Rumbelows and HMV could all work together for the greater good of the group. How utterly ridiculous! Laister was touring the room, stopping off at tables, picking people out and asking them to give him a summary of where we were. It was utterly laughable, and from the little world of HMV where I came from, I suddenly had an insight into a huge corporation and how it works.

Basically, to us, it appeared as though no one on the Thorn–EMI board had any idea what they could do with all these different brands, and they were hellbent on searching for money-making synergies that clearly didn't exist. I don't think anyone thought that the best way forward might be to leave everyone alone and let the management of these businesses develop them with support from the main board. Clearly judging from people's conversations on the way back to the conference hall, the conference and the lunch were a huge failure, and instead of showing the way and providing clear leadership to the various businesses they owned, everyone left the room deflated, confused and very disappointed. Even the summary after lunch by Laister and Co. couldn't lift our spirits, as everyone realised we achieved little that day.

Following the conference, David Johnston asked Ian Duffell and the other HMV directors to meet Jim Maxmin and Stuart McAllister. Maxmin, an energetic American, never stopped talking throughout the meeting. I realised after ten minutes he was speaking what is termed 'management speak'! Mostly bullshit, that no ordinary person such as I could understand. To give you an example, he said, 'Brian, you have to find out what your customer wants, and then love them to death.' Later in 1994, as Chairman of Laura Ashley he told a journalist from the *Independent on Sunday* that he proudly owned a special 'Bullshit' rubber stamp! This he fearlessly applied to 'deserving documents'. However, in the article the journalist Patrick Hosking wrote, 'The documents most crying out for treatment were Mr Maxmin's own mission statements, management slogans, marketing guff, and other jargon.'

This, then, was now the guy who would have a big say in HMV going forward and probably my career as well.

McAllister, on the other hand, said very little. A very tall man, and a chain smoker, he spoke much more slowly, and to give him his due, he listened intently to you. We discussed HMV at length, and they listened when I told them that we were beginning to get the business right operationally. We had stolen a march on our competitors with the new CD, and that time was ripe now to expand. I mentioned to Maxmin that I had heard rumours that Tower Records from the US were looking at opening a store in London.

Now, Tower was famous in the US. It had this iconic store on Sunset Strip in LA that everyone went to, ordinary buyers, but also artists, and record company personnel. In fact, in the US the record companies loved Tower Records, and its owner and founder Russ Solomon. Russ was one of the boys, and he socialised a lot with both record companies and artists. As a result of the success he was having in LA, he was expanding quite fast in the US, and not only was he looking at London he was also looking at Japan and beyond. Maxmin said I should go to the US, have a look at his operation and try and find out if he intended to open in London, and where. I said I would, but I wanted to take Chris Rimmer with me. That too was agreed.

On arriving in New York, we planned to visit all the Tower Stores – there were about six I believe. Particularly interesting though was the latest opening in Greenwich Village. We did the other stores, the one at the Lincoln Center was large, but blow me, the new one in Greenwich Village was just massive! Chris and I reckoned it was at least 30,000 square feet, compared with our Oxford Street flagship store at only 12,000 square feet. To say we were worried would simply be an understatement. It was not only a massive store, it was also one hell of a good record store. The range it carried was simply mind-blowing, and it was bright, fun, and packed out with customers. We decided to talk to one or two of the staff, introducing ourselves as big Tower fans, hoping one day that they would open a store like this in the UK. One of the guys said 'Hey, I hear we are opening a huge store in London within the next twelve months.' They didn't know where, but they said Russ loved London, and you can bet that it would be in a huge tourist area. Mission accomplished, we both thought! It wasn't the news we wanted to hear, but equally it was now a reality, rather than just a rumour, so we could plan accordingly.

On our arrival back in London, we got in touch with the guys from Thorn–EMI High Street Properties, our internal property agents, and asked them to call a meeting and dig out the two opportunities they recently mentioned. Namely, the big space somewhere in Oxford Street, and the new shopping centre in Leicester Square. Ian Duffell chaired the meeting and Chris and I briefed everyone on the reality of the Tower threat. In essence, although our store portfolio was still poor, we were nevertheless beginning to see some significant improvements that, along with our flagship store's profits, meant we were in better shape than we'd ever been.

Our recent new store openings were paying off, in particular the stores in Liverpool, Edinburgh, Blackpool, Nottingham, Leicester and Oxford, to name but a few. However, Oxford Street still accounted for a large percentage of our profits, and if Tower were to open a store the size of Greenwich Village, then we were all doomed!

Everyone agreed with this and we began to examine in much greater detail the two opportunities. The Trocadero development was not large, but it was bang in the tourist area of Leicester Square. As far as our agents were aware, this opportunity had only been offered to us, and no other record retailer. It was an attractive tourist trap, but for me it was only about 5,000 square feet, and the rent was huge. We then looked at the Oxford Street opportunity. Our agents by now had more details, and they told us confidentially, that a small run-down shopping mall, opposite Marks & Spencer was going to be closed down and the entire space was then to be offered to one retailer. Apparently, the current space was made up of several small market traders. The mall was called Oxford Walk, and allegedly Richard Branson started off his mail-order business out of there many years ago. When we asked what the total space was, we all fell over. It was 50,000 square feet at a rent of £500,000 per year.

Chris and I looked at each other and indicated that this was the answer to the Tower threat, it would also do immense harm to Virgin, whose Tottenham Court Rd store was not that far away. We discussed at length which of the two opportunities we should go for, and eventually Ian Duffell said we will go with Brian and Chris's recommendation, Oxford Walk.

To be fair to Ian, this was a huge decision for him to make, having only just been appointed MD.

We pushed all the buttons, David Johnston and Jim Maxmin signed off on Oxford Walk, our agents drew up all the legal documents, but then we hit a major hitch. The owners of Oxford Walk, the Royal Insurance Company, had to buy out all the leases of the small traders before they could offer us vacant possession. All went well, until one of the traders said no, he wasn't selling. He wanted to carry on trading until his lease expired in a few years' time. Clearly, he realised his powerful position, and he eventually left once the Royal made him an offer he couldn't refuse.

I have to say, we were all so excited and even more so when we heard that Tower had bought the lease to the old Swan & Edgar store in Piccadilly Circus. Apparently, it was about 25,000 square feet, but our intelligence told us that it was not an ideal retail store, more of a rabbit warren, and therefore they had massive problems to overcome. I had no hesitation in recommending to the board in 1985 that Chris Rimmer should become General Manager of the new store, which we decided we would call Oxford Circus. Our financial plan was signed off and Chris and I were confident with the sales projections we submitted – and in fact, secretly believed we would exceed them by some margin.

David Johnston and Jim Maxmin didn't hit it off. David was very much of the old school and, like me, frankly, had little time for Maxmin. Funnily enough, I got to like David a lot, he was a very wise individual and a decent and honest man. Inevitably he had to go, and I was very sad to hear this news. Although he was direct and tough, he believed in me and after we patched up our differences, we really got along very well.

In the chain, we were experiencing quite a lot of difficulty with a company called Revolver Records Ltd. They were beginning to cause us problems in several locations due to their discounting policies when we came up against them. The owner was a likeable guy and clearly, he was building this chain in the hope that someone would buy it from him. The word on the street was that yes, he would sell if the price was right. Duffell and Maxmin suggested that we buy it. I wasn't overly thrilled with the idea as we would end up with two stores in several locations, and you either keep them both or you must decide which ones to close, the HMV one or the Revolver one. Added to that, we were growing slowly, and by now had reached forty stores, with Oxford Circus to open within the year. I was also concerned about the potential clashes of culture that these takeovers bring, although I had never experienced one before. I am a fairly cautious individual, not a huge risk taker, unless I can see a cast-iron opportunity. And to be honest I never saw this as one.

In addition to the Revolver debate, we were approached by two Irishmen, Jim Aiken and Maurice Cassidy, who wanted to lease the HMV name from us. Both extremely likeable characters. Jim, in Ireland, was the equivalent of Harvey Goldsmith, the UK promoter, and Maurice was a very successful entrepreneur. Jim Maxmin asked me to sit in the meeting and we were both able to explain to them that we didn't lease our brand name. They explained that they, with a third party, had just bought the lease of two key retail sites in Dublin. One in Henry

Street, and the other in Grafton Street. Unfortunately for them, they had decided to open them as record stores, but they had just heard that Virgin was about to open a huge store in between the two sites. Their intention was to call the stores Mega Records Ltd, but they felt this was not strong enough to compete with a brand as famous as Virgin. Which is why they wanted to lease our name. We repeated our answer, it was a no. They went away, disappointed, but called again the following week. Were we intending to open in Dublin, they asked. We said no, so they asked, would we enter a partnership with them and call the stores HMV? They also said that if we agreed, we could manage the stores and charge a suitable management fee.

I was uncomfortable with this, Revolver looked as though it was going to happen and would involve me and my team in a great deal of work, and now we were being asked to enter into a partnership with people from a foreign country. Maxmin and Duffell again wanted to do it, and so we did a deal with the Irishmen, we would own a third each with HMV running both stores.

Unfortunately for me, I had no interest at all in Ireland, only Northern Ireland, but even that would be low down on my list, mainly because none of us understood the market there.

Our operational policies were improving all the time, we were building up a strong, talented bunch of managers and staff who clearly understood that we had to perform at the top of our game. Second best was never ever going to be acceptable to me. Our new stores were proving to be very successful; Virgin was not a threat. Fortunately, they didn't understand retail as we did, and as for Our Price, one day we would be ready to take them on too. Revolver and Dublin I did not need, but both got the go-ahead.

Maxmin became so excited about the Revolver purchase that he got a model built of 'The Revolver Store of the Future', employing an expensive agency to come up with an exciting new design. He even went public, telling the press the strategy behind the purchase – that it would be a separate chain to HMV and focusing on a very different customer. Retailers, he said, would all have to follow his lead and start targeting customers and their needs.

My initial thoughts were that I would be able to talk them out of running Revolver as a separate chain. They certainly had some excellent sites in which we were not represented, and where there was duplication, we would simply keep open the store with the most potential, irrespective of whether it was an HMV or a Revolver. However, this was not to be. Maxmin was hellbent on a separate chain and I was forced to appoint a General Manager to run it.

We were fortunate to have acquired several good managers and staff, Dave Marklew springs to mind as one of their most dedicated people, who turned out to become a very loyal HMV employee.

Eventually, after about six months, the experiment with Revolver failed, I got the go-ahead to rename the stores as HMV and we would dispose of the stores that were not going to be viable. Sean Coleman, the General Manager, left the business, and it wasn't long before most of the retained Revolver stores were exceeding our budgeted expectations.

Ian Duffell announced the date of our annual conference, which was 13–14 May 1985, and because of our growing sales and profits, it would be held in Marbella, Spain. It was such exciting news for everyone to receive, especially as we had all been working so hard for the past few years.

The record companies were also invited to Spain along with Lynne Franks and her team, Yellowhammer, our advertising agency, and Alan Zafer, the producer of the event.

The main speakers, which included me, arrived in Marbella a few days ahead of the managers to rehearse and get a bit of sun. I have to say I didn't particularly enjoy being surrounded by the PR and advertising people; they were just not my sort. From the outset, I realised most of them, including our marketing department, were not going to take this conference seriously and instead saw it as just one huge jolly. I was extremely impressed though with Ian's choice of producer, Alan Zafer. He was very thorough and extremely professional. He went on to work for us for twenty-five years. It was my privilege to work with such a consummate professional.

We agreed on the messages we wanted to convey to the managers, notably another complete instore new-look wallpaper, which we called 'Fax and Frottage'! I wasn't sure about it at first, but I warmed to it and I could see that this would be another major step forward for the chain. It was agreed that Ian, Tony and I would do the main speeches, and we would include Yellowhammer and Lynne Franks.

On the day before the managers' arrival, we agreed to rehearse the conference at 2 p.m. There was Alan waiting in the conference room for everyone as you would expect, with his team ready to start the rehearsal. Suffice to say it was a disaster. In fact, it was an utter shambles. We had people coming in and out, disappearing, and some of them were rather drunk from a good lunch by the pool. I became very anxious as it was important that the managers saw us as professional leaders, spurring them on to achieve their financial and nonfinancial goals. Ian was very embarrassed and told me not to worry, as everything would be all right on the night!

I finished my rehearsal and Ian said I had hit the right tone, in as much as that I was saying to the managers, enjoy Spain, see this as a huge thank you, but don't become complacent. When you aspire to become number one as I did, you can never take your foot off the pedal, you can never rest!

The conference went well considering, but I don't think a lot of our managers were that impressed with our 'creative people'. They were all knocked out though with the hotel, the Don Carlos, although the service was poor and the drinks at the bar were extortionate! A huge bonus for us all, was the fact that Billy Connolly had agreed to entertain us after dinner! We kept it a secret, you should have seen everyone's faces when Alan Zafer said, 'Please give a warm welcome to Billy Connolly.' He was just superb, a complete and utter pro, and had everyone in stitches from start to finish. He joined Ian, Tony and me in the bar afterwards. He was just as funny there, and to my surprise he said he didn't drink alcohol!

Overall, I think the event was hugely successful, and Ian deserves big credit for staging it in Marbella. For all my criticisms of him and the marketing people, I do believe through this conference he demonstrated that yes you can work very hard, as we all did, but if you're successful, you have to show people that you appreciate them. I took this on board very seriously and continued to take our managers abroad many times more after I became MD in 1987.

On our return to the UK, we were hit with the news that most of our suppliers were reducing our trading terms with them. Everyone, but especially us, were looking for ways to grow our margin, but what we hadn't foreseen was this attempt by them to actually reduce them.

Ian spent a great deal of his time in meetings trying to resolve the problems facing us, but in some cases, like EMI and Sony, we had to withdraw our cooperation in marketing their product in our stores. Polygram was no better, but after a short dispute our terms were reinstated as, eventually, they were with EMI and Sony.

One of my major disappointments as an important record retailer was that our suppliers never included retailers in any of their strategic planning. I constantly explained throughout all my term negotiations with them, that the healthier, the more vibrant, the retail sector becomes, the greater opportunity they will have to grow their sales, profits and develop new artists for the future. It was a constant battle and only a couple of senior CEOs in the record companies ever understood us and the important role we play in the industry. Generally, they failed to understand that we were in competition with the fashion and entertainment businesses. They were talented manufacturers sourcing creative talent, who, like the fashion and entertainment industries, had to have a strong retail sector to present and market their product. No matter how good the talent was, it doesn't sell itself.

All I ever heard was the risks they were taking, and that 90% of the artists they signed were unprofitable. What they failed to understand or accept was that when we signed a lease for a new store in the UK, it was for twenty-five years. So, for example, when we signed the lease for Oxford Circus, it was twenty-five years x £500,000, which equates to a liability of £12.5m.

HMV UK eventually had over 300 stores with leases of twenty-five years, making the maths very scary indeed!

Chris Rimmer proceeded with his plan to open Oxford Circus, and we appointed David Terrill, the tape floor manager at Oxford Street, to become the new General Manager at Oxford Street. Chris rarely impresses anyone that doesn't know him, as I said before, he's shy, very quiet and happy hiding in the background. However, I would not have chosen anyone else in the organisation other than him to run this important new store, which we would eventually market as the 'World's Largest Record Store'. His attention to detail was second to none, his memory was amazing, and he had a way about him that everyone wanted to work with him. His major fault though was he was not very assertive, and this always presented him with problems. I was the very opposite to him in this respect and I could get very frustrated if he failed to confront things as they needed to be. All in all, this flaw of his I lived with, because his other attributes were so vital and so needed in spearheading a project of this stature.

While Chris was meticulously planning the key operational requirements of the new store, Ian Duffell was working with Stuart Morgan from Thorn–EMI Electronics on the design. I was also involved but could sense early on that Stuart was keen on having an art deco shopfront, which Ian didn't dismiss out of hand. I must admit I didn't know very much about architecture or art deco as a design, but I did know that it didn't provide us with an operational solution. I kept saying, 'It's a shop, for Christ's sake! It's not the Natural History Museum we are buying.' Anyway, eventually, a very hurt and disappointed Stuart Morgan backed off and we eventually, with Chris Rimmer's input, arrived at a sensible attractive alternative.

Oxford Circus began to take up a disproportionate amount of Ian's time and I felt that some of his other responsibilities such as managing the shopfitting team were being neglected. We had undertaken to carry out several refits and we had a major new store opening programme. I have to say that I couldn't help but get involved in something so important, but along with my very demanding responsibilities, this additional worry was beginning to make me feel very tired.

At home, Sue continued to support me even though most other women would have left me long ago. I found the train journey increasingly frustrating, with its packed trains and constant delays. Having fought my way to Paddington, I then had to queue for the Number 73 bus to Oxford Street. Often several of those would pass my bus stop as they were full. Rightly or wrongly, I decided I had had enough of the train and instead would drive to Wardour Street. At the beginning this looked like a sound idea. I left home at 5.30 or slightly later some mornings and managed to be parked up in Wardour Street about 6.30–6.45. This was heaven, the office was empty, and I could get through stacks of paperwork.

Where it all went wrong was in the evening, it didn't matter what time I left the office, the journey out of London was a nightmare and it could often take two and a half to three hours to get home. At least when I eventually got home, I was happy.

We had lived in Woodcote for six years and our pay plus annual bonus continued to improve over that period. I found Woodcote a gloomy place to live, especially in winter, but we were now able to afford a bigger mortgage that meant we could move. Sue and I loved the surrounding area, the schools were good, we were near a train station and very close to the M4 motorway. We searched for a new home in Pangbourne and the charming little village of Whitchurch-on-Thames. Eventually we settled on a place on the High Street called Esk Cottage. We bought the cottage, which itself was charming, from a lovely old lady who had lived there for many years, sadly a number of them on her own. Although the rooms were small, the whole place had character and a lovely outdoor eating area with a separate annex. The other plus was that it was nearer to Pangbourne and the railway station and the sun seemed to shine much more there than it ever did in Woodcote.

The local people were very friendly, and I recall a knock at the door one night, to be greeted by several happy youngsters from the village introducing themselves to us and welcoming us to the village. We remain in touch with most of them, but a girl called Fiona eventually became the nanny for our youngest daughter, Katie. We remain close friends with her and her husband, Chris, and their two children, Olivia and Matthew.

I was so happy that we had Louisa and James so early in our marriage, and always hoped that one day we would have another one. Quite rightly Sue didn't, she was coming up to her fortieth birthday and therefore did not fancy motherhood again, especially the sleepless nights and the nappies! However, to my great surprise Sue announced to me that she was pregnant and our baby would be due in July 1987. I cannot tell you how thrilled I was to hear this wonderful news, I felt for Sue, but knew she would want the baby – but admittedly, not as much as I did!

I recall telling Ian Duffell about it, and typical him, he took me straight out to the pub and bought me a drink to celebrate. He was genuinely happy for us, and I thought it was a nice gesture.

In addition to this wonderful news, in the October 1986 we finally opened Oxford Circus, which was officially recognised by the *Guinness Book of Records* as the world's largest record store. Chris and his team had done an absolutely marvellous job, introducing a computerised stock control system and an offsite stock processing area in Banner Street. The store was officially opened by Bob Geldof, and there wasn't a day went by that there wasn't an article in some newspaper across the world trumpeting the opening of this great new store. Chris Rimmer and I felt very proud on our opening day, as we had made our trip to New York, seen the threat Tower posed to the whole company and responded almost immediately with the opening of this truly exciting new store. We only opened two out of the three floors for trading – we kept the third floor closed, believing that we would one day need it as the sales grew over time.

Our initial takings were significantly ahead of our budget, and it was, I believe, a point in our history when, for the first time, both our competitors and our suppliers began to take us seriously. Obviously, Ian was all over the papers and it would be fair to say that he took a great deal more credit for Oxford Circus than he deserved. Still, he signed off on the investment despite his concerns, and for that, we must be grateful to him.

We were now on a roll, we continued to trade well into Christmas and throughout December. Oxford Circus was packed out, the Revolver stores were successfully integrated, and our new stores were all performing well too.

I arrived back in the office in early January for our customary budget meeting only to be told that Ian was in Saint Lucia on holiday and would not be in for a few days. I wasn't happy about this, the window to get the budget done properly and on time for the start of the new financial year was tight, so I thought this wasn't a great move on his part.

I continued to drive to work and continued to get home very late, some nights, 9 or 10 p.m. and was getting very tired. Eventually, once we had put the budget to bed, Ian called me and Tony Hirsh into his office for a chat about our next managers' conference, scheduled to be held in Bournemouth.

Having seen Ian and Tony I returned to my office and immediately became unwell. I felt very faint, I was sweating and felt very lightheaded. My secretary rang Chris Rimmer in Oxford Circus and he sent over a couple of his security team who were trained in first aid. They were both very nice guys, and they got me to walk up and down the office, got me a glass of water, and said maybe

I've been overdoing things and should take the rest of the day off. I thought that was good advice and duly went home.

By this time in 1987, Sue was about five months pregnant, and I didn't want to worry her, given her condition. When she opened the door, she said I looked very pale and unwell and suggested I went to bed. This was about 4.30 p.m. and I slept until 6 when Sue came upstairs to tell me that Ian Duffell had rung. He didn't want Sue to wake me as I was unwell, but to pass on a message. The message was mind-blowing. He told Sue to tell me he had been to Marlow as planned to see Stuart McAllister, the newly appointed Chairman of HMV, and had resigned! I could not believe it! There he was sitting in his office this morning asking me for my thoughts on a conference he was never going to attend!

I spoke to him the next day and he told me that Richard Branson was so impressed with Oxford Circus that he wanted Ian to join Virgin and open a chain of stores for him in Australia. Ian said he was rather flattered with the offer and, as he wasn't getting on with Stuart, he thought it was the right choice for his career. He wished me a speedy recovery, apologised for not telling me his news the previous morning, but he felt obliged to tell Stuart first. He said he had no idea who would take over from him but suspected that Stuart liked Tony Hirsh and he was likely the favourite. We said our farewells, and to this day we have not spoken.

Chapter 17

The following day was the day that changed my life. Stuart rang me at home to discuss Ian's resignation and my health. I told him I was resting, and a few days off would do me the world of good. He was pleased to hear that and went on to say that part of his new brief as Chairman of HMV was to open new stores internationally. In fact, he was off to the US the next day to look at some stores and when he returned in a couple of weeks, he was minded to offer me the job of Managing Director! I couldn't believe what I was hearing! I think I said, 'Me, Stuart?' He said, 'Yes Brian, you! You've done a splendid job with the stores; you and I can work together to build a huge business both domestically and internationally.' He said, 'Get better soon, keep this under your hat until I return, as I expect Tony Hirsh and Mike Jones, the FD will both apply for the job, and at least I should see them.' I was literally shaking with joy at this amazing news, I kissed Sue at least a thousand times and the kids thought I had gone mad! Everything went through my mind at this point, but more than anything, the fear of failing, the fear of letting everyone down, getting the sack, not being able to pay the mortgage, not having enough money to look after my family. I was literally frightened to death that it was possible by taking this job, I could undo all my own good work over these past few years, everyone else's good work, and ruin the company at the same time. I confided with Sue on all of this, and she said it was all nonsense. She said I behaved and felt the same when JT promoted me to Operations Director and look how well that worked out! She was right, but I never had a lot of confidence in myself taking on any new role, until I was in it, and then I could measure whether I could do it. This feeling came with me from childhood – moving up a class at school each year used to bring about the same reaction and the same fear.

I felt much better after a few days off and went back to work. Wardour Street was buzzing with gossip and rumours regarding who the next MD would be. Tony Hirsh told me he had applied, and so had Mike Jones. I said I wasn't applying as I felt Stuart would want to see us all anyway on his return from the US.

My team were realistic, they didn't believe I would get the job, they thought Tony would. The ordinary guys like me from the shops don't get the big jobs was their view, and I never commented, I just said let's wait and see what Stuart decides when he returns. Of course, I knew who the new MD was going to be, but I was sworn to secrecy.

The suspense was killing everyone, except that if I was a bookmaker, I would have given the following odds:

T. Hirsh – 1/3 on
M. Jones – 33/1
B. McLaughlin – 6/1

Most people in Wardour Street agreed with that and apparently so did the suppliers.

We got notification that Stuart was returning the following Monday and wanted to see the three of us in our offices. He arrived at 3 p.m. and asked to see me first, confirming my new role as MD of HMV UK Ltd. We talked at length about Tony and Mike, and about press announcements, etc. So much so, that we had overrun our allotted time and therefore Stuart was running late by the time he got to see Tony, who was next on the list. By the time he got to see Mike Jones he was running about an hour late, and apparently, once he told Mike that I was his new boss, Mike looked very disappointed.

Wardour Street was just buzzing, very few people went home, waiting for the smoke to appear from the chimney! I emerged from my office to see Chris Rimmer, Jim Peal and Charlie McIntyre waiting for me. I had this enormous grin on my face, and they could not believe what had happened. They were convinced I would be overlooked again, and I have to say I have never seen three people as pleased as they were. I think Roger Reynolds, our Midlands RM, was there too, and he was beaming from ear to ear. Wow, I thought, we've done it! Us shop people have got the top job. No more arguments with marketing and PR people! We are the masters now.

Word soon spread around Wardour Street, and everyone came up to me to congratulate me. I have never felt as happy as I did then, and suddenly realised I hadn't phoned Sue! I called her and she literally screamed with delight, she was so happy for me, even though we both knew a fortnight earlier. She said, 'Don't come home, stay in London and celebrate with your friends, call me tomorrow, I love you.' I then broke down, I was just so proud of both of us, and so proud for my babies. Life had not been great for us, but everything we went through has now been rewarded with this amazing job and much higher income. At that moment, on that day, life didn't get much better. So, I booked into a hotel, so too did Chris, Jim, Charlie, and Roger. We had a few drinks in The Ship next door and then headed for the Thai restaurant in Frith Street. We drank and drank, laughed, and laughed. Leaving the restaurant wasn't that easy, it had a steep staircase down which I fell, and I also needed helping into a taxi.

I told Chris to meet me in the morning for breakfast at The Savoy. I woke the next morning with a thumping hangover, but the adrenalin was keeping me on a high following the news of my promotion. I headed over to The Savoy from my hotel to join Chris for our celebratory breakfast. I always loved The Savoy, it signified greatness and professionalism, just being able to eat there told me I had made it. It was also right that I should celebrate privately with Chris, we came a long way together from that Portsmouth store, and here we were now running the whole bloody company. I was on such a high, I could never ever remember being so happy or so excited.

I had unexpectedly been given the top job in HMV, and it meant everything to me because finally I had a chance to make this wonderful company great. Why Stuart chose me, I will never know – as I previously mentioned, I didn't look the part or have any qualifications except experience in running stores. Anyhow, it didn't matter to me. I got the job and I was so chuffed.

Having had the most wonderful breakfast at The Savoy and telephoned Sue to tell her I survived the celebrations, we walked back to Wardour Street. I don't know much about fate, but just as we were about to cross Shaftesbury Avenue into Wardour Street, the lamppost that one second ago I was standing under, dropped a huge piece of metal, crashing onto the pavement. There is no question that had I been under it, I would have been dead. And that top job I had just been appointed to would have eluded me again!

I got to Wardour Street safe and sound, and somewhat in shock. It began to dawn on me as we went up to the office in the lift that I had literally just avoided being killed. Talk about coming down to earth with a bang! As we walked through the offices, everyone was congratulating me, everyone was smiling and there was a great atmosphere in the building. I felt I should go and see Tony and Mike to commiserate with them and to hopefully receive their congratulations. I saw Tony first, while he was down and looking rather shellshocked, he nevertheless congratulated me and wished me good luck. He was unsure whether he wished to remain as Marketing Director, and said he needed a few days to think things through. I then went to see Mike Jones, and he too said he was considering his position. Mike went to Marlow that afternoon and resigned.

Dave Curnow came to see me – Dave was Mike's number two and Dave and I got on well. He was a thoroughly likeable guy with a solid head on his shoulders and I was willing to give consideration to Dave taking over from Mike. My mind was spinning, I had to get to grips with a lot of issues that Ian Duffell was dealing with and as each day went by, I became more and more scared. The press wanted to do interviews; the Chairman and CEOs from our suppliers wanted to meet me; decisions had to be made about areas of the business I wasn't up to speed with. Again, I missed Jane Smart, my previous secretary, I bet she would have taken some of the burden off me and helped calm me down. My heart was thumping away, and I really began to feel as if I was not able to do this job. My mind went back to the day I tried to persuade Jane to stay. I took her out to dinner and asked her to reconsider leaving. We had been an excellent team and felt we could try again. Jane was very upset, she clearly didn't want to leave, but I was unable to give her the role she felt she was entitled to. She would therefore not change her mind.

To confirm my fears, I went to lunch with Rob Dickins, the Chairman of Warner Records, in my favourite restaurant, Vasco & Piero's in Poland Street. I was nervous as hell, I didn't really know him that well, I tended to deal with the Sales Directors, and Warner's had a great guy called Jeff Beard. I was clumsy with the cutlery, dropping things that I picked up. He was intense, asking lots of questions, no small talk, and certainly not going out of his way to make me feel at ease. He specifically asked my views on discounting and pricing. To be honest I was so nervous, I didn't hear the questions and goodness knows therefore what he made of my incomprehensible replies. I could see he was aware that I was completely and utterly out of my depth and all I could think of was the film *They Shoot Horses Don't They?*.

This lunch knocked my confidence for six. On returning to the office, I was told that Jeff Clark-Meads, the senior *Music Week* journalist would be interviewing me the following week. I just thought, oh my God, how am I going to manage that. What if I say the wrong thing, what if I give out the wrong numbers? I was becoming a wreck, and I was more and more terrified as each day went by. I believed I had been promoted beyond my level of ability, as a lot of people are, I am told. I thought back to that wonderful morning in The Savoy and how happy I felt, I was overjoyed with pride. Now look at me, a nervous wreck, all I am experiencing is fear, fear of failing and fear of letting Sue and my family down.

At home that weekend, I put on a brave face. After all, Sue was heavily pregnant, and I didn't want to burden her with my problems.

On the Monday, I did the interview with *Music Week*. Jeff was a star, I have to say. He knew I was extremely nervous, and when rubbish came out of my mouth, he would say, 'Oh yes, I know what you meant to say, so I will write that instead.' He handled me very gently, sensing my unease and truly trying to help me get through this terrible ordeal, giving my first major press interview as MD. In the years to come Jeff and I got on very well and I will always be grateful for his kindness and understanding he showed me on that terrible day.

Stuart called in the next day, and was rather surprised to see me in my old office. Why had I not moved into Ian's office, the MD's office? I said I was more comfortable in my office, but in truth it was another sign that I wasn't up for this job, and therefore would have felt more of a fraud if I occupied the MD's office. Stuart wasn't having any of it and said I had to move in straight away. Demonstrate to everyone that you are now the boss, stop hiding away in your old office! Stuart told me that Tony Hirsh didn't want to work for me either and asked Stuart for a new role. Stuart gave his request some due consideration and came back to him offering him the MD's job of HMV Canada, which Stuart was in the process of starting up. So, I now had to find a new Finance Director and a new Marketing Director!

During my personal crisis, Stuart asked me to fly out the following week to New York with him and Stuart Morgan to view some potential new stores there. Personally, I thought the strategy to open HMV stores overseas was madness. We had not yet achieved the main goal we had set ourselves, becoming market leader in the UK. Any distraction from this was going to delay that achievement and allow the competition to benefit. Maxmin and the new Thorn–EMI Chairman, Sir Colin Southgate, were heavily into becoming global players, and they believed with its strong heritage, HMV could be highly sought after abroad. Unfortunately, the two biggest markets for music in the world, namely the US and Japan, would not allow us to use the Dog and Trumpet as it was licensed to RCA. I felt this was a huge problem as the Dog and Trumpet symbolised everything that HMV was good at. It was known throughout the world, whereas few people outside of the UK had heard of 'HMV'. Everyone though had heard of Nipper!

In those early days, it was best if I kept quiet about such things. These people were going to open HMV stores across the world, with or without my support, so I decided it was best to concentrate my efforts on the UK, which was what I was paid to do!

I flew out to New York with Stuart, and we got along well. He genuinely seemed to like me and gave me a lot of respect. We met up with various estate agents and visited a number of potential sites. It was March, and it was freezing cold, I didn't feel my feet for about three days! We sat in cafés with agents and calculators trying to work out the viability of the sites on offer. These US estate agents were foaming at the mouth at the thought of getting their hands on our money and yes, they too had worked out the lack of experience amongst our team. They were quoting ridiculously high rents, and given our lack of knowledge of the New York market, we were taking a huge risk. All I knew was that Tower was a serious record retailer. In fact, in those days I would say without doubt, they were the best in the world. Here we were, taking them on, without being able to use the Dog and Trumpet logo, and without a strong experienced team in place to run them.

We flew back to the UK with a few options to consider, and I guess Stuart sensed my heart was not in this venture with him, and subsequently didn't ask my opinion on anything to do with acquisitions.

A few days later he asked me to join him and a few others for a meal at the Tower Hotel. I told Sue it was likely to be a late one, so I decided to stay up in London, in Kensington I believe. It was a good opportunity for Stuart to spend some time with my new HR Director, Peter Renwick. Peter was a Saturday lad when I worked at the Co-op and we became very good friends, but lost touch. I had heard good things about him in the HR world and managed to poach him for HMV from Thames Television. That night was strange for me, as after one pint of beer I felt pissed, that doesn't normally occur until I have had several! Stuart asked if I was OK, and I said no, I was feeling very lightheaded and thought it best to have an early night. I got a cab to Kensington, went to bed and I had to be up early for a meeting in my office in Wardour Street. While cleaning my teeth, I became very faint, and had to sit down on the bed. I felt better, then checked out. And stood in Kensington High Street, trying to decide whether to wait for a bus or hail a cab. I couldn't decide, so stood there for goodness knows how long, until I decided to take a cab.

In the office, I felt faint again, and decided to ring Peter Renwick. He came around to see me and said, 'Brian you look terrible, we will need to get you to a doctor.' He called Tony Hirsh and they put me into one of their cars and drove me to Devonshire Place to see a doctor. I began to realise that I couldn't use my left arm, and I could hardly hear what people were saying. I felt very unwell and very tired. I went in to see the doctor, who gave me a thorough examination and said, 'I'm afraid you've had a brain haemorrhage, you will need to be rushed into hospital.' I said it can't be in London, my wife is heavily pregnant, and she won't be able to come up to London to see me. He told Tony and Peter that if that was the case, they needed to drive me home, and notify the local GP I was on my way, and that he should be there at my home to meet me. I thought, 'Oh my God what's going to happen to me? How will Sue cope with this news?' To this day, I'm still grateful for the concern Peter and Tony showed to me that morning and for driving me home.

I heard the doctor speaking to Sue and telling her about my condition. I just kept asking how is Sue? Is she OK? Please tell her I'm going to be all right.

With that, we drove home. Dr Wilson was waiting for me. I got out of the car and went into the lounge. Dr Wilson checked me out, said to Sue, 'I don't think it's a brain haemorrhage, more likely to be a stroke brought on by stress.' He called an ambulance to get me to hospital in Reading for tests. Sue came with me and still, to this day, tells everyone that I asked the ambulance driver to go through Friar Street in Reading so that I could check that the window display was OK! It's true, I did.

On arriving at the Royal Berkshire Hospital, I was keen to get the tests done, so I could be allowed home as my favourite football club, Portsmouth, were playing at Fratton Park against Millwall. It was a huge promotion game, and I didn't want to miss it! Sue said, 'You are not going to Fratton Park tomorrow, even if they allow you to come home. You are unwell and need to follow doctor's orders.' Sue left and they carried out numerous tests, I had never been in hospital before and I'm glad I hadn't, I didn't like it. It was very noisy, lots of coughing from everyone during the night, and the nurses never stopped talking! On the Saturday, the next day, I asked to be discharged as I was going to Portsmouth. Nurse said doctor would see me at 10 a.m. and decide. Doctor arrived, and said all tests proved inconclusive and that I should stay in hospital for a few days and rest. I made it quite clear that I had to get to Fratton Park – I felt much better, I could use my arm again. He asked me to get out of bed and walk up and down the ward. I managed to do this OK, and he said, 'Fine, you can go home, but rest, do not go to Portsmouth and do not return to work for a while.'

I rang Sue and told her, and she couldn't believe it. She said, 'But you are very ill, they shouldn't have discharged you.' I told her that basically I had discharged myself, something that did not go down well! By now, in her new assertive role, I realised Portsmouth was out of the question and did as I was told.

On the Monday, I telephoned Stuart, who was brilliant. He said my health was very important and I should only return to work once I felt better. I did rest a great deal, something I was not used to doing, but despite this my general condition deteriorated, and apart from just feeling unwell, my neck locked and I couldn't move it. Sleeping was a nightmare – you move without knowing, and I ended up in terrible pain. I went to see Dr Wilson who confirmed that I was suffering from overwork and stress. He was, though, concerned about my neck and sent me to see a specialist in London. After several tests, including a nasty lumbar puncture, he concluded that nothing was untoward, and that rest was the solution together with a neck brace.

I felt somewhat dejected, I have just been made MD of HMV and here I am, not well enough to do the job. The consultant said it could take six to nine months for me to recover and only if I rested throughout. Louisa was taking her A-levels and Sue was pregnant. They were both genuinely worried about me, but they had more important things to worry about. All of this was adding to my stress – would it affect Sue and the baby, and what effect would it have on Louisa's A-level results?

I had work sent from the office, and the phone from work never stopped ringing. But nothing I did made me feel any better. Eventually, I stopped taking phone calls or reading the mail from head office. I began to become quite emotional with my lot, fearing that I would lose my job because of my illness.

Then one day my dearest friend JT knocked on the door, took one look at me in my dressing gown and said, 'What do you think you're doing, you've got a company to run.' I explained my neck problem which, despite the brace, was not improving and any slight movement to the left or the right would bring on immense pain. He said, 'OK, you need to see a friend of mine, Dr Andy Watson in Wimpole Street, he will sort you out. He's an orthopaedic physician and a brilliant one at that.' The fact that James gave me his name lifted me out of my depression. Sitting at home, with nothing to do, just wasn't me, and I was beginning to feel very sorry for myself.

Sue and I visited Dr Watson. He gave me a thorough examination, sat me down, and said your mind and body have gone into lockdown. It's a form of protection – if, for example, if your neck hadn't have seized up, you may well have had a heart attack or brain haemorrhage. He said he could help me get back to full fitness, to talk about my new responsibilities, and he would also like to try acupuncture. I saw him every week from April until October in 1987, and he did indeed get me better. He helped me by talking through my poor management style at work, where I believed only I could solve all the problems, rather than delegating, and that I tolerated people who didn't perform. Every session with him brought about both physical and mental improvement, I was no longer depressed, and I could, albeit gently, begin to see movement in my neck without the accompanying pain.

In the middle of all this, Sue grew quite large with the baby, we even thought she was going to have twins at one stage. When we went out, Sue would struggle to get in the car, and she would have to navigate for me at road junctions as I couldn't move my neck! One day, a large print in the lounge collapsed to the floor, shattering all the glass. To this day, Sue and I still laugh at the memory of the two of us, in our condition, trying to pick up the glass. Eventually we just burst out laughing and agreed we would have to wait until Louisa got home!

On 21 July, Sue went into labour, and we got her into the Royal Berks at Reading. She had a wonderful midwife and the service at the hospital was just excellent. Louisa and James were very excited and me, the dad, as always was very nervous. Eventually, after a long tiresome day for Sue, at about 6 p.m. she delivered a baby girl weighing 10 lb 10 oz. I was at the birth and the kids were in the waiting room. As soon as the baby was born, I rushed out, in tears, to tell them they had a beautiful baby sister, whom we would call Katherine Francesca. Sue was just brilliant as she had been with the two others, never complaining, just grinning and bearing it, getting on with the job. I was so proud of her, it's no easy task having a baby as I can witness, and it's *really* no easy task when the baby weighs 10lb 10oz! We all hugged and cried together, we were all so happy, a truly loving family. We left Sue to rest. I told the kids I'd buy them fish and chips on the way home. Sue's mum would be anxious to see us. Sue's mum was delighted with our news and our fish and chip supper, washed down with a nice bottle of bubbly. Later Rod, my friend from the village, called in with some cigars and more champagne. I stupidly accepted a cigar, having given up smoking a year before, believing that just one couldn't do any harm. But to an ex-smoker, oh yes, one cigar or cigarette rekindles the craving, and next morning I went to the newsagents to buy a small packet of cigars. It was a huge mistake and it unfortunately kick-started me back into smoking, something I really didn't want to do again.

Sue came home with our gorgeous new addition. I couldn't help her much with the looking after, because I still had the neck brace on, but Katie was just delightful, slept through the night from almost the beginning.

Stuart wrote a lovely long letter to Sue, congratulating her on the birth of our new baby and also assuring her that everything would be OK with my job, 'He is the best choice and we want him back, but only when he's fit and well.' He even offered to pay for a two-week holiday in our favourite spot, Farringford, on the Isle of Wight, an extremely generous offer that we were glad to accept.

The letter was written in his own hand and Sue was nearly in tears reading it, as it removed the obvious anxiety about my position and our future.

However, a couple of weeks after sending this letter to Sue, he called me and asked me if I would interview a prospective Finance Director. I explained that I was making good progress with Dr Watson, but he advised me to stay clear of work-related issues until I was much better. He didn't seem very happy with my response and didn't seem to think that just taking part in one interview would be too taxing, or too risky for my health. I repeated what I said, and he asked if I wanted a Finance Director that someone else had chosen? I said that I was in no rush to recruit a new FD as Dave Curnow was a reliable guy and could continue to hold the fort until I returned. Then Stuart mentioned the forthcoming conference for managers in Bournemouth. Was I going to be available for that? I needn't speak but being there would be a morale booster for the managers. I said I would discuss it with Sue and my doctor and get back to him. By now, even though I was feeling a lot better thanks to Dr Watson, I began to see signs from Stuart that he was becoming impatient with me for not cooperating on a couple of his suggestions. I realised his dilemma, he needed an MD of his UK operation, so he was able to spend the necessary time abroad developing the international strategy. After seeing Sue's letter from him I had stopped worrying, but now I started all over again. Apparently, given the importance of my role, Stuart was legally entitled to replace me and treat me as a redundancy. This was what I was worried about. Nevertheless, we left all this behind us, and as a family went off to Farringford Hotel in the Isle of Wight, hiring a bungalow in the enormous grounds overlooking the Solent.

Sue used to continually badger me each year to find just two weeks to go on holiday as a family together, something I wasn't keen on until I arrived. If it wasn't for Farringford and having my family with me for those two weeks each year, I don't think I would be alive now. My life was just so intense, I had no room for them in it, and no room for me in it. It was all HMV. I was on a mission, and I owe Sue a deep debt of gratitude for forcing me to spend that time in Farringford. We had everything there, tennis, croquet, long walks, a swimming pool, we could barbeque, we could play golf and crazy golf. The hotel had a restaurant and bar, and my kids loved sitting there being served by the barman Franco. We knew the owners well and we always looked forward to meeting up with the families we had made friends with over the years. It was a marvellous place and those two weeks in August that Stuart kindly paid for were the beginning for me on the road to recovery.

Dr Watson saw an enormous improvement in me on my return. I felt so much better, and after our acupuncture sessions, I felt so invigorated, that I would walk to Paddington station from Wimpole Street. He said I should consider returning to work part time and that would help me with Stuart. He also thought swimming would be good for me, which it was. I let Stuart know that I would be returning to work for two or three mornings per week and he was delighted.

During my illness, I read a great deal and kept up to date with the world of business. I had great ambition still for HMV, we were building a solid operational base, we had a marvellous team of people and the competition was in disarray. Looking around, I was particularly impressed with Next, the clothing chain. They had over 200 stores, an exceptional operational base with great customer service, and growing profits. I asked myself, if we could choose our sites as well as Next, what is there to stop us having over 200 stores and becoming the most profitable record retailer in the world? For this to become a reality we would have to think big and manage our expansion differently. We had no problems getting the capital required, but we had to find a way of fast-tracking our management training and our physical store opening programme. Above all, I had to provide the leadership for this dream, something I was determined to do from the moment I returned to work.

At first, I found travelling to London very tiring. I drove to Coventry to look at the refit and on the way back had to find somewhere to park, so I could have a sleep. Each day I was asking myself, can I do this? Will the neck seize again? I was anxious, and this was not a good place to be in on returning to work.

Stuart invited me to a meeting in his office in Marlow to inform me that he had hired some external marketing consultants to look into developing the second floor of Oxford Circus as a Rock 'n' Roll Hall of Fame, similar to the one in the US. My initial reaction was no, and I asked him why he wanted to do this, as this was not retail business as we know it. Secondly, I was the MD of the UK business, and it was not something he should be getting involved with.

He said, 'Let's meet these consultants and I'm sure when you see their plan, you will change your mind.' I didn't! I saw their plan and didn't like it at all. We didn't have the skills to run a Rock 'n' Roll Hall of Fame, the business model they put up was far too optimistic for starters and was costly to set up. Oxford Circus was exceeding its profit budget, so there was no need for us to open something on a knee-jerk basis, alienating management and staff within the store. Stuart could tell during this meeting that this would be an issue of principle for me and once I had exposed the flaws in their business case he backed down. However, as we were walking to my car, he asked me when I was returning to work full time, and I explained that nothing had changed in as much as we should continue with two to three mornings per week to see how it went. He responded quite angrily, saying this business requires a full-time MD, and that he may have to find someone else if I could not do it.

Wow! I was so shocked, I said what about those personal assurances you gave me over the phone, and the letter you wrote to Sue. Did none of those mean anything? Stuart said, 'I'm under pressure, I need to spend more time developing my overseas strategy and this is something I cannot do without a full-time UK MD, I'm sorry.' I was devastated, I thought he genuinely would stick by me, but I felt he was angry with me regarding the Rock 'n' Roll Hall of Fame and decided to issue me with this ultimatum. I spoke to Sue and Dr Watson, and I told them I had to take the risk and return to work full time within the next two weeks. They both agreed, and I therefore wrote to Stuart confirming I would return full time by the end of September. I was definitely feeling a lot better, and I was itching to get on and run this company that I loved so much.

I owe a great deal of gratitude to my dear friend, JT, for putting me in touch with Dr Watson. He turned out to be my mentor and my doctor, a great deal of common sense that he passed on to me was put in place very quickly on my return.

It was time to get back to work!

Chapter 18

I had three priorities on my return to work, putting a budget together for next year, holding a managers' conference, and appointing a new board.

Dave Curnow had done a splendid job while I was away as acting Finance Director, but I felt that he would always be a number two and not the top guy. I saw several candidates for the position of Finance Director and, in the end, I appointed a guy called Laurence Campbell. Laurence had not held the post previously, but I could tell during the interview that he was very ambitious and hungry for the big job. He turned out to be an excellent choice and supported me for many years before being promoted to Group Finance Director working for Stuart at Marlow.

I also promoted Charlie McIntyre to be my new Operations Director. Charlie had previously been a regional manager with an excellent track record.

Stuart recommended a guy from within Thorn–EMI to be considered for the new role of HR Director. Mike Lymath and I hit it off from day one and he too, like Laurence, provided me with wonderful support before being promoted to Group HR Director working with Stuart. I owe Mike a great deal as he was a wise man and would always be available for me to offer advice and support whenever I needed it.

Finding the right Marketing Director was not easy. I felt I had found the right guy, but after I made him the offer, he changed his mind and went elsewhere. In a way I wasn't disappointed, as it gave me more time to consider whether there was an internal candidate who could do the job. I decided that there was, and his name was David Terrill. David was a bright, off-the-wall individual who had worked for us for several years and done a particularly good job in Oxford Street. He was heavily into music, and he had the necessary understanding of our store managers' needs, something that for years previously was sadly lacking. There was no contest for another newly created role, Store Development Director – that went to my great pal, Chris Rimmer. Having successfully opened and launched Oxford Circus, I needed him now to help me achieve my dream of opening 200 stores in the UK. Chris was up for the challenge, and ably assisted by the consummate professional, Jim Peal.

With the new board in place, it was time to meet all the managers and we did this at a hotel at Heathrow Airport. This would be my first speech as MD and I was extremely nervous, so much so that I went to the doctor and asked his advice. He prescribed a pill that you could take half of about an hour before the speech, I believe it was a beta-blocker. The only problem with it was that taking alcohol was unwise afterwards as I learnt to my peril on more than one occasion.

I asked all the directors to make short speeches outlining how they were going to help us become the UK's number one record retailer. We had big plans for the company, there wasn't an area of our operation that wouldn't be reviewed and then where necessary, radically improved. I made a passionate, somewhat emotional speech telling them that one of their own was now in charge and that we would be getting our company back! They loved this, because they knew I always batted for them and their staff, and even in this elevated role, I would always continue to do so. I knew most of them well, I employed many of them and I knew that despite their different backgrounds, different levels of talent and expertise, they wanted, just like me, to be part of something that was successful, and more importantly, to be part of something they could be proud of. Our company, I felt, was no different to so many others, its leaders were not either good enough or passionate enough, there was an 'us and them' culture, and frankly no one was interested in the little guy. Well, I was a little guy, and I made it to Managing Director, there would be no 'us and them' culture, our role on that board was to look after them, encourage them, train them, and turn them into successful retailers.

Next had a similar outlook, and look what they achieved, they became the best in UK clothing, overtaking M&S and delivering great value to their shareholders. We would do the same!

I did several store visits before chairing our first budget meeting. I wanted to hear at first-hand what our managers and staff needed to help them achieve their objectives. Time after time I heard that low pay was a problem, particularly in London, and it made it difficult for us to recruit the quality staff we needed. And in too many cases, the quality staff that we did have were taken for granted and continued to work for us despite this. Ian Duffell, when he was MD, would make an annual bonus award to all staff depending on our profit achievement. Generally, most staff picked up one or sometimes two weeks' pay as a thank you and it came in very handy for everyone at the year end. For some reason Stuart, our Chairman, was unaware of this and when we sat down with the draft budget, he asked me what it was. I explained it to him, and he immediately said, 'Oh so that's why last year's profits were depressed, we gave away all this money.' He said it had to stop, and I said that's going to present me with an enormous problem. Telling them last week that I'm standing up for the little guy, only for me now to announce the end of their annual bonus. I agreed with him that the scheme was too generous and left us open to paying out a substantial figure at the year end. I asked him for some time to go away and think through a solution. My great need was to get the basic pay increased significantly for our staff, particularly in London. I asked Mike Lymath to carry out a small survey of the top retailers in Oxford Street, to see how our wages and conditions compared with theirs. He confirmed what my managers had been telling me, we were underpaying people on the shop floor and in the stockroom by between 10% and 15% and the staff turnover of 70% per annum underlined this.

But where did I get the money to bridge the gap? I decided to see Stuart and suggest to him that I would agree to end the annual bonus scheme, which was too costly, but in return I wanted to take a chunk of that money to improve the wages of our hardworking people. He thought initially I was conning him, but I explained my dilemma. I couldn't remove the bonus and lose face with everyone, without taking a chunk of the money to address our biggest problem, very low pay rates for people on the shop floor and in the stockrooms. In the end, Stuart agreed. We both got what we needed. Stuart was able to reduce the year-end liability, and I was able to announce new rates of pay for our staff, including a 20% hike for London staff.

No sooner had this been announced, we were able to place ads in the *Evening Standard* with the new rates included. Within twenty-four hours of one ad appearing, Gary Nesbitt, the co-owner of Our Price, rang me to enquire whether our new rates of pay were a typing error! I said of course not, we are now able to pay people a decent living wage and we were proud to be able to do it. He explained to me that what I did was sheer financial madness, and that he would be under pressure to match these rates, something, he said, he couldn't afford to do. He said I was naïve and reckless, and these HMV pay rises would cost the industry millions. I explained to Gary that I was not running the record retail industry, just HMV, and that I must, and he must, set our pay rates to suit our individual needs. Basically, I told him, it was none of his business, but being secretly delighted that this was not something Gary would have wished for.

The news went down well with all our people, our London managers reporting that morale was through the roof and that applications for jobs had trebled. The same feedback was received via the non-London stores, and early signs that this new board are delivering what they promised, to look after everyone who worked hard and wanted to achieve the same goals. We already had a generous bonus scheme in place for store managers, Mike though improved that pretty quickly. Managers' wives, who I would meet from time to time, always made a point of telling me what their husbands' bonus meant to them. It was generally a new car, a new kitchen, or a long-haul holiday. These guys worked all the hours under the sun, and their wives disagreed with it, as mine did. But there was a tangible reward at the year end, and often as not, because of their efforts they could bank on it.

Our partnership with our Irish friends came to fruition, and we opened two fabulous stores in Dublin. Even these two stores had proved a distraction to me, but we signed the deal and so had to deliver. The whole arrangement, though, was frankly chaotic. Our partners going in and out of the stores, ordering our managers to change the window displays, or questioning why we didn't have enough stock of this CD or another. I spoke to them regularly to tell them that they agreed that we would run the stores and pay us a management fee. They had no right to interfere in the day-to-day operations of the stores. Thankfully, and to my relief, Stuart called me to tell me he was taking control of Dublin from Marlow. He would add these two stores to his list of other international stores such as New Zealand and Canada where EMI used to own them.

Back in Wardour Street, we had communicated our objectives to the company, formed a new board, tackled the huge low-pay issue, so it was now time to push the button to expand the number of stores rapidly. Because we only opened a handful of stores each year, we left the task of physically opening them to the regional manager and newly appointed manager. It worked well, although if they were all to open in the same region during the year the regional managers would be stretched. We had ambitious plans, which Stuart supported, to open a minimum of ten new stores per year. To do this we needed a central operation, separated from the regional managers' control.

New premises were purchased in the Midlands and the plan was to build the commercial side of the shop in these new premises, pack it all onto vans and deliver it to the new store. It would save hundreds of thousands of pounds as staff and other key people didn't need to be hired eight weeks prior to opening. Everyone loved it, we had a great team running it and Wakefield was the first store to benefit from our great new idea. However, like all best laid plans, it didn't go well! I arrived in Wakefield the day of opening and a sheepish Chris Rimmer and Jim Peal were avoiding my gaze, as things hadn't gone according to plan. The shopfitting people were also embarrassed, as jobs were not completed in time for opening and our base in the Midlands, for whatever reason, had fallen short. I didn't blow my top, they knew though that I was disappointed, and I was. But I took the view that Chris and Jim suffered, and they would never want to let me down.

This would not happen again, nor did it.

* * *

We held management meetings every Monday in the board room, with all directors present. We would review the sales for the previous week, and each week we dealt with a different set of issues. Our role was to keep on top of our objectives, support each other on a departmental basis and improve the lives of our key people in our stores. This drove me on, week after week, and I was never satisfied if we failed to deliver on something we promised. We were a good team, and I was learning so much from each one of them. I didn't have all the answers, but I chose people to join the board who were not HMV employees on purpose, so they could educate us all and help us develop new skills.

During one of our meetings, not long into my tenure as the new MD, my secretary told me there was an urgent phone call from Jeff Beard at Warner Music. I spoke to Jeff during our meeting, and he told me they were discontinuing our early payment discount with immediate effect. This was basically a bonus for paying your invoices early and was an important part of our margin mix. I was trying to plan and structure a business that was to become the number one player in the record retail industry. Stuart had supported my expansion plans and said the necessary capital would be made available. I had a happy, hardworking workforce who shared my ambition. However, what I didn't have was a supportive record industry, failing to see our strategy and how it would help them.

Although we were growing our market share, we were still not important enough at this stage and that meant you were fair game for the record companies. I was convinced that unless we expanded the chain rapidly, we would eventually go bust. Our overall gross margin was poor and after overheads, our net margin was less than 3%.

The support from Stuart was magnificent, every year throughout the 90s he approved every application I put forward for our new store programme. Having tended to invest more in the Midlands and the North, I believed it was now time to confront Our Price, who basically had control of London and the Southeast. Our London representation (apart from Oxford Street) was awful, and we set about closing the loss-makers, and identifying the towns and cities in London and the Southeast to take on Our Price. I knew quite a bit about them, I admired greatly what they had set up, but I also knew they were vulnerable. Their format was rigid and inflexible, which had huge plusses for them, but also it exposed a huge weakness which I would exploit. The stores were generally no larger than 1,500 square feet, the range was centrally controlled, and the local managers had very little say.

Our plan to take on Our Price was simple; we would begin targeting the affluent areas they were represented in and aim to open a store roughly 1,000 square feet larger than theirs. This proved to be a very successful strategy as we were able to dominate the sales of the new VHS videotape – they took up a lot of space compared to a cassette, and so Our Price just didn't have the room. I made countless mistakes throughout my career, but I always believe the one thing I got right was to appoint a small property agent called Jackson Criss. There were two guys that we dealt with, Andy Criss and Andrew Jackson. Two exceptionally nice individuals, who were well in touch in the property game, no airs and graces, and just decent and honest. I didn't want to appoint any of those big agents, as we would not get the attention or the property we were seeking. These two guys were hungry, and I just had a feeling that they would deliver the goods for us. Over the years, they exceeded my expectations, and I am thrilled that they became very successful as a result. Unfortunately, Andrew died before I retired, which I was very sad to learn. A consummate professional, a truly nice guy and I owed him a great deal.

With our property agents appointed, ably supported by our lawyer, Ian Christie, the sites we were seeking slowly became available in the Our Price stronghold. Virtually every store we opened was a success and although I guessed we hit them hard, and this was confirmed a few years later when Richard Branson, who eventually acquired them for his Virgin chain, commented in one of his many books about the damage HMV inflicted upon Our Price.

I knew the Our Price CEO, Richard Handover, very well and we got on. Our friendship was tested when I decided to hire one of his ex-senior managers, Glen Ward. Glen was a very likeable guy, very bright, but Richard decided he didn't need him any more. I needed someone at that time to write our strategic plan and over a good lunch I decided to ask Glen to join us on a temporary basis. This he agreed to do, wrote an excellent strategic plan, and as a result I hired him full time and appointed him as my Business Development Director.

Apart from our strategy to target Our Price, we were sufficiently strong operationally and, via our marketing department, strong creatively, that we decided to begin an additional store opening programme that would dominate the larger cities and, in the process, slow the growth of the Virgin chain. Prior to this we were opening stores up to 8,000–10,000 square feet, but due to our success, we became bolder, and more ambitious, believing we could make these huge sites pay. Included in this Our Price/Virgin strategy was a huge leap in market share for us and as a result a significant increase in our gross margin from our suppliers due to our size. In fact, the 1990s were dominated by major store openings in Manchester, Leeds, Newcastle, Liverpool, Southampton, Reading and Birmingham.

At home, we moved house again, just after Katie was born. We didn't move far but it was to a bigger house, with a lovely garden that was safer for our little one to play in. I was still working all the hours of the day and night, not seeing a great deal of Sue or the children. HMV just consumed me, and I couldn't slow down. I had no formal qualifications, a rough upbringing, lost my mum at fourteen, maybe I was still trying to prove something to myself.

Tensions were building between me and Stuart – his international strategy was, as I predicted, making demands on our workforce. As he continued his store opening programme, he would continually ask me for managers and other key personnel, and I had to explain to him that I needed these people for our expansion plans and for the achievement of our profit targets. Mike Lymath, my HR Director, was doing his best through our various training programmes, to deliver the people we needed but we couldn't produce enough for all our needs. Stuart, I feel, believed I was obstructing him due to his mission to expand HMV overseas, and although I did nothing intentionally to hamper him, that's how he felt.

We had a sizeable mortgage, we had just sent my son James to private school, so I began to worry that this ill-feeling Stuart had towards me would lead to me losing my job. I was in a hopeless no-win situation. If I gave in to Stuart and supplied his people's needs, I would slow down our expansion and ultimately that would have an adverse effect on our profits. Stuart would then complain about that, and maybe even that situation could have led to me getting the sack. I guess all of this was eventually going to make me ill again, but fortunately this time when I had to cope with pain in my shoulders and my back my amazing doctor, Andy Watson, was there with his acupuncture to help me, and thus I didn't keel over as I had done in 1987.

I had to attend quarterly international board meetings, in which the heads of all of Stuart's businesses would meet up for a couple of days. Stuart got on well with these guys, particularly Peter Luckhurst from US, Chris Walker from Japan, and Paul Alofs from Canada. We would be joined by Duncan Bell from Ireland and a small finance team. Later on, Stuart added three non-execs, Elizabeth Vallance, Len Govier, and Lord Arran. All exceptionally nice individuals, very bright and good fun. They were there primarily to scrutinise the decisions of management and to ensure good corporate governance was observed. The meetings were long and tedious, but Stuart was a good host in the evenings and, often, it was in a restaurant or bar where most things got resolved.

Chris Walker is an Australian and unlike us reserved Brits, takes no prisoners. He was doing an exceptional job in Japan, and not only did he like me, but he was also never backward in coming to me for advice. I liked Peter Luckhurst, too, but he had an uphill task managing our US business which, because of the high rents and low sales, was losing a great deal of money. I tried to explain to Stuart that I was having difficulty with my people explaining these heavy losses, as they would repeatedly remind me that in the end it would be HMV UK covering the shortfall. I explained to my people the longer-term strategy, and that we all had to be patient, but I agreed that this was not an acceptable answer, thereby increasing the tension between the UK and International.

As we continued to grow our market share through our successful store opening programmes, I began to raise the ante with our suppliers. My argument was that when we made these major investments, the suppliers, both music and video companies were huge beneficiaries, as wherever we opened, we grew the sales of entertainment at the expense of other goods. There was no escaping this fact, people lower down the ladder in these organisations confirmed this, but the Chairmen and CEOs didn't want to admit it, for fear I would become even more demanding for improved terms than I currently was.

I spent a great deal of my time negotiating improved terms with our suppliers. Our search for an acceptable return on our investments was largely down to growing our gross margin on an annual basis. All our suppliers were different, some had large market shares, others medium to low. Leaving that statement aside though, often as not what was eventually agreed on was their belief that we could deliver our promises to them and in a professional manner. This, I believed we did, both in terms of marketing and the range we stocked of their artists. It has to be said that, in addition to any improvement in our discounts that I managed to secure, they were extremely generous with their marketing support, which often gave us the edge over our competitors that we needed.

Maurice Oberstein, Chairman of Polygram, was an American from Brooklyn, whose father had also been in the music business. We all called him Obie, and to say he was eccentric would be an understatement. It's well known in the industry that at a Polygram conference he called a meeting to discuss a proposal from one of his execs. Apparently, there were twelve around the table, and Obie arrives to chair the meeting with his dog Eric. The proposal was not popular amongst the team, and they were all worried that Obie might accept it. After listening to him for over an hour, the guy sat down waiting for Obie's response. He thanked him for his presentation, put his head down towards Eric, started muttering under his breath to the dog, and then looked up and said, 'Thanks, but the dog says it sucks!'

This was typical of Obie, there would always be drama, farce, comedy, and all sorts of games when he was involved. But underneath all that disguise was an extremely intelligent man, who became a towering figure in the industry –

since his departure, no one has been able to fill his shoes. I never had to renegotiate terms with him, so we never fell out! But we had the utmost respect for one another, and I was honoured that I was one of two people who had the last opportunity to have dinner with him before, sadly, he died. Obie was undoubtedly king of the music industry. They may not have liked him, but they all looked up to him and respected him. He in turn had the utmost respect for HMV and, although not directly involved with me on a day-to-day basis, he did whatever he could to help HMV grow and prosper.

When Obie retired, Roger Ames took over and we too got along fine until it came to terms renegotiations. Roger was good fun and at a *Music Week* award ceremony – he may have had one or two drinks too many. I suspect I did too. He began shouting expletives at me a few tables away as he knew I would refuse to cancel our terms meeting at 9 a.m. the following morning. Upstairs in the lounge afterwards we continued arguing. I wouldn't budge on the meeting next day and eventually Steve Redmond from *Music Week* intervened to say if we didn't shut up, he would put our entire conversation in his paper the next week. Anyhow, he didn't show up on time the next day, but he did arrive about 11 a.m. He was not in a great mood; he had a major hangover as he had predicted. We never resolved our differences at that meeting but did so a few days later. I liked Roger, and still do.

Sony were a good record company. I got on well with most of their key people, John Aston the Sales Director in particular. John was hugely supportive of HMV and went out of his way to help me whenever he could. We loved music at HMV and so too did Sony, they had an enormous roster of artists – Michael Jackson, Bruce Springsteen, Barbra Streisand to name but a few. When Paul Burger became Chairman, we got on very well from day one and I was always keen to promote his artists if we could. I recall Barbra Streisand arriving in the UK for a short tour and Paul asked me if we could put a huge blow-up of her album cover on the frontage of our Oxford Street building. It had never been done before, but apparently they drove her down Oxford Street to see it after collecting her from the airport. Paul and I had several tough negotiations, often late Friday afternoons, that often worked because we would be under pressure to do a deal so that we could both get home at a reasonable time for the weekend. Paul, to get the deal done one year, hastily agreed to take back for full credit all my records without the sleeves. These had been stolen in the stores and were unsaleable to the public. It was to John Aston's dismay, he couldn't believe Paul had agreed to this and the size of the credit note was to have a major impact on John's profit forecast for that year.

I don't feel proud of walking out of my own office while negotiating with John Aston from Sony, but I did. John waited and waited for me to return, asking my secretary how long I might be. She said, I think he's gone home! John managed to dine out on the story for years to come, but we always remained good friends. Basically, I liked John too much to throw him out of my office, so I thought it would be better for our friendship if I walked out! I believe I did walk out of Paul Burger's office late one Friday night, when he went to the loo!

My dealings with EMI were strained, as we used to be managed by them at board level. Things had improved since this change, but they were tough to deal with. Mike McMahon, their Sales Director, was a great guy, but he had limited authority when it came to negotiating with me. I would have to then see the Chairman, J.-F. Cecillon, who came to my office in Wardour Street accompanied by an unknown individual who he refused to introduce by his title. I suspected it was his lawyer, who was not allowed at these meetings. I made an excuse to go to the toilet and I slipped into the marketing department to get someone to tell me what he did. Eventually, they came back to me, confirmed he was a lawyer, nicknamed The Butcher, and I threw him out. J-F, as he was known, took it well and we continued to have a good relationship despite this.

I liked John Preston at BMG, lovely guy, but we fell out after he sacked his Sales Director Dave Harmer. It was admittedly none of my business, but I felt

Dave didn't deserve the sack and wrote a letter to *Music Week*. John complained to Stuart about me and forced me to apologise, which I did.

I've been described as a tough negotiator, but I didn't think I was. I fought for what was right, and that we deserved what we were asking for. I only had three major disputes in my fourteen years as MD, one with Universal, one with Warner's and one with Pinnacle Records.

The dispute with Universal was serious. John Kennedy was the Chairman and a good one at that. John and I couldn't agree a deal so I said we wouldn't promote their new releases or chart product. They were market leaders, and we were close to becoming the same. The dispute happened near Christmas, and my executives said we couldn't risk going into Christmas trading in dispute with Universal. I called John and accepted a compromise deal, which I signed for five years. I was criticised for this, but John was running a powerful organisation and I couldn't take the risk that he wouldn't reduce my terms next time round. Our personal relationship, like so many of the others I had, was not affected, and I still enjoy our annual dinner with our respective wives to this day.

Warner's was the most difficult because we failed to reach an agreement, and this led to us banning their salesmen from our stores and not buying any of their new releases. Eventually the dispute was resolved and we agreed an acceptable compromise.

With regards to Pinnacle Records, Steve Prebble, the owner, and I had already agreed new terms following long drawn-out negotiations. However we couldn't agree on the detail and there was a real threat that we would fall out. Again, a suitable compromise was reached between us and we still remain friends until this day.

Like Steve, and other music industry executives I have referred to above, despite our professional differences, I got on well with most people in the music industry. I liked John Kennedy, Lucian Grainge, Roger Ames, and Nigel

Haywood from Universal, Bill Holland, Jimmy Mulvoy from Warner's, Roy Eldridge and Phil Cokell from Chrysalis, the great late Knocker Knowles, Paul Williams from *Music Week*, Adam White from *Billboard*, Chris Maskery from Pinnacle, Paul Conroy from Virgin, and countless others. They were all great supporters of HMV and I will never forget that.

I found terms negotiation extremely stressful, meetings and letters could go on for weeks and sometimes for several months. But although we worked hard as a board and a company, we played hard too. We were a good team, the HMV board, we went to all industry events together, and we all liked a drink.

* * *

Laurence Campbell, my excellent Finance Director, was promoted to Group Finance Director working for Stuart out of Marlow. The Thorn–EMI FD called me and said they had an excellent candidate from DER, a TV rental company Thorn–EMI owned. I duly saw Nigel Newlyn, liked him, but I needed to know that he was professionally capable, as I wouldn't have been the best judge of that. I was assured he was, so I hired him. Nigel was a polite, quiet individual who liked a drink, but very similar to my ex-FD, Laurence, he didn't drink as much as the rest of us.

Charlie McIntyre resigned as my Operations Director, and I was thrilled we were able to recruit an experienced retailer from Top Shop, Steve Knott.

A huge night out for us all was the *Music Week* Awards at the Grosvenor House Hotel. We were shortlisted to win the first Retailer of the Year Award in 1990 so we were all very excited. We had an excellent table in the room, and I remember Jim Peal was with us too, as well as the board. Amazingly, after years and years of solid hard work, we won. We were practically dancing on the table, absolutely thrilled, and I was so proud of everyone throughout the company for what we had achieved.

Our managers and staff were delighted to hear that we had won this prestigious award. It was hugely deserved because everyone was working hard to become the UK's No. 1 music retailer. We were all proud of what we had achieved and were still hungry and wanted to win this award every year.

There was to be no complacency, no let up, all I was interested in was continual improvement, throughout the entire organisation.

Our board Christmas lunches were also memorable, in a Soho restaurant one year we were drinking the lovely Talbot in magnums. When it ran out, the waiter climbed through a window, only to return ten minutes later with more.

We also loved the Nordoff Robbins Silver Clef lunch. An amazing charity, which used music therapy to enrich and improve the lives of mainly disadvantaged children. The whole industry would turn out, plus countless artists. It was the music industry lunch of the year. We always got pissed at this one, and one year I got badly pissed. I remember staggering out of the Intercontinental Hotel and grabbing a cab to Paddington. I was carrying a birthday present and I got to Paddington, looked up at the board, selected my train, called Sue and told her what time I would be home. Got on the train, fell asleep, only to be woken by the guard to tell me to get off. I said, 'Is this Pangbourne?' He said, 'No sir, you're in Paddington.' I said 'No, we can't be, I left ages ago.' He said, 'Yes you did, but you went all the way to Oxford and back again to Paddington!' I said, 'Oh my God, what time's the next train to Pangbourne?' He said, 'Ten minutes on Platform 11.'

I headed for Platform 11, still with the birthday present in hand, and the same thing happened again. I was woken by the guard to be told to get off. 'Are we in Pangbourne?' I asked? 'No sir, you're in Burnham!'

I thought, oh my God I can't do this train thing any more, I'm not sober or trustworthy enough to get home unaided. I decided to get a taxi from Burnham, I didn't have any cigarettes, but saw a tramp in the station smoking, so I asked him if he could give me one. With a huge smile he said, 'Shouldn't this be the other way around governor?' We both laughed and I asked a guy where the taxis were, he said straight ahead and outside the door. I get in the car, in the back seat, said to the driver, 'Pangbourne please,' he says, 'Who the f*** are you? I'm waiting here to pick up my f***ing wife! F*** off!'!

So, my day, after that, went from bad to worse. Eventually I got a taxi, kept the driver laughing all the way home as I told him about my journey! When we pulled up in my drive, I opened the back door of the car, and just fell out onto the shingle. Driver says to Sue, 'And the best of luck love.'

There's not enough space in this book to record how many great times we had together as a board, people may take a dim view of us, but frankly I feel it helped us all tackle the enormity of the jobs we were doing and helping us get towards achieving that accolade of Top Dog. We needed the banter, we needed the friendship between us, it was a good thing and kept us sane!

Thanks to the efforts of a key executive at Tower Records, Steve Smith, the British Association of Record Dealers (BARD) was formed. Unlike the record industry, we had no formal body to discuss or represent our views as retailers to the record companies.

Often as not, key decisions affecting the whole industry would be taken by the BPI representing the suppliers, with no input from the important retail sector.

Steve Smith became our first Chairman and did an excellent job of persuading the independent owners to join the big chains represented, such as HMV, Woolworths and WHSmith. To their surprise they found out that BARD was not just a talking shop for the multiples, and that their views would be welcomed and respected.

The first significant event that really put us on the map was the agreement to supply our sales information for chart compilations and analysis.This initiative was led by our outstanding Director General, Bob Lewis, formerly a very successful Sales Director for CBS, and Andy Gray, the owner of Andys Record Stores. Up until this point, our vital and important data was supplied free of charge.

As retailers, despite supplying the data, we had no say in how the charts were compiled or how our data could be marketed.

Thanks to their efforts, the industry recognised the importance of this data and eventually a new industry body was set up, the Chart Information Network (CIN), which BARD would be a key member of, and quite rightly was fully remunerated for the supply of its data. This helped us all, but especially the owners of the independent stores.

I had the honour of being elected as Chairman in 1990 and served a second term as Chairman in 1998. During my tenure, through the efforts of the BARD/BPI Committee, my Marketing Director, David Terrill, John Webster from the BPI, and Robert Chandler, a Creative Producer, worked together as an industry to find new opportunities to break new acts. After many meetings they came up with the idea of staging an annual live music event in a large hotel to showcase and reward those acts that had great potential. Funding the idea would not be easy, but they approached a company called Mercury, who were, at the time, hoping to take on BT in the world of communications, and they agreed to become our sponsors.

It was agreed that an award of £25,000 would be made to the best album released in the UK and Ireland. Winners included Primal Scream, Suede, M People, Portishead, Pulp, PJ Harvey (twice), Dizzee Rascal, Arctic Monkeys, Elbow and many more. The show is now staged at the Grosvenor House, Park Lane and is also televised by the BBC. It's been a phenomenal success for the industry and just goes to show what can be achieved when both sides of the industry work together. BARD, through its members, supported the BRIT Awards too, using instore and window displays to promote this successful annual charity event, managed by the wonderful Maggie Crowe from the BPI.

From being formed in 1988, BARD went on to have a major say in all the big industry decisions that I believe helped to strengthen our outstanding independent sector, which was so often at the forefront in breaking new artists in the UK.

It's known today as the Entertainment Retail Association (ERA) and in my opinion only continues to exist due to the efforts of one man, namely Bob Lewis. BARD was his baby, he put everything into it over many years and deserves our utmost thanks for what the Association achieved over many years.

In 1993, the Select Committee for Culture and Sport decided to hold an enquiry into the pricing of CDs. All the major record company executives and many of the independents were called to explain the cost of CDs compared with vinyl albums and cassettes.

The committee was lead by Gerald Kaufman, the Labour MP, who made it quite obvious from the start that he thought the record industry was profiteering, and thereby robbing the public and him personally, being an avid buyer of classical music.

I felt they all gave a good account of themselves despite the grilling they got from the MPs. They did their best to explain that higher royalties to artists was a major factor affecting the price, in response, one MP asked why, for example, can't you get someone else to sing Michael Jackson's songs, instead of being held to ransom because of his popularity?

To roars of laughter from the room, the record executive had to explain that there was only one Michael Jackson and that artists were not the same as washing machines!

As head of HMV, I had to give evidence, and I have to say, I found it the most stressful experience in my life! I had nothing to hide, because the committee had the record companies in their sights, not the retailers, we didn't set the cost price, the record companies did.

But, nevertheless, I was extremely nervous, fearing I would embarrass myself and then ultimately HMV. Apart from totally misunderstanding a perfectly good question from one of the MPs, I came away unscathed!

The predictable result of the enquiry was that the committee found that record companies were profiteering, and therefore, they would now be investigated by the Monopolies and Mergers Commission, a process that would take months to complete.

They rightly concluded that there was no evidence of profiteering, and the case was dismissed.

* * *

Having regularly attended the Nordoff Robbins Silver Clef lunch, I was somewhat embarrassed that as a major player we made no donations to this wonderful charity. This would all change in 1995, when Glen Ward, our Business Development Director, asked the board to join him at Enfield Town Football Club for a charity evening with dinner and Tommy Docherty as the after-dinner speaker. Glen's father-in-law was a famous footballer, Dave Bowen, who had passed away – he played both for Arsenal and Wales. It was a great evening and I suggested to everyone that maybe we, as HMV, could put on a similar evening to raise funds for Nordoff Robbins. It was clear that footballers loved music and the music industry loved football. Everyone agreed. Glen kindly invited us all again the following year, this time Jimmy Greaves was the after-dinner speaker. The room was full once again, and I admitted that I hadn't followed up my fundraising suggestion. The guy who organised the Enfield evening, Les Gold, told me he could help me put on a similar dinner for the record industry. He was still in touch with a number of ex-players, and he was sure he could get a good speaker for us. Les did just that, and continued to provide ex-footballers and managers for us for some time to come. Les is not only a consummate professional, he's also one of the most decent people I've had the privilege to meet. What he did for us and the charity will never be forgotten.

I approached the Grosvenor House in Park Lane and they suggested we take half of the Great Room as it was our first event. We sent out all the invitations, Jimmy Greaves was our first after-dinner speaker, and we sold 500 tickets and made £50,000 for Nordoff Robbins.

We were thrilled with the support and decided to repeat it next year. I asked Les to get someone we could honour that was famous in football. He said I can get the great John Charles, the striker from Leeds and Wales. We said, OK, let's honour the great man in the Grosvenor. Les called me to say John would be honoured to accept the award, but unfortunately he didn't have a suit to wear! I told Les to buy him a suit and send me the bill. We sold nearly 700 tickets and John Charles was amazing. A very special, very humble human being, the room melted in his presence. Another very successful evening. My pal at Sony, Gary Farrow, tells me, 'You've got something big here and I can help you achieve it.' Gary put me in touch with the Sky presenter Richard Keys, who was the face of football at the time. We had lunch, he said, 'I'm not the right guy for this, speak to my Sky pal, Geoff Shreeves, because he knows all the footballers. I met Geoff in Kettners off Wardour Street and told him about the dinner, the potential it had if we could attract big names without having to pay a fee. He did his due diligence on me, checking I wasn't in this for money personally, and after we shared several bottles of champagne, he agreed that him and Richard would help us. They asked for £5,000 fee, which I agreed to, but after their first year they said they wouldn't take a fee, either now, or in the future. Amazing gesture from strangers basically, who went on to help us raise over £8 million for Nordoff Robbins.

It must be said that these two guys were nothing short of sensational, utter professionals, and their dedication and enthusiasm for our event knew no bounds. They opened doors for us within the football industry, and they loved being involved, helping to raise funds for such a great cause.

We had a great team behind us, Karen Little, from our marketing department organised the event, and in my opinion what she achieved was beyond the call of duty. It's rare in life that you come across such a dedicated individual, and she was surely one of the best I had ever encountered. I would say the same, too, about Colin Culleton. He was my Head of Security at HMV, and Gennaro Castaldo, my Head of PR. They, too, did an outstanding job, freeing me up from worrying about those things that go on behind the scenes, and ensuring all the great and the good were looked after and shown the respect they deserved. Rare individuals indeed!

Gary Farrow, a true believer in the event and my pal from Sony Music, allowed us to hold our monthly meetings in their offices. We were joined by Steve Knott, Jim Peal, and Alan Zafer, who staged and produced the event with the tremendous Alison Webb for many years.

The meetings were fun, but we worked hard, searching for new ways to raise money, and turn the event into something we could all be proud of.

Les Gold continued to supply the recipients of our award, now named as the HMV Football Extravaganza Lifetime Achievement Award. He also supplied us with several after-dinner speakers, namely the late great Alan Ball. During his speech, you could have heard a pin drop in the Great Room of the Grosvenor House. He movingly talked us through his career, and the relationship he had with his father. I know I wasn't the only one in that room with a tear in my eye.

I wrote to all the Premier League managers asking for help, but at that time, only Alan Curbishley replied. Having met up with him for a drink, it was clear he loved the thought of being involved, so I offered him a free table as long as he invited some important guests.

He called me prior to our second event and asked if it would be OK to invite Sir Bobby Robson and Sir Alex Ferguson! I said I would need to think about it! Sir Alex became a regular guest, helping us to raise hundreds of thousands of pounds by hosting personal dinners that were featured in our auction prizes.

His presence in the room lifted the event to new heights, more and more footballers wanted to come each year, and it was an enormous compliment when Sir Alex told the press that this was by far the best football charity event in their industry, but sadly was not run by anyone employed within it!

Year 2, we honoured the wonderful Nat Lofthouse, and then the following year the great Stanley Matthews. We invited George Best as a guest on the top table that night, but after taking his seat on stage, he asked for the toilet. He got up and literally fell off the stage. It was very sad, as he was adored in the room and in the country. We went on from there to honour huge names in football, including Brian Clough, Tony Adams, Bobby Charlton, Jack Charlton, Sir Bobby Robson, Sir Alex Ferguson, Sir Kenny Dalglish, David Beckham, Eric Cantona, Denis Law, Alan Shearer and Pele, to name but a few.

The Great Room at the Grosvenor House in Park Lane was sold out every year and although Karen Little, our Event Manager, decided to leave after giving us so much, her replacement Rae Peal, carried the baton seamlessly, showing the same level of dedication and hard work for many years to come. They were both outstanding individuals, and this marvellous fundraising event would never have raised the monies it raised without them.

I continued in the role of Chairman for twenty-three years and was delighted to be able to hand over the running of the event to Geoff Shreeves, who was not only there from the beginning, but along with Richard Keys, put the event on the map, creating the most entertaining evening while at the same time, helping us year in and year out to raise the millions we did. I was indebted to Richard Scudamore and Peta Bestany from the Premier League who became our sponsors, donating over the years hundreds of thousands of pounds to the event.

To this day I am still involved with the dinner as Chairman of the Trustees, but I am immensely proud of everyone who gave up their time and made such an enormous contribution over many years. Universal Music, Warner Music, Richard Bernstein, Miles Jacobson and Peter Leathem from the PPL are still with us and still supporting us financially. Emily Philps and Maggie Peal continue to ensure the night goes off without a hitch.

Their hard work and support led to Nordoff Robbins being able to bring Music Therapy into the lives of so many people, who, prior to the HMV Football Extravaganza, would not have benefited. Nordoff Robbins is a wonderful, well-run charity and it was my privilege and honour to have worked closely with their CEO, Pauline Etkin. Previously a music therapist herself, she led that organisation for many years demonstrating an immense understanding and power of Music Therapy. She was an inspiration for me and several others and one of the kindest and likeable individuals you were ever likely to meet.

Chapter 19

My home life (when I was there) was nothing but stable. My son, James, was doing well at his school, the Oratory in Woodcote, and my daughter Louisa had left home to become what she always wanted to become, a nurse. Katie was growing up fast and we were fortunate we could afford to send her to private school, St Andrew's in Pangbourne. Louisa was enjoying life in London doing her nursing training and led an enjoyable social life with her many friends. She must have had a few boyfriends, but she only invited the one to our house for Sunday lunch, a policeman, John Nicoll. Sue and I took to him immediately, a kind, decent young man who eventually asked me if it was OK to marry my daughter. Sue and I had no hesitation in agreeing, they were madly in love and the wedding was booked for 20 August 1994, the day before my birthday. After a long search, we all agreed on the wedding reception, the Olde Belle at Hurley, and the actual wedding took place in our local church in Whitchurch-on-Thames. I was a very nervous dad on the day, but the weather was glorious, and everyone was just so happy. The whole day went off without a hitch, I admit though, I did shed a few tears when we were signing the register but then she was my first baby and I adored her.

The wedding reception was just wonderful, surrounded by friends and family, the happy couple had a day to remember for the rest of their lives.

At work we continued our expansion plan, opening up to ten new stores per year, every one of them a success. We also introduced, thanks to Glen Ward, an HMV gift voucher, following the closure of the EMI record token, and it proved to be one of the most profitable ventures in our history.

The annual *Music Week* Awards came round again in 1996 and surprisingly we didn't win Retailer of the Year Award. I have to say I was bitterly disappointed as like all previous years that we won it, we deserved to. That year the award went to Virgin, and I couldn't hide how sad I felt about it. However, totally unbeknownst to me, I won the most prestigious award of the night, The Strat Award. It was named after a famous and fun-loving record company boss called Tony Stratton-Smith. I was utterly speechless, I had no speech prepared as I would like to have done, as I'm not good without notes and preparation. I somehow blurted out how disappointed I was that we didn't win Retailer of the Year, but that I was totally honoured to receive such a prestigious award, from my industry peers. The citation, which was terribly embarrassing, read as:

> **It is fitting that the first retail recipient of The Strat should be a man who has done more to reshape the music habits of the UK public than almost anyone. Brian McLaughlin, has led the company's transformation into a powerhouse of the UK industry, and established the model for HMV's development into a global music, retailing brand.**

I'm not sure I deserved such praise, but I was terribly proud that night, for me and for Sue. She never stopped believing in me and she deserved this accolade as much as I did. I felt proud of what I had achieved over the years, the boy from Portsmouth, and felt so proud of what my team and our hardworking people had achieved.

That same year, 1996, HMV celebrated our 75th anniversary, and to make it special and memorable we flew all our managers and most of the record industry to Antalya, a wonderful resort in Turkey.

Everyone that was there still talks about that conference today, it was the most amazing venue and Alan Zafer and his production team excelled themselves not only with the stage set for the actual working conference, but also for the stunning outdoor gala dinner that they planned, organised and delivered. Our managers all dressed up for the occasion, suits and ties, and the ladies looked amazing in their dresses and evening gowns. After dinner, and once the speeches were over, Alan treated us all to a once-in-a-lifetime firework display. It was just stunning. One thing above all I remember was the wall-to-wall grins on everyone's faces. They just felt so proud, and I don't think there will ever be another occasion in our industry to beat that. The record industry turned out in droves, to celebrate and congratulate our long history and recent achievements.

As usual, we worked hard during the conference sessions, but everyone was encouraged to let their hair down on gala dinner night. Our popular finance controller, Richard Colyer, broke his arm around the swimming pool, and my Operations Director, Steve Knott, decided, very late in the night, to join me in my villa to give me an 'appraisal'. Both of us were very merry by then and we just couldn't stop laughing. I remember Steve asking for another drink and all I had was a bottle of red wine but couldn't find a corkscrew to open it with. Steve, showing signs of frustration, promptly snatched the bottle from me, went outside, and returned with the neck of the bottle smashed, thereby enabling us to partake, albeit with certain risks attached!

The following night was more casual, and everyone was encouraged to go into the beautiful town of Antalya. We decided to hire a coach to hold about twenty of us, and we would go to a bar and then find a restaurant later. The place itself was stunning, vibrant, fun, very loud and packed with people. We had a fabulous night and we decided to make our way towards our coach. We found the coach, the driver was asleep and as we drove down these shocking roads – somehow he managed to convey to us that we needed to stop for petrol. He didn't speak a word of English! We pulled in at this self-service petrol station, and we were all chatting amongst ourselves. I looked out of the window only to see our driver filling up with petrol, with a cigarette in his hand. I screamed out loud, 'Oh my God, you can't do that.' At this point someone ran out and snatched the cigarette off him. I had never been so scared, to think that that wonderful celebration could have resulted in twenty deaths, most of the senior management of HMV!

Apparently, our competitors were unhappy with our growth and the publicity we were receiving. We were receiving reports that many of them were in disarray. We were the beneficiaries, as we were thrilled to have hired the highly regarded John Taylor, the Virgin Marketing Director. I had known John for a few years and often suggested he may want to consider joining us, but we had to wait a few years for that to happen. John was a very likeable guy, who knew his music and was very instrumental in preparing us for the huge expansion programme to come. He was, unlike a lot of marketing people, quiet, down-to-earth and clearly understood the HMV core customers.

Although Our Price had an incredibly successful run, they were bought out by WHSmith. Virgin were also rumoured to be struggling and WHSmith eventually bought a majority interest in them, a move that would give them a leading market share. WHSmith continued to invest in Virgin under their new MD Simon Burke, who previously was their Business Development Director. Simon managed to persuade the powers-that-be to expand rather than closing it all down. They opened twenty-three new megastores, while closing nineteen Our Price branches. Even though Our Price had more outlets, over half the turnover then consisted of sales from stores trading under the Virgin brand, with their larger stores in locations with higher customer traffic. Yet, despite all this,

WHSmith in 1998 sold Virgin/Our Price for £145m to a division of the Virgin Group Companies in response to the stores losing £127m in the year.

As for us, we closed 1997 with the birth of our first grandson James, on 12 November. Sue and I and the whole family are thrilled.

Sir Colin Southgate, Chairman Thorn–EMI, had been busy over the past few years selling off the Thorn businesses. He apparently only saw a future in keeping EMI Music, and in 1998 we were the final business to be sold or demerged under the new name of HMV Media Group. This was all carried out in secret; I and my team knew nothing about this until we were called to a meeting in the city. We learnt that the night before we had purchased Waterstones from WHSmith. We had recently just acquired the failing book chain called Dillons, its jewel in the crown was the world-famous bookstore, Hatchards on Piccadilly. This purchase along with the acquisition of Waterstones was never part of any strategic plan I was involved with, so it came as a bit of a shock to say the least! The purpose behind the move was to have three strong retail brands that could eventually be floated on the stock market and help pay down the not inconsiderable debt we took on of £650 million. We were all in a state of shock as we learnt that not only was this debt a huge one, but the interest payments were also sky-high, making it very tough for us all going forward.

In addition to this, it was announced that Tim Waterstone, the founder of Waterstones, was to become Chairman of HMV Media Group, and Stuart McAllister, my Chairman, and Alan Giles, the MD of Waterstones would become joint CEOs. I was to become MD of HMV Europe taking over Ireland, Germany and Belfast from Stuart, in addition to my duties as MD of HMV UK.

* * *

It all happened so fast that we did not know what had hit us. We were surrounded that day by management consultants, lawyers, PR people and accountants. The new company that was being formed would take weeks, if not months, to put together on a legal basis and we would all be asked eventually, as HMV directors, to give our approvals and signatures. In the background, Stuart and I were not getting along well as he announced at one of our international meetings that, as he could not use and promote the Dog and Trumpet logo in the US, Canada and Japan, he would be discontinuing its use in HMV. Obviously, I was shocked and argued that his biggest and most profitable business was HMV UK, and that logo underpinned all the values of that company. He was not up for listening and told me that furthermore, he was going to develop an international design for all stores and everyone, including me, would have to adopt it. There would be an international design committee established under his Chairmanship and the international execs would all be members of that committee. I could only think of one response, and that was to resign. To ask me to operate, manage and lead the UK business without its famous logo was pure madness, and to force me to accept a design for my shops (every single one profitable) from a committee, that in all honesty did not have the knowledge or the experience I had, was just unfair and deeply disappointing.

In the restaurant in Soho that evening, I told him I would resign, and he said that's not what he had desired from this, but I should calm down and come and see him in Marlow in a couple of days' time. I made an appointment and went to see him. We had never fallen out before, we got on pretty well, but I could tell he was angry, and he was also brusque with me. He said, 'If you want to resign, you can come here and tell me, you can even write to me, but I don't accept resignations in a Soho restaurant.' I explained that there were two major changes he was introducing, and I had no prior notice. I was upset and very disappointed. He said that it would take time to unwind the use of the Dog and Trumpet and it would also take time to develop the new design. Don't rush these things, talk it over with Sue and we'll talk again soon, he said. Sue and I talked it over and decided it was wrong for me to be driven out after all I had achieved.

Secondly, we believed Sir Colin Southgate would not allow the Dog and Trumpet to be removed from HMV UK and I could, in time, appeal to him to override Stuart's decision.

As far as the new design was concerned, I tried my best to have a huge, influential say on this committee, but it was not to be. Many of my colleagues owed everything to Stuart for their positions and lifestyles, and none of them would support me. I even tried to acquire additional votes on the committee, given I made all the profit for the entire group. That was refused. The committee met monthly for a while, beginning with choosing a new design company. I had only recently employed a new one, and they did a splendid job with our new Manchester store, and that new design we intended to roll out to other stores. Stuart wasn't impressed, he preferred a US-based company in Boston, and they were appointed after giving a presentation to the committee. I was the only one who didn't vote for them.

My team in Wardour Street were stunned, and I think they knew that the end was in sight for me. I had lost my authority on the International Board, and I just had to go along with these decisions. We fought hard to get the best design we could from this debacle, but to no avail. My other colleagues knew that Stuart wanted to win this battle with me, and therefore supported him. We ended up with a poor design, but it had to be implemented. Stuart even appointed Laurence Campbell – the Group FD, and my former FD – to act as police officer to ensure we complied. There was a set of instructions issued, Laurence said he would enforce them. I just couldn't believe what was happening. I felt sorry for my people, especially my lovely secretary, Emma Allen. She had to bear the brunt of my struggle. She had worked with me for some years, happy, fun, tremendously loyal, good at her job and very supportive. She could see how down I was, but there was nothing she could do. I missed her greatly when she left, but we remain good friends.

We chose the newly acquired Milton Keynes store to implement the new design and I told my people that where certain aspects of it didn't work in the UK or we just felt were wrong, we would ignore instructions and make our own substitutions. We made the best we could out of a bad job, and then Laurence called to say he wanted to visit the store with me. I was furious with him; how could he do this to me after the loyalty and respect I showed him? On arrival at Milton Keynes, I said to Laurence we had certain difficulties with the design and therefore took it upon ourselves to change things for the good of the store. Oh no, he wasn't having that! He insisted I reverse the changes and if not, he would make a report to Stuart. I can't remember what expletive I used in response, but it was very unpleasant! Obviously, Stuart would get in touch soon with a letter ordering me to comply. The letter duly arrived, and I ignored it.

Wardour Street was swamped with the lawyers and management consultants. We all had to put a new forecast together that would be used to demonstrate to the banks that we were good for this enormous debt. Alan Giles and I met at a function, he was very supportive of Tim Waterstone and looking forward to becoming joint CEO of HMV Media with Stuart. Mike Lymath the Group HR Director was very helpful to us in the UK business, always there to explain or answer any questions we had. Mike joined me from Thorn–EMI on Stuart's recommendation, and he turned out to be an exceptional HR Director. He was financially astute and was very effective in the compensation and benefits areas. He also established an in-house training facility at our Nottingham store and acted as a mentor and counsellor for me! We remain good pals until this day.

Steve Knott, my Operations Director, had left and taken up the new position of MD of HMV Germany. This was a blow to me as Steve had become a very effective Operations Director. His previous career was in the fashion business, working for Burtons and Top Man. Culturally, at first, he wasn't a good fit with our managers, but in time he proved himself to be very effective, and gained a great deal of respect from them. I believe he taught us how to effectively merchandise the product instore and in the windows, something I knew little about. This had a major impact on sales and was head and shoulders above anything our competitors were doing. He also took upon himself to seek out and develop the immense young talent we had in the business, coaching them, developing them for future management roles. There were a great number of people who owe their careers to Steve and many of them went on to hold important roles within the company. Like Mike he was great fun, and they both helped keep me sane!

Steve and I, though, continued to clash over stock levels within the stores, something we still laugh about today!

I promoted a very talented guy called David Pryde to replace Steve as Operations Director. David worked his way up from Sales Assistant, eventually becoming the Buying Manager – a massive responsibility, as he and his team were solely responsible for what was stocked and marketed in an HMV store. Under David's leadership I had finally achieved what I set out to do when I became Operations Director in 1980, which was to build a stock profile for the business that didn't have to rely on the musical tastes of the local manager and staff.

The only way we could expand swiftly and profitably was to concentrate the knowledge in the hands of a few experts, with the help of technology in our head office and spread best practice across the chain. We adopted a strategy that most large retailers use, and while I admit this was a huge radical and cultural shift for the business, we could never have achieved our ambitions any other way.

David turned out to be an excellent Operations Director, gaining the respect of everyone in our business and in the industry as well. David and Steve, I thought, would go far, and we will find out later, they did.

The due diligence on the creation of HMV Media was going through and we learnt that we had two equity partners in this new company, Advent International, a US venture capital outfit, and EMI Music. I believe they both had an investment in us of around £80 to £90 million. Steve Tadler would represent Advent and Simon Duffy the EMI Group FD would represent them on our board.

Late one afternoon, a lawyer phoned me, acting for Advent, asking if it was correct that the Dog and Trumpet was not to be part of their deal. I said, 'Who told you that?' She said, 'Stuart McAllister, he sees no need for it as he can't use it overseas.' I told her in no uncertain terms that Advent would be diluting their investment in us if they didn't ensure they, HMV Media, retained the rights to use the logo. We didn't own the logo, EMI did, but they never charged us, believing it was good for them to have this famous logo that they owned being used throughout the UK and Europe. She said, 'OK, message understood, I will alert Steve at Advent.' I was stunned, the logo was going unless I could do something to stop it. Immediately, as Sue and I had previously agreed, I called Sir Colin, desperately hoping he would take my call. Amazingly, he did, and I relayed the lawyer's conversation to him. He said it would be madness to do away with such an asset and said, 'Leave it with me.'

A few days later, Sir Colin called me and invited me, Stuart, and the EMI board secretary to a meeting in his office. I met Stuart in the lift on the way up and he never said a word. Colin wanted us to outline the for and against of keeping or not keeping the logo. Stuart and I did that, and after carefully listening he said, 'Brian's right, we should keep it, he needs it Stuart, and you don't.' When we left, Stuart was fine, no hard feelings between us. I broke the news to my team, and we celebrated long into the night!

The final paperwork for the demerger was ready to be signed and our sales and profit forecasts had to be ready too. With £650 million of debt, there wasn't much room for error, we had to hope we got our figures right and so too did everyone else.

As things progressed, HMV were achieving their forecasts and Waterstones wasn't. In fact, they were miles off target and we were likely to be in breach of our financial covenants with the banks. Our Group FD, Neil Bright, was rightly very concerned, and he said that the banks were demanding a meeting with the HMV Media Board to hear our explanations and future plans. This was serious and we all knew it.

* * *

In July of 1999 I called Stuart to tell him I was off on holiday at the beginning of August. He said we had a lot to discuss on my return, but anyhow he too was going to be away the same two weeks as me. As usual, we went off with the family to Farringford in the Isle of Wight and had a wonderful time as we always did. It was the only time I really felt well in myself, in fact while walking over Tennyson Downs, I believe life couldn't get much better. On our return home, Sue and I went out for dinner on our own and that's when I broke the news to her that I had decided to resign from HMV. The holiday had taught me that I couldn't go on with this daily pressure and I was fearful that my health would suffer again, but this time would I be so lucky with just a frozen neck? I didn't have to convince her that this was the right thing for me to do. I think she saw the difference in me in the Isle of Wight, and yes while we were becoming well off, it wasn't much fun if I was going to be seriously ill. I told her I would take a couple of months off, and we would need to cut back on most things so we could pay the bills, and that would have to be done from our savings. I had never felt better in making that decision. We knew I may never ever get as good a job elsewhere and that we were likely as not, to have to downsize the house and move to a cheaper area than Whitchurch-on-Thames. All in all, it was a risk we were prepared to take, and I would inform Stuart of my decision on the following Monday.

I called his office at 9 a.m. and asked to speak to him. His secretary said, 'Stuart? You mean you didn't know?' I said, 'Don't know what?' She said Stuart suffered a brain haemorrhage on holiday in Florida, and was flown home after having surgery. Doctors were unsure whether he would survive, but we had to be optimistic, people do. Others have survived these terrible things. I was in a state of shock, I never gave it a thought that anything like that could happen to him, although I constantly told him to give up smoking Benson & Hedges cigarettes. He was a heavy smoker, with a bad cough at times, and these cigarettes, in my opinion, were far too strong. Stuart's secretary said she'd phone me with any news, and I said, 'Thank you and please pass on my best wishes to his wife, Lynne, and the family. I would be praying for them, that he made it.' The next day I was told that the operation went well, and that Stuart would pull through. That was wonderful news, but he would not be returning to work for some time.

Tim Waterstone, our new Chairman, called in to see me at my office to ask if I would take Stuart's seat on the board representing HMV. Alan Giles would for the time being become sole CEO and both businesses would report to him, including me. At our first board meeting Simon Duffy, the EMI FD and board member, asked Tim how long Stuart was likely to be recuperating and were we sure we could as a group cope in his absence. Steve from Advent International was also concerned and felt we should keep in touch with Stuart on a regular basis to check on his condition and ascertain if he wanted to return to work. After a lengthy absence we were told Stuart had decided not to return, and as a result, Alan Giles was confirmed as the sole CEO of HMV Group. I had decided to stay on as MD of HMV Europe as I felt, after talking to Alan, that the issues concerning the new international design were not on his agenda and that I could adapt it to suit the needs of the UK business. He made the point, quite rightly, that for better or worse, we had paid for the design, and we were financially now obliged to implement it. This was an enormous relief to me as I was sure Stuart and I were not going to agree on the implementation, hence my decision to resign.

Alan took over the Chairmanship of the HMV International board, which met quarterly but was now to include Waterstones as well and their new MD, David Neal. Friction began to build within this group, as the Waterstones performance was not achieving budget or the forecasts we had given to our lenders. At HMV Media board level, Simon Duffy resigned and was replaced by Eric Nicoli, the new EMI Chairman, following the retirement of Sir Colin Southgate.

I had the honour and privilege to be invited to Sir Colin's retirement dinner at Hatfield House in Hertfordshire. Prior to that evening, I had been very busy with giving speeches to various HMV personnel and was looking forward to a night off relaxing with Sue. This was not to be, as on my arrival at the front door a young lady approached me and asked if I was Brian McLaughlin. I said, 'Yes, I am.' She said, 'Would you be kind enough to make a tribute speech for Sir Colin?' I thought oh no, but it was an honour to be asked and I couldn't let him down. Unfortunately, throughout dinner, I was frantically writing notes as reminders for my speech after dinner. I felt sorry for Sue, but then she was used to these things happening! My speech was well received, except I made a joke about Simon Duffy, the EMI FD, only to be told by him afterwards that he was not amused. That night I had the pleasure of meeting Eric Nicoli for the first time. He was the new Chairman of EMI, and as it had been with Sir Colin, we hit it off immediately. He has a wonderful sense of humour, no airs and graces and I thoroughly looked forward to working with him.

Eric hadn't long been an HMV Media board member when Tim Waterstone offered his resignation. It didn't take the board long to agree that Eric should replace him, a decision, I should point out, that turned out to be just marvellous for me, HMV and Waterstones.

Sadly, in the September of 2000 we learnt that Stuart McAllister had died at the age of 53. It must have been an awful blow to Lynne and his family as he was a devoted husband and father. Looking back, Stuart was my boss for twelve years and goodness knows how I survived in my job. For some unknown reason, he saw me as a threat and would always see the future of HMV as overseas, relying less and less on HMV UK. This was never going to happen as our overseas businesses continued to lose a great deal of money and we were finding it more and more difficult to establish the brand in several new markets. If I leave all of that to one side, I owe him a huge debt of gratitude for appointing me as the UK MD, when most people would have chosen Tony Hirsch. Secondly, he supported my team and I by providing the capital, which was literally millions of pounds, to enable us to become such a huge success story. Unfortunately, by the time Stuart became ill, our personal relationship reached an all-time low, hence the phone call I was about to make to him to resign. I wished him no ill feeling as another human being, and I was very sad to learn of his passing. However, I decided not to attend his funeral, which to this day I regret. His personal commitment and support for me in 1987 deserved recognition, and so too did his contribution to HMV UK. I wear my heart on my sleeve so I'm told, so I suppose I couldn't square my conscience by attending his funeral after fighting battle after battle with him. His family were unhappy with me at the time – with hindsight I don't blame them.

Towards the end of 2000 I achieved my dream of learning that the music industry body, the BPI, had officially recognised that HMV UK had become the market leader in UK music retailing, and the most profitable music retailer in the world. It had taken us nearly twenty years to achieve this objective, but with so much to be done and so much to be changed and improved, it was always going to be a long haul, and the whole company was thrilled and deserved all the congratulations they received. The Oxford Circus store and its size played a significant part in our achievement alongside the implementation of the Our Price strategy and the massive stores we opened throughout the UK. The Tower threat never materialised as the site they acquired, the old Swan & Edgar store in Piccadilly, was basically a rabbit warren and not suited to retailing. I guess they never made any money, but Russ Solomon just loved telling people he owned a store at No. 1 Piccadilly in London. To add to their woes, and Virgin's too, we were fortunate to be offered a huge store opposite our original store in 363 Oxford Street. In square footage terms it was double the size of 363 at about 25,000 square feet. We had been overtrading out of 363 for years and it was not a pleasant shopping experience for our customers!

The new store was to be known as 360 Oxford Street. We asked George Martin, The Beatles recording manager, if he would unveil a blue plague that we were allowed to affix outside of 363, stating that it had been there since 1921 and that the store was officially opened by Sir Edward Elgar. In May of 2000, we opened the new store, trading over three floors, and we threw a lovely party for key HMV people and record industry executives. The night before we re-enacted, with the creative skills of Alan Zafer, the famous lunch that Sir Edward Elgar hosted the day 363 opened. We had a small select guest list from across the industry and we drank wonderful wines and told wonderful stories.

Although the new store was twice the size of the original one, it was a substantial financial investment in shopfitting and rent. A rent which, like most leases we signed, meant we were locked in for at least twenty-five years. Fortunately, after just a few days' trading, we all knew the store was going to be a great success, and it was.

In May of 2001, we took all our managers and the record industry for our annual conference in La Manga, Spain. However, before La Manga, huge drama unfolded within HMV Media Group. Friction between HMV execs and Waterstones continued to build, with a serious threat developing of the Group potentially breaching its banking covenants and going bust.

Stuart, before he resigned fell out with Mike Lymath, the Group HR Director, and fortunately for Mike, I had fallen out with my HR Director, thereby enabling Mike to return to HMV UK in his previous role. Mike was to play a significant role in the drama about to unfold.

Chris Walker, MD of Japan, and Peter Luckhurst, MD of US and Canada, were increasingly concerned, as I was, of the deteriorating financial position of the Group. Basically, HMV were achieving the forecasts we agreed with the banks, but Waterstones wasn't. The situation was so critical that many of the banks were asking for their money back, which would clearly lead to our total demise. In fact, a few days after the next international board meeting, the banks had summoned Alan and his board to a meeting to explain how we were going to fix the issues facing us. The planned flotation was cancelled due to Waterstones' performance and that in itself rang alarm bells in the city.

* * *

Eric Nicoli decided to make some changes to reassure our lenders that we could meet our sales and profit targets. He asked Alan Giles to give up the day-to-day running of the Group and hand it over to me in a newly created role of Chief Operating Officer. Alan would remain as CEO, but concentrate his efforts on managing the City, something Alan was very good at. I would therefore take control of all the HMV stores across the world, plus Waterstones.

I called Sue, who wasn't sure whether to laugh or cry! She knew I had taken on a huge responsibility that would involve significant overseas travel plus the managing of a book chain, something I had never done before! In fairness, Eric, I told her, had given me a big pay rise that would all count towards our pension, and provide us with even more financial security as a family.

There was clearly lots to do, and I relished the challenge. We had to get to work immediately, and the first thing I had to do was appoint my replacement at HMV Europe and begin fixing Waterstones. At our next Monday management meeting in Wardour Street, I announced my promotion to COO and said that I would be giving serious thought over the next week to who was going to be my replacement. Nigel Newlyn, my FD, had left due to personal reasons and was ably replaced by John Clark. John was the best FD I had ever worked with, technically sound and a thoroughly likeable guy. David Pryde, who like me had come through the stores, was a very capable Operations Director and was my choice to replace me. David was first and foremost a music man, he had worked tirelessly for some years slowly building a template for the stores that would finally remove the hit and miss of our range and the purchasing of new releases. Managers loved him, suppliers respected him, and he was an HMV man through and through. I decided to give David the job and to promote John Clark to Deputy MD, HMV Europe. Not sure John was happy with this, but David was and so too was the business. These appointments allowed me to get stuck into HMV International and Waterstones.

I spent a couple of months touring the Waterstones stores, after which I met up with Mike Lymath and told him that both David Kneale, the MD, and Brian Worrell, the Operations Director, would both have to leave.

We survived the day with the banks. Alan, Neil and I gave them a solid presentation, with me promising them that I could fix Waterstones. I sincerely felt that the managers were mostly competent, very enthusiastic, and they wanted to be as successful as HMV was. There was a lot for me to learn, as the dynamics of Waterstones was very different to HMV, big competition from WHSmith and the emerging Amazon.

I went to Brentford to see David and Brian and asked them to leave, both were very disappointed, but both behaved professionally.

Chapter 20

I decided for the time being to run Waterstones myself, it was the only way I was going to understand it, and more importantly, the clock was ticking to start demonstrating that this business could be fixed. I decided to hold a managers' conference, so they could all see me and listen to what I had to say. Waterstones, I told them, was a retailer – yes it sold books, but it was a retailer. In any business you have standards, and you have to have a unique selling proposition that ultimately leads to success. I felt from the outset that we would tackle the basics, first-class in stock position, then appraise and train all the staff, make changes if necessary, know your weekly sales targets, get the stock from the stockroom onto the shop floor. I also told them how great their brand was, how impressed I was with so many of them, and did they want to be the poor relation in HMV Media Group, or did they want to be seen as the cavalry leading us to our flotation?

I appointed some excellent people to the board, in particular Sarah Trota, the HR Director, who was my rock in those early days at Waterstones. Nick Williams was also someone I could rely on as he tried to work through the operational issues facing the business. Our agenda as a board was huge, we had numerous HR issues to confront for the longer term but while Sarah was tackling those, I concentrated on getting the sales and profits up.

Our first conference at Hammersmith Novotel was deemed a success by most people. I'm a straight-talking honest individual who wants to get the best out of people, and in Waterstones they had great people who needed leadership and support. I felt that I had become a good leader. I know people in HMV followed me, I tried to get more things right than wrong, and both feet were very firmly on the ground. I left the Novotel that night with a high degree of optimism. The managers seemed to warm to me, and I knew they were good people who needed direction and consistency. We had a big job ahead of us, I obviously had a lot to learn, but I was excited that we could turn this business around.

Time to take a break from Waterstones and join the HMV managers and David Pryde for their annual conference. La Manga was just brilliant. The first night was madness, everybody catching up with everyone, drinking, laughing and just having a good time. I didn't stay up late as I had been working on my speech for the next morning and I'm always tense and very tired before this.

In the morning at breakfast, it transpired there had been some late-night entertainment in the bar. I asked who it was, and was told it was some bald geezer, but he did have a great voice! I suddenly thought, oh my God, that would be our Chairman, Eric Nicoli. I had invited him as I knew he loved La Manga, and I had heard he often sang down there when he's on holiday. Anyhow, thankfully, the managers I spoke to all liked him, which was just as well as he was their ultimate boss!

We let the managers and record execs have the afternoon off, most of them playing some form of sport or other. I liked to play tennis, not that I was any good at it, but it was fun and my old mate from Pinnacle, Steve Mason, would partner me in doubles. The courts were wonderful, and we had two opponents that on paper looked easy to beat. We started off well, me, typically, at the net and running for everything. Steve was on the baseline due to his height and that he was a better player than me. After several games he took off his top to reveal another T-shirt with the words 'Yours' written across the back. This was reference to my tennis playing, where every ball that came above my head at the net, I would shout 'Yours'. Everyone melted with laughter although it was a slight exaggeration, and it's gone into conference folklore now.

The gala dinner was wonderful as usual, I would host the awards to our manager and head office personnel, followed by the announcement of the night's highly prestigious award, the Dave Wilde Award. Dave, you may recall, promoted me to Regional Manager and became a great friend. He left HMV a sad and disappointed man but so much of what I learnt about music and music retailing came from him. He had died a few years before La Manga and although most of our employees would not have worked for him, I wanted him to be remembered and respected for what he did for HMV.

Steve Mason, Eric Nicoli, Paul Williams from *Music Week*, and I shared a table at the gala dinner. I didn't notice at the time but Steve kept Eric's and my glasses topped up throughout. Eric got up to make a speech, opening with 'The last time I was in a room like this we buried my brother-in-law . . .' didn't go down as well as Eric had hoped but he continued. He then thought I might be fair game for his jokes and that didn't go down well either. The serious part though was excellent, and everyone was thrilled when he heaped so much praise on us for what we had achieved. Eric was clearly tipsy, but I believe I was drunk! I got on stage and first called Eric the 'C word' apparently! I have no recollection, but in the morning, I found out I was the only one who couldn't remember. Apparently, there was a sharp intake of breath in the room, as no one, not even me, who would swear a lot, ever used that word. I managed somehow to present the awards without falling over and managed to announce the Dave Wilde Award without notes! When I sat down, Paul Williams said my remarks about Eric would be in Monday's edition of *Music Week*. I asked what remarks he was referring to. He said, 'You called the Chairman a C!' I said, 'I certainly did not, I've never used that word in public and never would!' Paul said, 'I can assure you Brian you did, and it will make most of our readers chuckle on Monday.'

Eric and I met with Steve for breakfast, none of us looking or feeling great. Steve mentioned that Paul was going to print what I called him. Immediately Eric turned to me and said, 'You had better make sure he doesn't, Brian. It was a private party, he was not invited as a member of the press, he was invited as a friend of HMV.' Eric was clearly angry, and I decided to go and find Paul. After searching the hotel for at least thirty minutes, I found him checking out. I put on a big smile, and said, 'Paul, how are you?'

'Fine Brian, just going to post the copy for Monday's edition.'

I said, 'Paul, I need a favour, please don't publish my speech, Eric is unhappy, and I am likely to get into trouble if this gets out.'

Paul, looking disappointed, said, 'It was the best bit of the two days and it's a shame you don't want to go with it. Typical.' Paul continued, 'You're a good mate Brian, you owe me one!'

In October that year, I received a phone call from David Munns, the Chairman of the Music Industry Trust Award. I was a member of the organising committee, and had been so for years. The BPI (British Phonographic Industry), the industry body, wanted to introduce an annual award to those people who had made an outstanding contribution to the music industry. Former winners included Maurice Oberstein, John Deacon, John Barry, Sir George Martin, Sir Andrew Lloyd Webber, Alan Freeman and Ahmet Ertegun, to name but a few. The award ceremony would be held in the Grosvenor House Hotel, Park Lane, and the proceeds from the dinner would be split between two industry charities, the BRIT School in Croydon, and Nordoff Robbins Music Therapy. David, our Chairman, said, 'Brian, the committee have met without you to decide that you will be this year's recipient of the Music Industry Trust Award.' I was literally speechless, as I had no indication I was even on the long list, let alone the short list. Of course I accepted, I was humbled and honoured, not just for me but everyone in HMV and Sue and my family that between us had worked so hard to make this happen. I was on Cloud Nine – imagine me going to join a list of such famous people as Obie, John Barry (who I idolised), Sir George Martin, and the music man himself, Ahmet Ertegun. Sue was in the kitchen at home when I told her, and we both shed a tear. Such amazing recognition made what was a huge personal struggle for both of us so worthwhile. Our kids too were thrilled that they were going to the Grosvenor House with their dad to collect his award.

On the night, I felt very strange, and realised that there were 1,000 people in the room to witness my award. Furthermore, to add to my embarrassment, there were huge photos of me all around the room and on the main screen. Paul Gambaccini was our regular host, and as the evening went on I became more embarrassed and more nervous. When we all arrived for drinks beforehand my family and I were lined up for several photographs by different photographers. It was surreal, I'd never experienced anything like it before.

On our table, Sue and I decided that along with our family, my long-suffering PAs and Events Manager, should join us. That was Cathy Coackley, Emma Allen and Karen Little, known as Brian's angels! They were such fun, and so loyal and supportive to me over the years, it was my way of recognising what they meant to me.

I didn't say a lot to anyone and going to the toilet was also a challenge. As I approached the urinals, people were nudging each other, whispering is that Brian McLaughlin? My mentor, friend and ex-MD, James Tyrrell, and his wife Jill were invited, as too were our best friends Billy and Shaun McNamee. JT warned me that he would walk out if I gave him any credit for my success, 'This is your night Brian, not mine.' As it turned out, typical James, he left before the award was given, to get the last train home! He never accepted that without him I would not be receiving this award in the first place.

Gambaccini started the ball rolling as he always does, but for some reason this year instead of talking about the achievements of the recipient, he talked for quite some time about the horrors and destruction of 9/11. I believed, like him, and the rest of the world, that this act was brutal cold-hearted murder and most of us were still in shock. I just wondered at one stage whether he would even get around to announcing why we were all there tonight. I think eventually he did, but swiftly left the stage and handed over to Lulu. She kindly went through my career and then was joined on stage by various artists, John Lodge from The Moody Blues, Sophie Ellis-Bextor, Bruce Dickinson from Iron Maiden and many others. They gave me my award. I held it up high and pointed it in the direction of the tables occupied by the HMV managers. It reminded me of a player winning the World Cup – as he lifts it in the air, everyone cheers. There was a huge roar from my people along with a long-standing ovation in the room. I made my speech, which I hear went on too long! I had never felt so special, so proud and so very humbled. Eric Nicoli came over to me and gave me a huge bear hug, saying, 'Brian you are a genius!'

Meanwhile, throughout the course of 2001, Waterstones' sales started to rise, and we recorded quarter-on-quarter and year-on-year sales increases. Clearly, I was no bookseller, but I was a good retailer and Waterstones was a retailer. I focussed my attention on the basics, reducing the overstocks, maintaining a high in stock position, training all our managers and staff, and marketing our chain effectively to the public. I felt I had won over a large percentage of the managers, albeit I don't think I ever made much of an impact on the booksellers themselves. Excellent as they were at their jobs, they didn't see the need to understand a profit and loss account, that was seen as something for people like me. However, I continued in association with Sara Trota and Nick Williams to try and educate them in the realities of funding a business.

Unless the sales in each store reached a certain level, we couldn't operate profitably. This relentless focus on sales eventually started to bear fruit, and the board and I could see light at the end of the tunnel. Despite my achievements, I admit to making many mistakes, particularly removing a lot of buying autonomy from the store managers. Although it was necessary for Head Office to have a big say in buying decisions at HMV, with hindsight, it was too soon to force Waterstones down this road.

I was however relieved to learn that the current CEO, James Daunt, reversed that policy, giving the managers more say in the buying decisions. No wonder, then, that Waterstones continues to flourish under his leadership. He has done an outstanding job, and he is in my humble opinion to be congratulated for the huge success they are enjoying today.

In HMV it was announced that DVDs would be launched in the autumn, ready for the huge Christmas trading period. HMV UK, under David Pryde, was doing extremely well, exceeding its targets, and well on course for another great year. However, with the news of the DVD release we had the opportunity, if we moved quickly, to steal a march on our competitors, and grab a huge amount of market share. David and his team mapped out how much space we could afford to give over to this exciting new product. Once that decision was made, David galvanised the company to roll out the plan as soon as the product became available.

While all this was going on Louisa, my eldest daughter, gave birth to a lovely little baby girl called Amy, on 7 December. Sue and I were absolutely thrilled, so too were Lou and John and all our family and friends.

Sue and I after many months of discussion, finally decided to buy a dog. We agreed it would be a Bichon Frise, and through the Kennel Club we found one in Gosport, which is fairly close to Portsmouth where we were born.

Literally, from the moment we set eyes on this lovely Bichon puppy, we fell in love with him and decided to call him Jazz. The family too fell in love with him.

For thirteen years Jazz gave us all great enjoyment, and when he died we were all heartbroken.

* * *

Throughout December, reports were coming in of an amazing Waterstones performance, and because of the DVD plan, HMV UK exceeded its budget by miles. It was a tremendous feeling. So much had gone wrong earlier in the year, with so much stress attached to it, but now, here we were, about to announce in January quite staggering HMV results, followed by another impressive performance from Waterstones.

At our board meeting in January, Eric was thrilled with our results and with me personally. He was so good to me, and his support made the hard work worthwhile. After reviewing the results and quizzing me on the outlook for 2002, Eric announced that our situation was good enough for us to float the business on the stock exchange. This was an amazing and momentous statement for Eric to announce, as he had seen off every attempt by the so-called 'non-believers' to sell the company for a song. Private equity companies queued up to buy us on the cheap, City advisors told us that we wouldn't float and that we should take what was being offered. Time after time, to Eric's credit, he refused to sell, believing, as he put it, 'That my hairy arsed friend over there, Brian, will fix it.' He had enormous faith in me, but it was a huge gamble for him to take as it so easily could have backfired on him.

We made the announcement, and now we had to prepare for the flotation with a roadshow to sell the shares to the City. I thought Alan and Neil would do this but I was told I needed to be included to inspire people with the Waterstones' turnaround. It was something I dreaded, I didn't care much for these people anyway and to be on the road for nearly two weeks with them filled me with horror. Alan and Neil put together the script we would need to present at all our roadshow meetings, including my section. I read it through and was unhappy with it, but few changes were allowed. Prior to hitting the road, we had to have a dummy run-through at our brokers' offices in the City. The idea was to test us and ensure the messages we were getting across were consistent, and compelling enough to encourage investors to buy.

Alan is a born natural in their company, and the environment in which it is delivered. Neil was good too. I'm like a fish out of water with these people, and I'm afraid my lack of education and qualifications raises its head and I develop a huge inferiority complex as a result. I know they are not better than me, but I lose all confidence in their presence, and I am then hopeless as a presenter. As I feared, my run-through in front of about thirty UBS executives was a disaster. It contained a lot of graphs and numbers, and I only had notes to explain them, rather than having it all written down. Once I finished, the mob tore me to pieces, tearing holes in everything I said, deriding my posture, deriding my clothes and my beard. I was terrified, and absolutely furious. I had to keep my temper, something I found very difficult to do, but was determined not to lose it and give them the satisfaction of totally humiliating me.

The thought of going through this ordeal for two weeks was frightening, but so much was at stake. We still were carrying over £600m of debt, which the flotation would reduce significantly. It would also take the pressure off the management and the HMV Media Board. Added to this, I knew EMI was keen to crystallise its investment in us – another key reason for it all to go well.

Apparently, we would do several meetings in the City, and then go overseas. We were being accompanied by two UBS executives, basically to hold our hands and make sure the process worked – and ultimately to make sure we sold enough shares. All the key execs in HMV and Waterstones had shares, so you felt an obligation from that standpoint too, not to let them down.

The first few meetings in the City of London were horrendous. It made the run-through we had appear like an easy fireside chat with some friends compared to presenting to these utterly hostile potential investors. I was a nervous wreck at all of them and we were on the go from 7 a.m. to 6 p.m., meeting after meeting, question after question. A *Financial Times* article halfway through the roadshow cast doubts on our numbers and plans, which led to even tighter scrutiny in the meetings and a fall in the share price, on what was called the grey market. We were offering shares at £1.92, and it was important for the float and for our future that we achieved this number.

From London we went to Boston, San Francisco, San Diego, Milan and Paris. I was exhausted, still a nervous wreck, and never regained my confidence throughout the trip. I was not helped by the UBS guys who were with us, who would sneer at me during a presentation, increasing my nervousness and making me even more incoherent. After one lunchtime presentation, I had had enough, and let them have it with both barrels. They obviously denied they were doing this to me, but I made a point that if it happened again, I would walk out during the meeting.

It didn't!

On the final meeting in Milan, we all got trapped in a lift, and once we got out an investor at the meeting accused us of lying. Why, I do not know, we weren't lying! All the numbers we presented could be challenged, but we didn't lie.

I couldn't wait to get the plane home, and finally when I arrived indoors to be greeted by Sue and the family, I just broke down in tears. I was emotionally exhausted.

The next day was D-Day, we went to the offices of UBS, and they were all actively on the phones selling. The drama began early. Several investors were not going to pay £1.92 and EMI, via Eric, were threatening to pull the float. Eventually, through the skill of these UBS guys, we got there and achieved the price we needed. It was such a relief, the feeling was unexplainable, but I was elated and very proud. Alan and Neil had done a great job, and despite my lack of confidence during the trip, I felt I was able to confidently predict that we would achieve our forecasts for both businesses. And we did.

Although I didn't have a significant shareholding compared to Alan and Neil, I made quite a lot of money from the float and gave a large proportion of it to my children. I felt somewhat bitter and disappointed that having been the architect of the turnaround I was never given a bonus or any form of financial thank you for what we achieved. I did ask for something, which was unusual for me, but the board turned me down.

Once the float was put to bed, I decided it was time to give up the acting MD role at Waterstones. I couldn't keep up with the demands of that and be an effective COO. Steve Knott who had become MD of HMV Germany decided to leave once his contract expired and he returned to the UK to join World Duty Free.

I wanted someone I knew to run Waterstones, someone I could trust, so I decided to offer the post to Steve. Thankfully, he accepted and now I could turn my attention to HMV International.

Fortunately, Neil Bright, our Group FD, was able to provide monies in the accounts following the flotation to help us exit certain international markets. Our main problem was the US, where most of the stores were unprofitable and the two stores in Manhattan and the store in Harlem were haemorrhaging cash. Our leases in New York were long, and the rents rose every year whether we were trading well or not. The HMV board gave me permission to try to exit any of these unprofitable markets without incurring huge costs in the process. Basically, we desperately needed to exit the US. Chris Walker, our Hong Kong MD, recommended an Australian property guy who specialised in helping companies across the world with failing property investments. This guy was not cheap to engage but he had an excellent track record, so we gave him the brief to negotiate an exit strategy with the US landlords. After several months, and again thanks to the skills of Neil Bright, and our property guy, we successfully negotiated settlements with all the US landlords and finally we were no longer in the US and the drain on our profits would cease.

In Canada, we had about one hundred stores in total and we made a small profit. After the departure of Peter Luckhurst, I employed an ex-Sony retail guy called Humphrey Kadaner. Humphrey proved to be an excellent appointment and continued to run our business there very successfully.

Our Australian business unfortunately was losing money, despite having Chris Walker in charge. Chris, an Australian himself, eventually, after setting up our Japanese, Hong Kong and Singapore businesses from scratch, was asked to add Australia to his charge and stem the losses. We had previously sold our New Zealand business and Len Govier tried during his tenure at HMV Group to sell Australia too. Chris had done a fantastic job. With no music retailing experience, he had opened numerous stores in Japan as well as establishing a small business in Hong Kong and Singapore.

Japan was an impressive chain of stores and after many years of investment began to make a small profit. The business was subsequently sold after my retirement for an eye-catching figure. Canada too was subsequently sold, along with Australia, Hong Kong and Singapore. On reflection, I strongly disagreed with Jim Maxmin, then CEO of Thorn–EMI Electronics, with his policy to open HMV stores overseas. I was never consulted, and if I was, I would have pointed out that competition in all the major markets across the world were tough to overcome. Furthermore, record companies would always tend to support the local guy rather than any foreigner who just turns up on their doorstep. Margins were too low, and costs too high. Given his brief, I believe Stuart McAllister did his very best, but the strategy was doomed from day one for the reasons I have already given.

The new arrangement, with Alan remaining as CEO, Neil Bright as FD, Mike Lymath as HR Director, and me as COO was working well. Alan bore none of us any grudges and we all got along well. The businesses benefited as a result.

In 2003, Eric Nicoli, our Chairman, decided to stand down and a search began for his replacement. It was a personal blow to me as Eric had supported me through thick and thin, and had the courage and skill to promote me to COO, a move that could have badly backfired on him. He was, in my opinion, responsible for saving HMV Media Group and for protecting the interests of shareholders, staff and management. He stood up to everyone who wanted to either buy the group on the cheap or Waterstones on the cheap. An outstanding executive and an outstanding individual, the like of which I had never come across in my nearly forty years in business. I am proud to this day to call him a very dear friend.

Eventually, after a long search, we appointed Sir Robin Miller as Chairman of HMV Media Group. Robin spent most of his business life in EMAP, a very successful company, publishers of countless sought-after magazines. He had been with them twenty-five years and was a highly regarded CEO.

Our first board meeting with him was interesting. As Sir Robin walked through the building, passing managers and staff on his way, I noticed he was carrying a WHSmith carrier bag. That's strange, I thought, our new Chairman walks in carrying a competitor's bag! I mentioned this to him at the end of the meeting and I got the impression he was not at all impressed with me.

But Robin was a likeable, down-to-earth guy and enjoyed meeting up with his directors either for an evening drink or for lunch. Unfortunately, he would use this time to launch into lengthy interrogations about your job, kind of like an ongoing appraisal or as someone else described it, micromanaging. It wasn't just me, he wined and dined most of us, and we all went through the same intense questioning.

* * *

The highly respected David Pryde, our MD of HMV Europe, called me requesting a meeting. We met up for a drink in Wardour Street and he told me he was resigning for personal reasons that he didn't want to discuss. This was a major blow to us all as David had the potential to be an outstanding MD. I discussed the situation with Mike Lymath and we decided to move Steve Knott from Waterstones and promote him to MD of HMV Europe. Steve would be a popular choice; he was highly respected within HMV and I was sure he was the right choice. I agreed that I would go back temporarily to run Waterstones again, which I knew I would enjoy, it was unfinished business for me as their MD and I was looking forward to it. Steve was delighted with this news; it was a job he always wanted, and he relished the challenge.

Waterstones once again began to take up a great deal of my time. Nick Williams and Sarah Trota were the two key executives who worked well together and continued to make great progress within the business. The store managers were beginning to respond to the messages we were sending them, especially regarding stockholding. Unlike the music business, purchases from publishers were sold on a sale-or-return basis, which I believe led to bad practice on both sides. Managers and buyers became lazy, there was little skill required. While all of this was going on – clearly not good for our business – I discovered that most of the stores were not even returning unsold stock as they were entitled to do. This was nothing short of crazy! Immediate attention to this would not only improve our stock turnover, but also our working capital.

The trade paper, *The Bookseller* would be often on the receiving end of leaks from some of our employees who disagreed with me on this, leading to it questioning or highlighting our new stock turn goal or target. My aim was never to dumb-down Waterstones as some people accused me of, my aim was to retain all its great brand values and ensure it became more efficient. The company was becoming happier with itself under the HMV leadership.

We held managers' conferences abroad, like we had with HMV, and I remember the impact they made when we held them in Paris and Sorrento.

They told me we treated them with respect, this had never happened to them before, and they were literally overwhelmed that management would go to these lengths to show them our appreciation of their efforts. Profits were never ever going to be great at Waterstones, unlike HMV, but there was a gradual increase year after year, proving that this was a good company with great potential.

In 2004, I decided to start a search for a new MD for Waterstones as, after lots of soul-searching, Sue and I agreed that I would retire at the end of the year. The last few years had been relentless, and I owed it to her and the family to slow down and spend some quality time with them. We had acquired a significant amount of HMV shares; we had earnt bonuses for several consecutive years and I was told by my accountant that I had a good pension.

In all honesty, I was looking forward to retiring, as my heart had gone out of the business since we became a public company. For good corporate governance reasons, you have to appoint senior heavyweight directors to the board. We had the Chairman from EMAP, the finance director from Cadbury Schweppes, the CEO of AVIS Europe, a director from BUPA, and a banker.

Frankly, although I understood the need for good corporate governance, all these people tended to spend most of the board meetings dealing with operational issues, which was my responsibility. They had no retail experience between them, which meant that I spent most of the time explaining to them how our business worked! I didn't resent outsiders joining the board, but it would have been much more sensible, given the massive threats we were facing from the new download technology, the supermarkets and Amazon, if we appointed experienced retailers. I would have welcomed this, for I am certain HMV would not have suffered as it did if these people been on board. All retailers were to face the uncertainty of the new digital world, and I am certain that between us we would have found better solutions than we did.

In the March we appointed David Gilbert from Dixons to become the new

MD and I decided to make my announcement publicly at the managers' conference in Spain. Obviously, I informed the board and I asked if they would consider retaining me as non-executive Director. I had been with the company for thirty-seven years and felt I could still be of service to them. Robin Miller said he would give my request some consideration and let me know.

I made my announcement to the managers and the suppliers in May in Spain, I was very nervous and very emotional. The response in the room was staggering, and I was shocked. Everyone got to their feet applauding me, and despite my efforts to get them to sit down, they just wouldn't. I even left the lectern and went to my table, but they continued applauding. I felt just wonderful, all these fabulous people in one room, taking the trouble, through their applause, to thank me for my contribution to HMV. It meant the world to me, and my only regret was that Sue and the family were not with me to share in the moment. I was literally overwhelmed and thought myself very fortunate to have been given the opportunity to lead this great company and its people. I know I will miss them, but I had decided that now it is time for me, Sue and the family.

Robin Miller told me that the board had decided not to offer me a non-executive role once I retired. He believed it would be wrong for my replacement to have to be on the same board as me and it would likely to lead to differences of opinions. I didn't agree with this at all, I was capable intellectually in distinguishing between an exec and a non-exec. The new person would be running things and I wouldn't. I would be there if the board needed my advice, nothing more. I wasn't doing it for the money, I didn't need the money, it was, I felt, a nice way for me to retain links and an interest in the business I had given a huge part of my life to.

I have to say I was pretty angry with them after all I had done. Then a solution raised its head. My old friend from Virgin, Simon Burke, was putting a bid together for WHSmith and he rang me to ask if I wanted to become their new MD if the bid succeeded. Frankly, I didn't want to, but if I was to make this offer known to the board maybe they would change their mind and offer me that non-exec role I was seeking! I guessed right, WHSmith was a massive competitor of Waterstones, and they didn't want me there plotting the downfall of Waterstones! They agreed a three-year contract and I was delighted. Furthermore, Simon's bid for WHSmith failed to materialise, and they must have felt pretty low at HMV when they heard the news.

* * *

I took my team to Venice for our annual meeting/thank you, with our wives, and we had a great time. On the Monday after we got back, David came to my office in Maidenhead to break the news he was resigning due to ill health. His back problem was making it too difficult for him to carry out a full-time job as important as MD of Waterstones, so he was leaving. This was a severe blow to me, as this was October 2004, and I was due to retire in December. I discussed it with Sue, and she knew I couldn't just walk away in December leaving HMV without an MD for Waterstones. I then discussed with the board, and they asked me to stay on for another year, and during that time recruit a new MD. I felt very embarrassed having to announce this news, it seemed as though I was having second thoughts and didn't really want to leave. Although this wasn't the case, I knew that would be what people might think. In fact, staying on for another year and having to be part of this board, convinced me I had made the right decision to retire. Our listing on the stock market changed the company that I knew and was brought up in. The culture changed, too, and the fun was gone.

In the outside world we were reading daily of the dotcom boom, with all these questionable internet businesses attracting huge investments and valuations. In HMV, competition was increasing as the supermarkets decided to expand their space to include music and video, and they heavily discounted both. This was costing us a great deal of lost sales in the Top 30 CDs and videos. In some cases, the supermarkets would price so low we couldn't compete. Steve Knott and his team in HMV were doing all they could to find a solution, but their efforts were hampered when Amazon joined in.

At Maidenhead, our Group HO, Alan Giles, our CEO, told me he was resigning and had given the board twelve months' notice, as he was contracted to. Alan felt the time was right for him to move on, and he expected to take up a few non-exec roles. Later that week, Robin Miller called me and invited me out to dinner. He told me the board would like to offer me Alan's job as CEO and cancel my retirement. While feeling very flattered, it was the top job after all, I had a sense of fear go through my body at the thought of dealing with the City. Alan was good at that, and I knew I wasn't. It was a huge honour though, after thirty-eight years from the shop floor to become Group CEO, but I said I would want to talk to Sue. We went out to dinner, went over and over it, and in the end, we agreed the answer was no. I had done enough, the City wasn't for me and I wasn't happy with being part of that board.

I rang Robin. We met up in a café in Wardour Street, and I thanked him for the offer, but told him Sue and I were ready to retire, it was our final answer. Robin understood and he wished me well for the future.

I hired an executive search company to find a new Waterstones MD and in September 2005, we appointed Gerry Johnson, previously MD of Bookers. A truly nice guy, very commercial, and came to Waterstones at a critical time with the increasing influence of Amazon and the supermarkets offering heavily discounted Harry Potter books.

As we moved into December, Alan asked me how I would like to spend my last day in the business, and I said, 'How about lunch at the Waterside Inn?' Alan, taking a huge gulp of air, said 'Yes, why not?' I invited, Alan, Mike, Neil and my dearest record company friend Bill Holland. He was one of the most likeable people in the industry and we had become very close friends. We had an incredible lunch, laughing throughout about how many retirement do's I had

had. Alan even allowed me to choose the wine, but nearly suffered a heart attack when the bill came!

I had a brilliant retirement dinner at the Landmark Hotel in London, a few days earlier. The entire music industry turned out and several key execs from the publishing world, Lulu performed live, and to cap my evening Sir Colin Southgate, ex-Chairman of EMI Ltd, was there, as was my dear friend, Eric Nicoli, who made a very funny speech retelling the story of me using the 'C word' in La Manga, which didn't go down well with the CEO from Random House!

Sir Colin being present at my retirement dinner was something I will never forget. The ultimate boss for years at EMI and HMV Group, he was my guardian angel through the stormy periods with Stuart McAllister, my Chairman. He saw something in me from the outset, and never failed to show his support for me when I needed it. I owe him a great deal, but unfortunately, never saw him again prior to his recent passing.

It was a fun evening, surrounded by my family and great friends from the music industry. While I did enjoy the lovely tributes, it was also a very sad evening, as I was leaving a company that I had built over many years, supported by the best people in the world. It was an enormous honour to have served them for thirty-eight years, and I will never forget what they did for me, and what they still mean to me now. Together, we became the most profitable and the most successful music retailers in the world, a journey that was hard work, lots of fun, and something, I feel certain, we will always be proud to have been part of.

Meanwhile, apart from being a non-exec for HMV I agreed to become Chairman of fundraising for Nordoff Robbins Music Therapy, a charity very dear to my heart and I was looking forward in my retirement to helping them continue with their excellent work.

I had a lot to look forward to.

Chapter 21

Outside of the mad world I lived in, my real hobby was supporting Portsmouth Football Club. Sue and I were born there, her parents were supporters in the 40s and 50s, my dad was an armchair supporter, but a supporter nonetheless. My brother-in-law, David Lea, encouraged me to take my young son James to Fratton Park when he was about seven or eight years old. I was never interested in football, and I had never been to a football match before. I will always remember our first game, it was against Burnley, there were 18,000 people in the ground, and we were in the bottom of the league, Division Four. The crowd were amazing and so too was the game. I think Pompey won it 4–3. I was hooked! So too was James. We went to most home games with David and the excitement was the same for every match. Over time we climbed our way out of the lower leagues, I remember we became champions of Division Three under manager Bobby Campbell. Alan Ball got us promoted to the old First Division and the whole family, when we lived in Harrogate, travelled to Anfield in an FA Cup tie that we lost.

My favourite time though at Fratton Park was when Harry Redknapp and Jim Smith ran the club. We got promoted to the Premier League and the quality of the football was just outstanding. I remember vividly our first home game that year was against Manchester United, and I thought we had little chance of beating them! To our shock, we matched them man for man and in the end, we beat them 1–0. We stayed in the Premier League for eight seasons, with Harry and Jim doing the most amazing job. It was huge compensation for Jim who under his management he took us to the semi-finals of the FA Cup against Liverpool. We drew 1–1 at Arsenal's ground and drew 0–0 on the second leg at Aston Villa. The game went to extra time and penalties, and we got a lesson from Liverpool how to take penalties and end up at Wembley!

Years later, Harry got us to the quarter-finals of the FA Cup and we were drawn against Manchester United! A terrible away draw, we were sure to get a hiding! On the day we were magnificent! The game reminded me of the film *Zulu*. Manchester United threw everything at us including the kitchen sink. They even had a good penalty shout turned down! They somehow could not get the ball into our net and then a couple of minutes before the end, our striker, who rarely threatened the opposition goal, headed into their penalty area and was brought down. Penalty says the referee. Their keeper was sent off, so they had to put a defender in goal – Rio Ferdinand. Our Sulley Muntari, steps up, ball in back of the net, 1–0 to Pompey, and referee blows the whistle, end of game! We beat them at Manchester United, we are now in the semi-finals of the FA Cup.

Then we drew West Bromwich, and the game is held at Wembley. Kanu scores and we win 1–0.

I'm there at Wembley, freezing cold and to our utter amazement we were in the FA Cup final, yes, us, Pompey! Through a friend I organised a wonderful box for us to watch the game against Cardiff. We all had our family there and friends. We also had one of Pompey's all-time great strikers with us, Paul Walsh. A lovely man who always kept in touch with us. The hospitality was superb, great food, drinks on tap and the best seats in the house. I was so keen to acquire this box for the day that apart from the cost of hiring it, I had to buy two Wembley seats for ten years at an annual cost of £1,500. Boy, it was an expensive day out, but wouldn't have missed it for the world! Everyone there was so excited, and my son, James and I would have been very nervous. It wasn't a great game in all honesty, but the Pompey supporters cheered their hearts out throughout. It was all worthwhile in the end when Kanu slipped past a defender and popped the ball into the back of the net. We were ten to fifteen minutes away from winning the FA Cup! Last time we did this was 1939, ten years before I was born! To our absolute delight, Pompey hung on, the final whistle went, and we were dancing around the box. We have won the FA Cup! It was the most wonderful feeling, and I was so happy for everyone who was with me that day. The players celebrated by running around the pitch with the cup, and Harry Redknapp was close behind! This was an enormous day for my son James and I. When he was small, he used to stand on a wooden box on the terraces at Fratton Park cheering on his beloved team. Yet here we were years later, in a private box cheering them on again, but this time, we won the FA Cup. Magical times, wonderful memories.

We got to the semi-final again two years later against Tottenham, bizarrely Harry had left Pompey and was now managing Spurs! We didn't hire a box this time, but we had a lovely table in a restaurant and great seats in the stadium. It was an appalling, boring game and Pompey were the underdogs that day. Spurs were the better side on form, we were nearly bankrupt as a club, and couldn't win a game! Extra time was needed and would you believe it! We scored two goals and we were on our way to another cup final at Wembley. Unfortunately, we had to face Chelsea in the final who were just outstanding that year, and therefore we made a family decision not to trust our luck any further and decided to watch the game at home. We've all been to Wembley twice and never lost; it was a wonderful feeling. We didn't want to risk going a third time, having to experience losing. We got it spot on, we did lose, but only by a penalty and one goal. From those heady heights Pompey got relegated and eventually went into administration.

I got to know Harry and Jim through the HMV Football Extravaganza and they kindly invited me and my son James for a drink in their office after every home game. It was a fascinating experience, always getting a chance to meet the opposing manager too. Not so good though, when we lost, but great fun when we won!

Sir Alex Ferguson, a great supporter of my football dinner was there for our first Premier League game, and he was normally a truly charming guy. With Pompey winning against Manchester United by one goal, he was clearly fuming, and used a few expletives to sum up the result!

We had eight wonderful seasons in the Premier League watching top-class football. After that I decided to call it a day, I couldn't go back to watching the low-quality football pre the Premier League. The club was bought by its fans and then by the ex-boss of Disney, Mike Eisner. They are doing well and one day I know they will make it back to the big time.

Throughout my crazy time at HMV, the world was going on still and when the craziness stopped you realised how much you missed spending time at home. Louisa, for example, completed her training to be a nurse in 1991, becoming a staff nurse in the oncology ward at Westminster Hospital and then became team leader at both Charing Cross Hospital and Duchess of Kent Hospice. All her wonderful efforts were then rewarded by being appointed Ward Manager at our local Royal Berkshire Hospital. After a long break, she returned to nursing via Oxford Brookes University Hospital and then joined Sue Ryder Hospice as Clinical Nurse Specialist. From there she was promoted again to the position of Ward Manager. I am immensely proud of her and her achievements. I am in awe of her too, because I would be unable to demonstrate the level of care and devotion she has given to so many people over the years.

My son, James, left the Oratory School and from there went to Henley College. He then decided to go to university to study retail and business studies. The university was Bournemouth and James achieved his degree, which we were all delighted with. His love of football saw him joining Southampton Football Club in charge of their retail store, specialising in the club's merchandise. From there he went to Watford Football Club in a similar role. From football to cricket, James joined Edgbaston Cricket Club as Sales Manager, he is now CEO of Cure Leukaemia, a successful charity based in Birmingham. James is personally instrumental for the large amount of revenue they generate, taking part himself in many of the fundraising events. The monies raised helps to fund research that can identify cures for leukaemia.

James married Donna Alos, surrounded by family and friends, in October 2009, at a splendid venue in the Midlands. I have fond memories of James arriving in Del Boy's three-wheeled yellow van, which was just so funny and utterly amazing.

Katie, my youngest daughter, decided to leave university early as it wasn't for her. No sooner had that decision been made, she was determined to find work as soon as possible. She applied for a job as a temporary PA with PepsiCo. That job soon became permanent, and she became a highly respected and sought-after PA. She was later promoted to an events role where she managed their large corporate events and then into Shopper Marketing & Sales Planning. Katie was hugely popular throughout PepsiCo and spent ten enjoyable years there. After Max was born she went on to work for Johnson and Johnson, and has recently joined Bayer. Her career achievements to date are incredible, given she had no experience and no university degree. Like James and Louisa, we are so proud of her.

We have the most fabulous family memories to look back on, holidaying together in Cannes, Puerto de Pollensa, Corfu, Barbados, and sharing the most wonderful Sunday lunches at Pangbourne Lodge and more recently at Icknield House.

During this time my sister, Frances, and I became a good deal closer, and I have enjoyed spending time with her and her partner Shawn, and their lovely family. Sadly, dear Shawn died in 2016.

I don't see my brother Tom as much, nor my sister Enda, but they are both very happy and it's wonderful when we can all get together for big family celebrations. Being taken into care, all those years ago, didn't damage them, in fact being loved and cared for by foster parents was the making of them as individuals.

My first board meeting as a non-executive director was in January 2006 and it was the first meeting under the Chairmanship of Carl Symon – Sir Robin Miller had resigned. On arrival at Maidenhead, Alan Giles introduced me to Carl, and it was obvious from the outset that we were not going to get along.

In the summer, Sue and I decided to sell Pangbourne Lodge and move to the Isle of Wight. With hindsight, it was a very impulsive and ill-judged decision. We saw this wonderful house in Seaview in *Country Life* and we made an appointment to view it. We fell in love with it immediately, so the decision was made to move.

My instincts proved correct, after only a few months in my new role as non-executive director, Carl called me and said it would be better for both of us if I resigned and took up a new role as a consultant. Obviously, this would mean I could no longer attend board meetings, but the directors were free to consult me on an ongoing basis, given my lengthy experience. I never received a call from anyone in the one remaining year of my new role.

Frankly, I was bitterly disappointed as I felt that I still had a great deal to offer, and given the technological threat to our business I wanted to be there and help in any way I could. Nevertheless, I had to accept that my thirty-eight years at HMV was now over.

I was honoured to be asked to become Chairman of Fundraising for Nordoff Robbins Music Therapy. Although I was now retired, I was still heavily involved with the HMV Football Extravaganza on their behalf and also had the time to help raise even more funds for them.

It's only a small charity, but it's a wonderful outlet for all of us in the music industry to put something back using the power of music. It made everything we did so worthwhile when you witnessed the results of the therapy sessions at the Nordoff Robbins Centre in North London. At that time, it was mainly small children who benefited, most of whom had autism, which often made it difficult for them to communicate with their friends and family.

Our fundraising efforts were mostly channelled into training and developing the therapists who were absolutely dedicated to the cause.

The founders of the charity, Clive Robbins and Paul Nordoff, discovered a link between autistic children and music that could help them express themselves and communicate effectively. Thanks to the generosity of the music industry, thousands of children have been helped and, recently, the therapy has been effective in helping older people with dementia and cancers. I worked for a period under the exceptional Chairman, Derek Green, and Pauline Etkin, the CEO, both ably assisted by Audrey Hoare, who worked tirelessly to keep us on our toes.

Julie Whelan replaced Pauline, doing a splendid job in a short space of time and has now handed the baton over to Sandra Schembri. We continue to be fortunate throughout this period of change to have the services of David Munns as Chairman – an extremely successful music executive, who has for twenty-seven years staged the prestigious annual Music Industry Trust award in aid of the BRIT School and Nordoff Robbins. He has dedicated most of his time to guiding the charity through choppy waters, but above all ensuring that Music Therapy is now reaching more people than we could ever have imagined all those years ago.

The burden of driving from the Isle of Wight to London to fulfil my role at Nordoff Robbins began to take its toll on me. Coupled with the fact that Seaview was very quiet in the winter, and we made very few friends there, we decided to sell and go back to the mainland.

The main complication with this decision was that we brought our gardener Dave over with us to Seaview and he lived in a cottage in the grounds. Sadly, his wife Angela died not long after they joined us, so having to tell him we were selling was not something I was looking forward to. He was effectively homeless, but as luck would have it, he met a lovely lady called Karen at a bereavement counselling evening, and eventually became an item together, living in the Isle of Wight.

Dave has been our gardener and very close friend for over thirty years, and it was no surprise to us to learn that he would be prepared to travel to our new home in Goring every week to look after our large garden. Something he still does to this day!

A very private man, he means the world to all our family.

Like all families, we have our ups and our downs. I lost my dad in 1993, my brother Pat in 2014, and then my dear sister Christina the following year. But in January of 2011, we were blessed with another grandchild called Samuel and then, in January 2019, a fourth grandchild called Max.

Sue and I have recently celebrated our golden wedding anniversary and our life together over that period.

She has been my rock throughout my career, encouraging me when I had lots of self-doubt, raising our family while I was away, and loving me no matter what. No man could ask for a better friend or a better mother/grandmother to my children and grandchildren.

They say luck plays a big part in your life, well how lucky was I to meet and marry Sue?

We are both in our seventies now, enjoying life, but we will both find it difficult to get over the loss of our son-in-law, John Nicoll, to a really rare and aggressive cancer called sarcoma.

John battled courageously for nearly five years and had his leg amputated to try and rid himself of this awful disease. The amputation failed to halt the spread of it to his lungs, and he subsequently passed away on my birthday, 21 August 2020.

We are all devastated as John was the life and soul of our lives. A truly decent honest man, a loving father and husband, and friends of countless people – both inside the police force where he worked for many, many years, and outside, in the towns and villages he lived in.

Our daughter Louisa supported him and cared for him throughout those last few years of his life, and he left this world knowing that no one could have loved him and respected him more than she did. He leaves behind two wonderful children, James and Amy, who are a credit to both Louisa and John, and like all of us, they will never forget him.

Sue and I both enjoy relatively good health, and we are surrounded by a wonderful family and friends. We enjoy our lovely house in Goring and being fortunate enough to spend the winter in Barbados. We celebrated Katie's unforgettable wedding to her husband Ben Roberts there in 2012.

We celebrated fifty-four years of marriage this year, and we often look back on those difficult times at HMV. Whatever I achieved during those thirty-eight years, I couldn't have done it without her, I owe her everything.

Chapter 22

Thirty-eight years! I would never have guessed that applying for a position at HMV all those years ago would have lasted a week, let alone all that time! Looking back, I find it hard to remember the person I was before I started at HMV, and yet he is still inside me, sometimes bold, often shy, and always so astonished that he has been able to live his dream.

I sometimes wonder what would have become of that little boy from Portsmouth, who had no proper education, if I hadn't got that first job way back when. Would I have been with Sue, and had all our amazing children, and our grandchildren who bring me such delight every day? Knowing Sue as I do, I don't doubt she would have stuck by me whatever happened, but I do feel proud that I was able to make her choice a good one. In spite of all the hours we spent apart, in the end the reason I did the job was for her, and if she'd ever told me to walk away, I would have in an instant. That she never did, and that she supported my every step of the way just shows how right I was to ask her to marry me. I hope her dad thinks he was right in saying yes to me, even if I got in front of the telly when he was watching the football!

For my parents, I can't imagine what they would have thought about my journey. I think it would be incomprehensible to them. Whatever their faults, I never forget that I am their son, and perhaps they might have had the luck I had, and a few doors might have opened for them too. All of us, I believe, have a huge potential inside us, some get lucky, some don't, but it is down to everyone to make sure that if opportunity knocks, we are ready. And as I've learnt through my charity work, if you know someone where the door has not been opened, the best thing you can do is help put your shoulder against it and push.

I have been so lucky to have made my career in music. When you are doing the things I have done, a lot of it comes down to dealing with people, figures, looking at stock, and negotiating terms. This can happen in any business, whether you are selling real estate or pens. When I took over at Waterstones, as I said, the fact that it was selling books didn't scare me. It was still retail. But, like music, books enhanced people's lives and gave them tremendous enjoyment.

Looking back, I can't help remembering a young man – a boy in fact – who had fallen in love with The Beatles' 'Please Please Me', and even more so, with Billy Fury. As I printed out my Billy Fury fanzine, who would have thought that the passion I brought to that money-losing enterprise would be the same passion I brought to running the UKs biggest music retailer?

The truth is, from the day I first set foot in HMV 363 Oxford St, I fell in love with the company and the famous dog, Nipper. Chris Rimmer, my first manager in Portsmouth, gave me the chance to work with them. Because of this passion, I steadily worked my way up the company, eventually becoming its Managing Director. We had a brand in music retail with the same reputation as Rolls-Royce, and I was determined that we would, one day, live up to that reputation not just in the famous store in Oxford St, but throughout the UK.

My wonderful team hired thousands of people over the years with the same drive and passion we had. Our aim was always to employ people whereby music dominated their lives, mirroring that of our customers.

The record industry, to their great credit, put up with me relentlessly trying to improve our discounts, so that we could achieve our dream of becoming the best in the world.

I know in the long run, they too became beneficiaries of this aim, and so too did their artists and their managers, but I will always be eternally grateful for their friendship and their amazing support.

* * *

Even now, I still get a thrill when I walk into a store and see those lines of albums or CDs. Perhaps another young boy or girl will pick one up and fall in love with the music. They won't be printing out a fanzine, like I did with Billy Fury, it will be online. But if one kid, with a mum who died, and a dad who couldn't cope, and a family struggling to keep it together, can dream that they would go on the same journey I did, it shows that with a lot of good luck and hard work, anything is possible. Sadly HMV isn't the force it once was, but thanks to the new owner Doug Puttman, the Dog and Trumpet still stands proud to this day. Thanks Nipper, I hope I did my best to keep your place in history alive.

As the DJs say, thanks for listening.

Index

G

H

M

N

R

S